W9-ASP-242

# SPECIAL OP: BOMBER

## DARING MISSIONS THAT CHANGED THE SHAPE OF WWII

### STEVE DARLOW

David and Charles

SILVER BAY PUBLIC LIBRARY

*Dedicated to the memory of the RAF and American airmen*
*who sacrificed their lives for my ongoing liberty.*

A DAVID & CHARLES BOOK
Copyright © David & Charles Limited 2008

David & Charles is an F+W Publications Inc. company
4700 East Galbraith Road
Cincinnati, OH 45236

First published in the UK in 2008
First published in the US in 2008

Text copyright © Steve Darlow 2008

Steve Darlow has asserted his right to be identified as author of this work
in accordance with the Copyright, Designs and Patents Act, 1988.

All rights reserved. No part of this publication may be reproduced, stored in
a retrieval system, or transmitted, in any form or by any means, electronic or
mechanical, by photocopying, recording or otherwise, without prior permission
in writing from the publisher.

A catalogue record for this book is available from the British Library.

ISBN-13: 978-0-7153-2782-1 paperback
ISBN-10: 0-7153-2782-8 paperback

Printed in Finland by WS Bookwell
for David & Charles
Brunel House, Newton Abbot, Devon

Commissioning Editor: Neil Baber
Editorial Manager: Emily Pitcher
Desk Editor: Demelza Hookway
Art Editor: Martin Smith
Designer: Eleanor Stafford
Assistant Designer: Joanna Ley
Project Editor: Marie Shields
Production Controller: Kelly Smith

Visit our website at www.davidandcharles.co.uk

David & Charles books are available from all good bookshops; alternatively you
can contact our Orderline on 0870 9908222 or write to us at FREEPOST EX2 110,
D&C Direct, Newton Abbot, TQ12 4ZZ (no stamp required UK only); US customers
call 800-289-0963 and Canadian customers call 800-840-5220.

9-17-08 OCLC
940.5442 DAR
Gift

# CONTENTS

# INTRODUCTION

Is life so dear, or peace so sweet, as to be purchased
at the price of chains and slavery? Forbid it, Almighty
God! I know not what course others may take; but
as for me, give me liberty or give me death!
*Patrick Henry, 1775*

There had been nothing like it before and there has been nothing like it since. The air battle over Europe during World War II was exceptional: thousands of airmen flew the fight, thousands died, thousands were injured, thousands fell into captivity and thousands survived to tell their stories. Key to victory in Europe was the contribution of the American and RAF bomber crews who put into practice the strategic air offensive. These men transferred the air battle from the skies over England to the airspace over Germany, placing Luftwaffe air policy on the defensive. These men's efforts directly contributed to the final victory in Europe. They deserve to be remembered. Their sacrifice deserves reflection and commemoration.

This book tells of certain specific bombing operations, or in American parlance, missions. The chosen raids are 'special' in respect of the tactical nature of the operations, the way they changed the course of the air battle, or the way they highlight certain aspects of the air war. Not all met with success in terms of fulfilling entirely their respective objectives. But they all highlight technical skill, bravery, courage and determination, and new tactical ploys.

This is not a book of strategic discussion, tactical detail or aircraft specifications; although each will be touched on to give context to the main narrative. It is a book that concerns the experiences of the aircrews. I have enormous respect for what these men did. Some of the language in the book details the horrors of the air battle and I make no apologies for such inclusion. I fear that any sanitation of the representation of the actual air fighting and bombing results may lead to a romanticism of the act of war. The act of war is horrific and is not for celebration. I have been studying the bomber war for over 10 years now and have yet to speak to a veteran who celebrates war. I have read of the truly terrible experiences of those suffering beneath the Allied bombers. Although they will not be retold in this book, which will focus on the experiences of the aircrews, the reader must always bear in mind that the Allied bomber offensives resulted in extraordinary suffering on the ground. Civilians were in the front line and there was death and destruction of an unprecedented level.

However, I have still to find any argument that I can accept that suggests an alternative. The absolute need to win the fight against Germany, crush Nazism and liberate the occupied countries, forced the development of the bomber offensive. To lose the war would have been the greater moral failing. Therefore, the Allies had no option but to use the blunt instrument, limited by technology and available weaponry, which was the bomber.

How have the operations been selected? When Neil Baber at David & Charles asked me to put this book together, I was keen to uncover a mixed variety of experience as told by the Allied aircrews, and the majority of these accounts are hereby in the public domain for the first time. I have chosen a varied selection of operational types. There will, of course, be argument for other raids that should have been included, but the physical constraints of the book limited the choice. By the end of the book, the reader will have experienced the multifaceted nature of the air war and hopefully will have developed an appreciation for the bomber airmen who flew the fight directly against one of the most evil regimes in history.

Please note that there are slight differences in the American and British spellings of certain words. With respect to first-hand RAF stories and my narrative I have used British spelling. The spelling of first-hand American accounts will remain true to their source.

# PROLOGUE

M. Jean Barclay of the Women's Auxiliary Air Force was commissioned in August 1941 and posted to the Royal Air Force bomber station at Waddington, Lincolnshire (part of RAF Bomber Command's 5 Group) to act as an intelligence officer. On 25 August 1942 she put pen to paper, reflecting on her experiences to date:

Exactly a year ago today I arrived at Waddington. It seemed one of the greatest thrills of my life, and still does, to stand on the tarmac of an operational aerodrome and know it to be your home and your life for – how long? And today I can still look around me and feel the same excitement and admiration at the scene; so much the same as on that day and yet how different. Gone are the game, war-torn Hampdens that seemed so colossal and in their place the vast magnificent Lancasters . . . The hangars have shrunk to a more normal and less impressive size. My eyes could hardly take in their vastness a year ago, and the whole station has acquired through the months a friendly and familiar aspect.

But since that day how many faces have come and gone and how few can be seen here today that I first saw then. So many ghosts wander round Waddington now. You meet them at odd times and places, perhaps in the deathly silence of the ops room during the hours before dawn when you are waiting for the aircraft to return and you fall to remembering those who used to wait with you or for whom you waited so often. Perhaps in the clamour and bustle of a Mess party on a Sunday morning and a chance name crops up, whose owner seems suddenly, dreadfully and overpoweringly absent. Often at the end of a flarepath as the evening darkens and aircraft loom up out of the dark and speed away into it again as they have done so often. Looking through old operational records, too, now and again something inside you jolts and you close the book hurriedly and come back with a jerk to a seemingly empty present.

In a way, perhaps, their greatness is too near, these deeds of the present. One is surrounded by them, day and night, almost one's whole existence is wrapped up in the microscopic part one plays in the preparation of an operation order that will send people out to fight and live or die as chance wills it. One watches them go, racing down the runway and into space, and one by one they reappear hours later, the everyday familiar faces. The great story is briefly told and briefly written down. 'Next please. Get a photograph, do you think? Oh, good show. Oh, bad luck. Yes, I'm afraid the tea is rather foul, we can only get condensed milk. Did the 109 open fire? What a break. Have a good sleep. You next? Oh, it was you we heard on the R/T [radio telephony] describing Flying Control in such original and exotic phrases. Oh? No wonder . . . He's in sick bay, is he? Will he be all right, do you think? Yes, I'll ring you when the doc comes if it isn't past your bedtime. No trouble. Flak accurate then – obviously.' The last crew goes off to breakfast and bed. One re-reads the raid reports and, now that the room is quiet, each report comes to life as a story. It never occurs to one at that moment that some of these pencil-scribbled stories will probably find their way into tomorrow's history books.[1]

# 1
# THE BOMBER BATTLE OF BRITAIN: BLASTING THE BARGES

*In the summer of 1940, with Hitler's all-conquering armed forces poised across the English Channel, the British people braced themselves in defence of their country. The Royal Air Force's Bomber Command was at the forefront of the Battle of Britain, notably carrying out special operations bombing the German invasion barges assembling in the Channel ports. National survival was on the line.*

On 15 August 1940, at an RAF Bomber Command station in Yorkshire, England, home of 77 Squadron, airman Richard Pinkham, having cleared away the rubble, found himself being lowered through the emergency hatch on the top of an air raid shelter. Minutes earlier German bombers, Junker 88s, had deposited their explosive cargo on his station, RAF Driffield. Minutes prior to that Richard, having returned from operations, had been finishing off his afternoon meal:

After lunch we retired to the ante-room for coffee and to listen to the news on the wireless, when this was interrupted by the air raid sirens of the town of Driffield. Apart from me, no one in the Mess appeared to take much notice of this, probably because our own station sirens were silent. I turned the volume of the wireless down amid a howl of protest from my brother officers, who demanded that I return the volume to its previous level. I retorted, 'You chaps can stay here if you want but I am getting out.' For a moment I hesitated, wondering whether to go out of the front of the Mess or make a dash for the east wing, in fact to the nearest air raid shelter. Instinctively I made for the shelter and I am quite sure that I would easily have qualified for the Olympic record, just as the first bombs were falling.

As the Junker 88s attacked, Richard recalled that:

Local ack-ack batteries were useless and our own station
defences were quite inadequate. This consisted of one
.303 Vickers machine gun perched on top of the water tower.
The airmen manning this gun put up a spirited response
throughout the attack but were totally ineffective.

We cowered in the air raid shelter as several bombs fell
uncomfortably close and a quarter of an hour later we
heard the 'all clear'. Emerging from the shelter to view the
damage, we found that the Germans had done an effective
job. One stick of bombs had fallen across the front of the
Officer's Mess and the west wing had been hit. My bicycle
was a tangled mass of metal. I shall always be aware that
had I gone out of the front door instead of the east wing
I would perhaps have never written this narrative.

The damage was extensive: four hangars had been hit and the number
of Whitley bombers lost went into double figures. Lives had also been
lost:

We had been totally unprepared for this attack, and after
the initial shock we wandered around in somewhat of a
daze to view the damage and to render what help we could
where it was needed. We had not had any first-aid training
or drills for such an emergency and we did not consider
the possibility of any delayed-action bombs going off.
A group of us came across an air raid shelter which had
received a direct hit. We passed by this but having done
so I felt quite unhappy and I therefore returned to the
shelter where another group of airmen were standing.
It was thought that perhaps someone was trapped within
the shelter, the entrance to which was completely blocked.

The airmen located the covered emergency hatch and pawed away the dirt and debris. Owing to Richard's lean physique, they decided to lower him through:

> This was my first real taste of war and I was feeling just a little apprehensive, but once inside the shelter I looked around and in the poor light I saw, there in front of me, the body of an airman whose head had been squashed flat. I was surprised at my reaction on seeing this gruesome sight, for I felt absolutely nothing.
>
> RAF Driffield had been put totally out of action and there was little we could do. The operation scheduled for that night was of course cancelled and the next morning the squadron was dispersed to Linton-on-Ouse, where we equipped with new aircraft. Briefing was set for 13.00 hours and at 14.00 hours we took off for Abingdon where we refuelled ready for ops that night.[1]

Richard's account is a detail from a nation under attack. In the summer of 1940 the cause of freedom and democracy in Europe was at stake: dictatorship and oppression had run amok. The British Isles now had the choice of accepting the whim of the dictator, Adolf Hitler, or stubbornly fighting on. The British Army was licking its wounds following the evacuation of France, the 'miracle of Dunkirk', and now the Nazi war machine was mustering its forces across the English Channel preparing for operation *Sealion*, the invasion of Britain.

## THE BOMBER BATTLE OF BRITAIN

When the Nazi war machine scythed into Holland in May 1940, the Luftwaffe proved the potential of the bomber through the concentrated bombing of a city target. Bomber Command pilot Wilf Burnett, flying with the RAF's 49 Squadron, was a witness to the devastation of one such Dutch city:

When the invasion of Holland took place I was recalled from leave and went on my first operation on 15 May 1940 against mainland Germany. Our target was Dortmund and on the way back we were routed via Rotterdam. The German Air Force had bombed Rotterdam the day before and it was still in flames. I realized then only too well that the phoney war was over and that this was for real. By that time the fire services had extinguished a number of fires, but they were still dotted around the whole city. This was the first time I'd ever seen devastation by fires on this scale. We went right over the southern outskirts of Rotterdam at about 6,000 or 7,000 feet, and you could actually smell the smoke from the fires burning on the ground. I was shocked seeing a city in flames like that. Devastation on a scale I had never experienced.[2]

British cities were yet to suffer under German bombardment, though such an ordeal was only a few months away. So by June 1940 Britain stood alone; the English Channel was all that stood between Nazism and freedom. Key to German invasion plans was the neutralization of the Royal Air Force. The Luftwaffe and Fighter Command would be battling for control of the skies over England, but the 'Battle of Britain' was not just about the 'fighter boys', Churchill's famed 'few'.

Although it is the Spitfires and Hurricanes and their pilots that are rightly remembered as the heroes of the conflict, RAF Bomber Command had a special and largely unheralded contribution to make to the historic Battle of Britain: the Battle of the Barges. It is a campaign that is much overlooked by history, yet it is special in that it played a crucial part in the defence of Britain; a defence from which the springboard to victory was established. Hitler was planning a seaborne invasion of England once air superiority had been seized from the RAF. To ferry an invasion force across the Channel, he needed boats, and to this end thousands of barges were being assembled at the Channel ports. If British bombers were able to keep sinking these boats and disrupt German preparations for an invasion, it would buy precious time to re-arm and prepare, and perhaps thwart the invasion altogether.

The defence of the islands hinged on the ability of the RAF to persuade the German Command that passage accross of the English Channel would be costly, too costly. The Germany Navy was not going to risk a crossing unless there was protection from the air against the RAF's intervention. Fighter Command was busy ensuring that the RAF did not lose air superiority and Bomber Command was going to prove that such superiority was essential.

The latter half of August 1940, and into September, was a time of intense fighting during the Battle of Britain. Attrition rates were stretching Fighter Command's resources to the limit. Indeed, the Germans believed that Fighter Command was close to defeat. With this in mind, the Luftwaffe went for the English capital on 7 September 1940. There was tangible fear that the Germans were going to attempt an invasion any day: a Channel crossing appeared imminent. The Allies were certainly aware of the German intention to launch a seaborne invasion. Through the summer months of 1940, Allied reconnaissance revealed the build-up of sea craft along the Channel coast – notably, the rows of invasion barges filling the Channel ports. This had to be opposed and the task was given to the Blenheim, Whitley and Wellington crews of Bomber Command. Jim Moore served with 18 Squadron, flying Bristol Blenheims, and recalls being made aware of the threat building just a few miles across the English Channel, and his squadron's state of readiness:

The Germans started moving hundreds of barges along
the canals of Western Europe towards the North Sea and
Channel ports. These enormous barges were essential to the
invasion force, which they intended to land on the shores
of our embattled island. On the squadron we were briefed
as to the type of attack we would be required to make on
German naval vessels and troop-carrying aircraft . . .
As soon as we landed after a raid, an aircraft was immediately

refuelled and bombed up, some of the groundcrew being at the dispersal points with the aircraft 24 hours a day. Further, there were always a number of aircrew on standby.[3]

Wilf Burnett also became aware of the threat and noted the sense of foreboding, and yet determination, in his fellow airmen:

> The station commander gathered all officers together
> one morning and told us that it appeared invasion was
> imminent and that we should be prepared for it.
> I remember the silence that followed. We left the room
> and I don't think anyone spoke, but we were all the more
> determined to make certain that we did everything possible
> to deter the Germans from launching their invasion.

Wilf goes on to briefly outline the type of flying required on the anti-invasion raids:

> At the time we were bombing the invasion barges in the
> Channel ports, undertaking operations almost every other
> night. I remember one operation in particular against the
> invasion barges. We had part moonlight, which was very
> helpful because navigation in those days depended entirely
> on visual identification. We flew to the north of our target so
> that we could get a better outline of the coast. We followed
> the coast down towards our target, getting down to about
> 4,000 feet so that we could get a better view of what was below,
> and to increase the accuracy of the bombing. At that height
> light anti-aircraft fire was pretty heavy and fairly accurate,
> so we didn't hang around after dropping our bombs.

Ernest Chuter served as a pilot with 75 Squadron, flying Wellington bombers. His first operations took him to Channel ports to counter the barge build-up. Ernest also describes the nature of the anti-invasion operations, which he contrasts with the nature of RAF Bomber Command operations later in the war:

> We went to Le Havre and it was fairly effective as far as I could tell. These were nice short trips: you were there and back in 4 to 5 hours. In those days it was all very individual, not like it was later in the war. You took off at intervals and everybody was on their own, did their own thing. Having been briefed, you knew your target and you were given a take-off time, but in effect our squadron would take off in intervals of 3 or 4 minutes. You decided on your own route, your own method of attack and decided on your own return route. It was all delightfully sort of unorganised. You entirely did your own thing and picked up experience as you went. No organization as they had with the mass raids later on. We just used to drift over and bomb.[4]

Mike Henry flew Blenheims with 110 Squadron and recounts his experiences early in his operational career, opposing the German barge build-up during those desperate days of survival. He also witnessed from the air the suffering the Luftwaffe was inflicting upon London:

> Our fourth trip took place on the night of 7/8 September. We had been briefed to attack the docks at Dunkirk. 'Recce' aircraft had brought back photographic evidence of a build-up of invasion barges there and at all Channel ports . . . On that night as we flew south over the North Sea, there was an ominous glow in the western horizon.
>
> This time it wasn't the moon, but came from the direction of London, 100 miles to the west. A Londoner myself, I became anxious for the safety of my parents, relatives and friends, but the full realization of what happened was not felt until the following morning when the BBC announced that the onslaught against the capital had started . . . When I heard the news, any feelings of guilt I harboured about dropping bombs on others

were swiftly replaced by a grim determination to fight back, and the ensuing attacks on invasion barges were carried out with an added sense of purpose by all, wherever they lived.

My fifth trip, on 9 September, was to Boulogne . . . This was followed by attacks with my own crew, on Calais (twice), Dunkirk and Boulogne, on 11, 14, 16 and 18 September respectively.

The Channel ports in late 1940 were amongst the most heavily defended targets I can remember. Hitler's intention of preserving his invasion fleet was made clear as his minions threw up everything but the kitchen sink. What made matters worse for us was the altitude at which we had been briefed to attack: between 6,000 and 10,000 feet. At that height light flak was at its deadliest. It came up like an inverted monsoon of vivid colour: from all directions it poured to culminate at the apex of a cone of searchlights. They were at the time some of the most terrifying experiences of my life. 'How any aircraft can survive in that lot,' I thought as we made our bombing run, 'is a miracle.' But as we found out, the age of miracles was not past and we came through unscathed. Many, of course, didn't, and were seen to plummet, flaming pyres, earthwards. Those targets made our first two sorties look like a poor man's Guy Fawkes night in heavy rain.[5]

As Mike mentions above, there were losses on those raids, but during the summer months, when Bomber Command was fighting at night, the loss rate was actually quite small and manageable; although that can only be accepted in hindsight when compared to the losses experienced later in the war. Nevertheless, operating at this time was still a dangerous business: on the night of 8/9 September 1940, in attacks on Channel ports, eight Bomber Command aircraft failed to return and twenty-six airmen lost their lives. The bomber airmen were certainly in harm's way in defence of Britain. On the night of 15/16 September, one 18-year-old airman went beyond the call of duty on a raid against invasion barges. Below is the extract from *The London Gazette* of 1 October 1940 relating the experience of John Hannah of 83 Squadron:

On the night of 15 September 1940, Sergeant Hannah was
the wireless operator/air gunner in an aircraft engaged in a
successful attack on an enemy barge concentration at Antwerp.
It was then subjected to intense anti-aircraft fire and received
a direct hit from a projectile of an explosive and incendiary
nature, which apparently burst inside the bomb compartment.

A fire started, which quickly enveloped the wireless
operator's and rear gunner's cockpits, and as both the port
and starboard petrol tanks had been pierced, there was grave
risk of the fire spreading. Sergeant Hannah forced his way
through to obtain two extinguishers and discovered that
the rear gunner had had to leave the aircraft. He could have
acted likewise, through the bottom escape hatch or forward
through the navigator's hatch, but remained and fought
the fire for 10 minutes with the extinguishers, beating
the flames with his log book when these were empty.

During this time thousands of rounds of ammunition
exploded in all directions and he was almost blinded by the
intense heat and fumes, but had the presence of mind to obtain
relief by turning on his oxygen supply. Air admitted through the
large holes caused by the projectile made the bomb compartment
an inferno and all the aluminium sheet metal on the floor of this
airman's cockpit was melted away, leaving only the cross bearers.

Working under these conditions, which caused burns to his
face and eyes, Sergeant Hannah succeeded in extinguishing the
fire. He then crawled forward, ascertained that the navigator had
left the aircraft, and passed the latter's log and maps to the pilot.
This airman displayed courage, coolness and devotion to duty of
the highest order and by his action in remaining and successfully
extinguishing the fire under conditions of the greatest danger
and difficulty, enabled the pilot to bring the aircraft to its base.

For his unselfish bravery that night, John Hannah received his
country's highest award for gallantry, the Victoria Cross.

## DAY VERSUS NIGHT

The operations related so far were all carried out at night. There was a simple reason for this: to restrict the loss rates. To oppose a German invasion, the British still had an undefeated and formidable presence at sea; and a depleted yet potent defensive force in the air: Fighter Command. In addition, the Royal Air Force's bomber force, Bomber Command, was poised for offensive and defensive action. But as history would show, its capabilities were severely restricted when exposed to the operational rigours of warfare; particularly in daylight. Through the Battle of France and the Battle of Britain, Bomber Command did its utmost to fight back: crews regularly went into a daylight battle where the odds were stacked against them. Many a Bomber Command aircraft fell at the hands of the Luftwaffe on day operations. Ken Dobbs's story provides a case in point. Ken served as a pilot with 114 Squadron, and, as many young men did when away from home, he often wrote to his mother. In a letter of 18 August 1940, amidst the news of family members, there are signs that Ken was feeling the strain of life on an operational bomber squadron:

Horsham St Faith, Norwich, Norfolk

Dear Mum,

Thanks very much for your letter and I have only just replied because I have only just received it owing to being away for a few days. I can't tell you about it in a letter but I have been having some hectic times. Thanks for the photograph of Marion – it is very pretty isn't it? If you don't make her have pigtails and boots she'll be a good-looking girl when she grows up. I'm glad you managed to get a bit of a rest during Dad's holiday and I hope he is getting better. Thank Phil for his letter and I am sorry I have not sent Brian anything yet but as I said before I don't know whether I have been standing on my head or my feet for the last few days. I have been meaning to send you some money for some while but I can't get out to catch the Post

Office open to register a letter. It shuts at 6.30 pm here but I'll send some as soon as I can get to the P/O and include some for Brian. We are not at Horsham now, we are living in a large mansion in the country that used to belong to Anne Boleyn and her ghost still haunts it, but the place is secret and our letters must still be addressed to Horsham and they are brought here daily by car. We all wish we could get some leave or we shall crack up under the strain – seeing your friends disappear one by one each day. Well bye bye for now. I will keep worrying for leave until I get it and I'll desert if I don't. Love, Ken.[6]

This would be the last Ken's mother heard from him. The next day he was posted missing, failing to return from an operation to Bremen. Ken's fate remained a mystery, and on 25 March 1941 his family received a letter from the Air Ministry stating that they had reached the 'conclusion that he lost his life'.

In time, eyewitnesses to the crash of Ken's Blenheim came to tell of the last moments of his life. A Dutchman by the name of Jan de Wolff was working in a barn on 19 August 1940:

Then I heard a number of shots, machine guns stuttering, up in the sky. I looked around the corner of the barn and I saw a burning plane coming at me, very fast. The German Messerschmitt which had shot it down was gone. A moment later there was someone hanging up, in the air under his parachute. It was an awful scene and I thought that it would come down exactly on the farm. Then it made more or less a half turn, and it landed smack in the orchard. It was burning.

A Mrs Van Kempen, née Van Splunter, had also watched the Blenheim crash:

A short time later Germans arrived, including the pilot who had shot it down. The doorbell rang . . . it was the butcher, and all of a sudden this silly little man walked up with a few others. 'I did that,' he said. I thought, 'Not much to boast about, killing two youngsters and then boasting about it, saying, "It was I who did it."' It was awful. I could have thumped him. Then came some more officers and they were very kind. They were decent people and I said to them, for I may have said too much sometimes, I thought it was a horrible thing. One patted my shoulder and said, 'This is only the beginning.'

It was terrible, seeing such a thing, and you never get it out of your mind, not as long as you live.

A few years after the war, in May 1948, the Air Ministry could confirm Ken's fate:

The Research Office located your son's grave, which is situated in a meadow at the scene of the crash, at Midden Beemster, 2 miles west of Purmerend, Holland. An attempt was then made to recover the remains for transfer to a British Military Cemetery where the grave could be cared for, for all time, but unfortunately this was unsuccessful, as the grave had been constructed over the wreckage of the aircraft beneath which the remains of your son and his companion lay. The grave has been well cared for and is surmounted by a cross, but in addition to this commemoration your son's name will be recorded on one of the general memorials to the missing.

Ken's story is one of many recounting the fate of Bomber Command airmen lost on operations in 1940. Ken's Blenheim was one of the 66 aircraft that Bomber Command lost on 1,885 daylight sorties in the period from 26 June to 12/13 October 1940; a loss rate of 3.5 per cent. This can be compared to a night-time loss rate of 2.0 per cent; 180 losses from 8,804 sorties.[7] These statistics clearly demonstrate that the early months of the war had highlighted weaknesses in Allied air policy. In particular, any plans the RAF had for daylight bombing raids were exposed as flawed; losses to German fighter opposition were too high and could not be sustained. The darkness of night became Bomber Command's protector for much of the war, but it also limited operational efficiency.

UNRELENTING PRESSURE

As September 1940 progressed, whilst Bomber Command fought the Battle of the Barges, the Luftwaffe kept up the pressure on Fighter Command and inflicted further misery upon Londoners, the details of which were regularly fed through to the men of Bomber Command, whether through the press or on the radio, or from information supplied by friends and family. In October, Douglas Mourton would begin operational flying with 102 Squadron. Just prior to this he received letters from his family telling of the situation in London. On 17 September, Douglas's mother wrote:

> Things are very uncomfortable here at present, but we are getting used to it, but they don't give us 5 minutes' peace. Beat's [Douglas's aunt's] house was bombed and they have come to live with us. There is 14 of us sleeping in the cellar, including the cat. We haven't had any gas since last Sunday. Poor old Eric [Douglas's brother] has to run home quick from work every evening about seven o'clock and then we are in the cellar until breakfast time.[8]

On 24 September, Douglas's father wrote:

> I am sorry to tell you your car has been severely damaged by incendiary bombs although it was in Jager's garage. I cannot get any satisfaction from the insurance company as they have been bombed out.

How were Londoners to deal with such conditions? Morale is, of course, an all important factor in war: maintaining the hopes of the besieged populace. Douglas Mourton makes his feelings clear about the importance of the RAF, in this respect, at this stage of the war:

> The factor that turned morale upward was the performance of the RAF. Our fighters had begun to get the upper hand in the sky. Bomber Command was bombing Germany almost nightly, which gave great consolation to the victims of the Luftwaffe.

British Prime Minister Winston Churchill had also tried to keep spirits up through his rhetoric:

> This is the time for everyone to stand together and hold firm, as they are doing . . . All the world that is still free marvels at the composure and fortitude with which the citizens of London are facing and surmounting the great ordeal to which they are subjected, the end of which, or the severity of which, cannot yet be foreseen. It is a message of good cheer to our fighting forces, on the seas, in the air and in our waiting armies, in all their posts and stations, that we send them from this capital city. They know that they have behind them a people who will not flinch or weary of the struggle, hard and protracted though it will be, but that we shall rather draw from the heart of suffering the means of inspiration and survival, and of a victory won not only for ourselves, but for all – a victory won not only for our own times, but for the long and better days that are to come.[9]

Words spoken to raise morale, for sure, but Churchill was clearly stating what was at stake. The newspapers also brought to public attention some of the measures in place to counter a German invasion. Headlines in the *Daily Express* of 12 September cried out, 'Terrific London Barrage Meets Greatest Raid, while Navy and RAF pound Nazi invasion fleet.'

RAF Blast Docks: Earlier it was announced by the Air
Ministry that for hours, up to dawn yesterday, RAF
bombers unloaded high explosive and fire bombs on
Hitler's invasion harbours, causing heavy damage.

A large part of the dock area round the Carnot Basin at
Calais Harbour was left in flames. One fire alone blazed along
200 yards of the waterfront. Bombs were dropped clean on to
barges tightly packed along the whole east side of the basin,
and the explosions threw debris high into the air. Barges in
another basin were hit, and then a large merchant ship suddenly
burst into flames. For 3 hours the pounding of the dock
area went on. A railway was hit and fires were started round
lock gates. Our pilots dived low through thick cloud to pick
out their targets, braving fierce shelling from the ground.

Six E-boats, fast motor torpedo boats, at Dieppe were bombed,
despite heavy fire from the ground and a patrol of Messerschmitt
fighters. After the explosions two of the E-boats had disappeared.

Ostend harbour was continually bombed for 8 hours.
Heavy loads of high explosive straddled barges in the
port and direct hits were made on a number of ships.

German ships in Boulogne harbour were attacked and other
bomber squadrons unloaded on to the docks at Flushing.

Enemy fighters tried to find the raiders but the RAF pilots
gave them the slip in the clouds. From all these raids, and
an attack on Berlin . . . four of our planes did not return.[10]

The press and the country's leaders certainly fought the war of words
with all their strength. But those in the know were fully aware of how
close they were to defeat. With the nation's survival on the line, the
fighter arm of the RAF was stretched to its limit. Similarly, the Bomber
Command airmen fought to their limits, sometimes conducting
more than one sortie per night. George Parr flew as a navigator/
observer on Blenheims with 18 Squadron, and recalled the night of
17/18 September 1940:

We bombed Dunkirk. All the Channel ports were full of barges in preparation for the invasion. At that stage Hitler was quite keen on it. His Navy wasn't. On this occasion we went over and I put my bombs across a quay, across the barges, and set alight a large hangar; a great fire started. When we got back to base it so happened that there were a few spare aircraft; and the first ones back were given the chance to pick up one of them. So we went out again the same night to the same target. When I got into the Thames Estuary I could see this fire burning in Dunkirk; the one we had started on the previous visit. So we bombed it again. That was fairly satisfactory.[11]

George's account is full of optimism, with respect to the damage he and his colleagues were causing, but there would be no let-up. Throughout the last few weeks of September and into October, Bomber Command kept up its targeting of the Channel ports. Although the airmen did not know it at the time, their efforts had paid off. On 17 September, the German Naval Staff made note that, 'The RAF are still by no means defeated: on the contrary they are showing increasing activity in their attacks in the Channel ports and in their mounting interference with the assembly movements.' Following the raids of 17/18 September they took toll of 'very considerable losses':

At Dunkirk 84 barges were sunk or damaged, and from Cherbourg to Den Helder the Navy reported, among other depressing items, a 500-ton ammunition store blown up, a rations depot burned out, various steamers and torpedo boats sunk and many casualties to personnel suffered. This severe bombing plus bombardment from heavy guns across the Channel made it necessary, the Navy staff reported, to disperse the naval and transport vessels already concentrated on the Channel and to stop further movement of shipping to the invasion ports.[12]

A few days later and the German Naval High Command became aware that 21 transports and 214 barges had been lost to enemy action; 12 per cent of the invasion fleet. Such an attrition rate was becoming unacceptable, and Hitler ultimately resigned himself to cancelling any further build-up of the barges and dispersing those that had not already been sent to the bottom of the sea by the RAF.

However, the German High Command was not prepared to make their adversary aware of the change in plan, and Bomber Command maintained the anti-invasion bombing, which met with further success, but also claimed the lives of more crew through enemy action and accidents. Mike Henry of 110 Squadron relates one such incident, which further highlights the perils of operational flying:

I crewed up with Flight Lieutenant Lyon . . . our first op together began at midnight on 7 October 1940. The target was Boulogne. It was a trip which didn't differ much from previous ones until we got back to base. It had been my tenth sortie and I was still in one piece. In the usual way we had identified ourselves and had been given a 'green' to land. There was some ground haze but nothing to worry unduly about. We made a long, low motored approach, the pilot lining up the aircraft with the row of gooseneck flares. When about a mile from the airfield boundary, he switched on the landing lamp (set in the port wing leading edge). Always keen to watch the approach, I noticed that the angle of glide indicators were showing red, we were coming in too low. I looked down and saw the dim outline of trees whipping by beneath the wing. They looked too damn close for comfort and a feeling of impending disaster began to creep through my bones. It was uncanny how one sensed real danger. However, we managed to reach the 'fence' without hitting anything, but by the time the aircraft had over flown the approach it was off course and we were no longer in line with the flare path.

A burst of power indicated that the pilot had decided to go around. Phew! I had, by then, managed to get all my fingers and toes crossed. I prayed that he wouldn't pull the flaps up too soon since we had lost several crews and aircraft that way. Not until reaching about 500 feet should the flaps be lifted as the Blenheim (and most other aircraft too) had the tendency, when doing so, to sink rapidly.

Meanwhile, we were racing low over the airfield, the landing lamp carving a path of light across the grass. We were so low that I could have almost picked up a flare as we crossed the 'path'; there was still no indication of the nose being pulled up to gain height. I repeated my prayer about the flaps in 48-point bold italics. It was still dark and I had no idea in which direction we were heading. Would we hit the hangar or the trees at the far side of the field? At the height he was maintaining it could be either and soon. Still gaping forward, I suddenly saw and felt the port wing drop. This was it. A sudden blinding flash, a few stars, then stillness.

I found myself sitting in the fuselage with my feet in the turret cupola, which was on the ground. It had become lighter, the reason becoming horrifyingly apparent when looking round I saw flames licking their way down the fuselage. Through the turret Perspex I saw bits and pieces burning on the ground outside my 'prison'; for I was trapped. The ladder was wedged across my back, barring the exit through the camera hatch. There was no way aft. My immediate thought was, 'The only chance I've got is for somebody to start cutting from the outside, but quick.'

Looking round to my left I noticed a jagged hole in the fuselage side. It was big enough for my head to go through. Through it went and with strength lent by desperation, I braced my feet on the facing wall and pushed. A gallon of Guinness wouldn't have bettered my efforts. My shoulders were fortunately protected by a thick leather Irvin jacket

and parachute harness webbing. The metal skin gave and
I fell out into the night air then lit by a raging fire. I saw
two men running towards me: the duty medical officer and
one of the ambulance crew (they and the fire crew were on
the spot very smartly and went about their work without
thought for their personal safety). They grabbed me by the
arms and hurried me to the gaping doors of an ambulance.
Any moment the fuel tanks would explode and throw their
blazing contents in all directions, as would the oxygen bottles
and my ammunition. Before getting into the 'blood wagon'
I noticed the pilot staggering from one side of the blazing
wreckage and the navigator from the other side. Both had
faces covered in blood but they were alive and on their feet.

THE DEFENSIVE VICTORY

Historians now recognize that the last of the Channel port bombing
raids, with respect to countering the imminent invasion threat, took
place on the night of 12/13 October 1940. The fighter battle lasted
a few more weeks, although not at the intensity of the previous
two months. The Battle of Britain is considered to have officially
ended on 31 October 1940. The daylight air battle over England had
clearly diminished and operation *Sealion* was on 'hold'. However, this
can be somewhat misleading. Some commentators on the period
consider that it did in fact continue through to May 1941, with the
Luftwaffe's night Blitz of British cities. Throughout this period,
Bomber Command looked to build strength, whilst maintaining some
direct offensive action against Germany. In addition, further attacks
were made on the Channel ports, just in case Hitler once more sought
to muster his seaborne invasion force.

Rod Rodley flew with 97 Squadron at Coningsby in Lincolnshire
and that winter was involved in further persuading the Fuehrer
that invasion would be a costly exercise. The German invasion had
effectively been abandoned by this stage, but his experiences provide a
vivid example of the navigational difficulties of operating at night:

Having joined . . . we had to wait a while until a few Avro Manchesters were delivered to us. We did some training flights and then came the night of our first operation . . . My first raid was to bomb the docks at Calais . . . It was an easy navigational trip because it was only 20 miles across the Channel. Leaving from Beachy Head I steered a course for about 20 minutes and sure enough up came the coast.

It was a moonlit night; we could even see the fingers of the docks. I said, 'This is too good a chance to miss. Let's get some of those barges. We'll drop just one bomb at a time.' The bomb aimer went down to his bomb sight and lined up some of the barges. We were bombing from about 15,000 feet, and with a bit of 'left, left, steady and right and steady', I felt a little leap of the aeroplane and number one bomb went. I proceeded inland and did what was called a procedure turn: 45 degrees to one side for about a minute and a half and then a turn back and you come over your old track. On the way out we did 'left, left, steady, steady, bomb gone', and that was two bombs. There were 13 to go.

I began to notice in the Perspex of the cockpit little flashes, like someone lighting a cigarette down behind me, and I asked the rear gunner, 'Can you tell me what that light is behind us?' He said, 'There's some flak behind us, captain, but it's well behind us.'

We did three or four more runs and all the time these flashes were getting brighter and brighter and I was beginning to hear a crump each time. I became suspicious and said, 'Jack, are you sure that flak is safe?'

He replied, 'Oh yes, skipper, it's a good 25 yards off yet!'

On that run I said, 'Drop the lot,' and off we went, back across the North Sea.

We were so inexperienced. I didn't know what I was doing. I was sent the next night to Calais again as a punishment for being so stupid. This time the weather wasn't so kind. From the English coast you could see underneath a layer of cloud the lights of Calais and the searchlights, but as you approached you came into the cloud and the target was hidden. I realized we weren't going to be able to bomb visually and unless you could see the actual target you had to take your bombs back to base, which was a dangerous thing. I said to the crew, 'We're not going to be able to drop these on the barges at Calais. Let's go home.'

I turned north, got the coffee thermos, and the smell of forbidden cigarettes began to waft up the fuselage from the back. I lost a bit of height and said to the navigator, 'What time do you think we'll reach the English coast?' With a tone of utter surprise, he said, 'Have you left the French coast then?' 'Yes,' I said, 'I told you we were giving it up.' 'How long ago was it?' he asked. I couldn't imagine – half an hour, quarter of an hour. I told him 20 minutes. 'Right,' he said, 'we should be coming up to the coast in about 5 minutes' time.'

I'd lost height from 15,000 feet down to about 8,000 feet by then and sure enough a coastline came up dark velvet against the silvery sea. I didn't recognize the huge river mouth, with large islands. Panic hit me then, because we simply didn't know where we were. It was certainly not England. I didn't realize that in losing height the scale of everything had gone up and that the mouth of the river I saw looked like the Emden or the Rhine. The navigator came up to look at the coastline with me and as we came in over it to my horror guns started firing at us and searchlights waved around in front of us.

I turned out to sea to give a bit more thought to this. I asked to have any maps passed up to me and I looked at the coastline from Scotland to the Bay of Biscay trying to find this river mouth. We used to have an emergency frequency on the radio which was called 'D for Darkie', which you could call for help. I pressed the button and called, 'Hello Darkie, this is Lifebuoy A for Apple calling, do you read?' A voice came back, 'Allo, Lifebuoy A for Apple, zis eez . . . vill you land pleeze?' This proved they were hostile down there – there was no question of an RAF character talking like that!

We were utterly lost and in German territory. The end came when my gunner called, 'Skipper! I think I can see a beacon.' There were networks of beacons flashing all over the country at night, and we had been given a code on a sheet to identify them. I set a course north from there and much to my pleasure our own home beacon came into view and we were able to land.

Now my wing commander was very unhappy about this whole procedure because he'd had to wait up for 6 hours, unable to go to bed because he had a missing aircraft. He tore me off a strip. I said, 'But sir, Darkie, I'm sure it was a teutonic accent.' 'Yes,' he said, 'there's a Polish squadron down there!' So that explained that.[13]

When Hitler turned his attentions east, to Russia, in the middle of 1941, Britain could finally breathe and take stock. Fighter Command had successfully defended the skies over England in the summer of 1940. Bomber Command airmen such as Richard Pinkham, Mike Henry, Ken Dobbs, Wilf Burnett, George Parr, John Hannah, Rod Rodley, Jim Moore and Ernest Chuter had persuaded the German Navy of the futility of a seaborne crossing without air superiority. The victory from the defensive struggle that was the Battle of Britain belongs as much to the Bomber Command crews as to anyone else.

# 2
# THOUSAND BOMBER RAID

*In May 1942, the Royal Air Force made a historic statement.
The extraordinary and special 'thousand bomber' raid to the
city of Cologne sent a tremor through the Nazi hierarchy. It was
a demonstration of the blunt destructive power of the bomber,
unprecedented in the history of international conflict.*

As the second anniversary of the outbreak of war approached, the war-winning bomber dream seemed to be just that – a dream. Since the Battle of Britain, the RAF had embarked upon an escalation of the bomber offensive against Germany, including a campaign to counter the growing U-boat threat in the Atlantic. But put quite simply, the aircraft, technology and experience of the aircrews fell short of requirements. A damning government report of August 1941 indicated that Bomber Command's offensive was falling short of expectation. The Butt report analysed just over 4,000 photographs taken by individual aircraft on raids in June and July of 1941. One of the main statistics proving Bomber Command's inefficiency was that only one in four of the respective crews that reported bombing a German target had been within 5 miles of the aiming point.

Following the revelations of the Butt report, a review of the future of Bomber Command was carried out, culminating in a new general policy adopted in February 1942. The key summation in this directive stated, '**It has been decided that the primary objective of your operations should now be focused on the morale of the enemy civil population and in particular of the industrial workers.**' In addition, a new commander took over the RAF bomber force: one of the most determined and controversial commanders of the entire war. Air Chief Marshal Sir Arthur Harris remained in command of the RAF's heavy bomber force through to the end of the war.

## SHOW OF STRENGTH

Shortly after his appointment, Harris felt that a point had to be made. The worth of continuing the bomber offensive was indeed still under serious scrutiny. Harris's statement would be to call upon all the resources in his command. The enormous destructive potential of the RAF's bomber force was to be tested, and hopefully proved, with over 1,000 aircraft to be sent to a German target. Harris's post-war memoir *Bomber Offensive* recalled his plans. He was going out on the proverbial limb, extending his resources to the limit:

> At that time, as it happened, I did have a force of well over 1,000 aircraft in my command; if the crews and aircraft at the OTUs [operational training units] and conversion units were added to the front-line squadrons we could easily raise our strength to that figure. They were half-trained crews, of course, but the OTUs had already undertaken the task of dropping propaganda leaflets over France, often on a large scale; it was useful training for them, it relieved the front-line squadron of this task, and they gained some knowledge of what it was like to be shot at by flak or even intercepted by nightfighters. If there were great risks involved in a high concentration of aircraft then these risks would be increased by sending out large numbers of new crews, but if, on the other hand, this high concentration was a definite protection against fighters and flak then I should not be calling on new crews to run so grave a risk as the front-line squadrons had habitually taken. The dangers were many and obvious. If anything went seriously wrong – and this was to be in many ways a wholly new type of operation – then I should be committing not only the whole of my front-line strength but absolutely all my reserves in a single battle.[1]

Harris trawled through the entire command to find the aircraft to support his historic venture. Hamish Mahaddie, one of the most well-known Bomber Command pilots of the war, with two tours of operations to his name, recalled:

This raid proved to everybody that wanted to have proof,
that the strategic concept was something that could be a very
very important aspect of our war effort. I was an instructor.
I had finished a tour of bombing and was instructing at
Kinloss. We stopped training, we had to produce every aircraft
and send them down to the bomber bases in the south.[2]

Alex Shaw had completed a tour with 99 Squadron and then took up
a role training fledgling crews:

To find 1,000 crews they had to rope in instructors. We had
an all instructor crew. We went up to Snaith, taking our
training aircraft. The unit there had modern, up-to-date
Wellingtons. After the raid was over our ground staff flight
sergeant, who went with us, told us that his opposite number
was laying bets that none of us would get back, because of our
clapped-out aircraft. In point of fact we all did and they lost
some of theirs. We wondered whether or not we were going
to meet any other aircraft because there were loads there.[3]

Bomber Command airman Ian Robertson recalled the use of some of
the command's most war-torn aircraft to make up numbers:

To muster 1,046 bombers, aircraft from training units had
to be used to supplement the operational squadron of the
RAF. These aircraft were mostly old Wellington bombers
relegated to training duties, obsolete for operational use. We
took off from Upper Heyford in Oxfordshire in one of these
Wellingtons with a full load of fuel and incendiaries.[4]

Peter Ward-Hunt had operational experience behind him, and
received the call to add one more operation to his tally:

I was temporarily in charge of a training flight at Scampton at the time, training crews to transfer from Manchesters to Lancasters. We got the call that a special raid was on, and that all crews were to be involved. Well I didn't get a Lancaster, I ended up with an old Manchester. Just as we were about to leave, the squadron commander came and joined us as his plane was u/s [unserviceable].[5]

Tom Tate was a wireless operator with 75 Squadron, and was initially asked to fly with an unfamiliar crew in a Handley Page Hampden:

The Hampdens were almost ancient Britons in the war. I said, 'Well I would prefer not to.' I couldn't refuse. The commanding officer took a sympathetic view and he said he had managed to get a replacement for that crew.[6]

Tom would still fly on the raid, with another crew. 'I remember that day because it was clear, and the sky was absolutely full of aircraft. It was fantastic.'

THE BRIEFING
Before the sky could fill with aircraft the crews had to prepare and be briefed on the plan for the raid. Victor Martin was with 1652 Conversion Unit when he received the call to take part in the Cologne raid. Prior to the briefing Victor, like thousands of other airmen all over England, checked his aircraft:

Raid details are not yet known but aircraft reliability must be checked and routine armament testing carried out, all essential for a successful operation. Flying across to the North Sea, aircraft checks are carried out and over the water the gunners can concentrate on the efficiency of the guns by firing into the sea. All is well and return to base for refuelling and 'bombing up' with up to 6 tons of high explosive or with a mixture of incendiaries.[7]

Gordon Mellor's first operational flight was to be the thousand bomber raid. He was allocated to an experienced pilot, who had already passed the 20-operation mark. Gordon recalls attending the main briefing for the raid:

We all sort of bundled into this large hall, rows and rows of chairs. There was a curtained off area and the CO [commanding officer] was there, the group captain, the gunnery leader, navigation leader and bomb leader. The CO largely took control. First of all they whipped the curtains aside and there was the big wall map, the whole of Europe. The target was pinned up with string leading to and from it. As a navigator I already knew (having attended a navigator briefing prior to the main one). There were some sharp hisses and 'Ooh look at that', sort of thing from those who didn't know.

Having the view of the map, everybody now knew it was Cologne. From the front one of them made the point this was a special raid, 'Everybody is taking part.' We knew that because we had aircrew come in from the operational training units with their aircraft; we had aircraft stacked around the aerodrome. We were told that we were putting up 1,000 aircraft in one raid, lasting an hour and a half. There was a great big cheer.[8] We quietened down and then got on with the business of the briefing and the various specialists went through their spiel.[9]

Tom Dailey was a wireless operator/air gunner with 158 Squadron:

A collective sigh of relief eddied through the flight briefing room of 158 Squadron in Driffield, Yorkshire on 30 May 1942, as the squadron leader identified our latest mission. 'Your target for tonight,' he announced, 'is Cologne.' The port city on the Rhine was in relatively easy reach, just 2 or 3 flying hours away and therefore less time for being shot down. A gasp followed his next utterance. 'It will be a big one. We intend to send over 1,000 bombers.' No air raid on this scale had ever been conceived before. Air Marshal Sir Arthur Harris, head of Bomber Command, was out to make an impression. Before we took off there was the usual banter, 'Can I have your bacon and eggs if you don't come back?'[10]

The plan for the raid entailed an opening attack by Vickers-Armstrong Wellingtons and Short Stirlings, over the course of 15 minutes, unloading a considerable number of incendiaries on the centre of the target, lighting the way for the crews in their wake. These 'Pathfinders' would be followed up by the rest of the force, with the four-engine Lancasters and Halifaxes unloading their explosives during the last 15 minutes of the 90-minute attack. As the operation order stated:

> The stage of the war has been reached when the morale of the German people is likely to be seriously affected by an unprecedented blow of great magnitude in the West at a time when they are experiencing difficulties on the Russian front. We were in a position to deliver this blow from the air . . . Apart from the effect on morale of such an attack, the unprecedented damage which will be caused is bound to have a considerable effect on the issue of the war.[11]

At the end of the briefings at the RAF Bomber Command stations, a message was read out from Sir Arthur Harris, a last rallying cry to his men:

> The force of which you form a part tonight is at least twice the size and has more than four times the carrying capacity of the largest air force ever before concentrated on one objective. You have an opportunity, therefore, to strike a blow at the enemy which will resound, not only throughout Germany, but throughout the world.
> In your hands lie the means of destroying a major

part of the resources by which the enemy's war effort is maintained. It depends, however, upon each individual crew whether full concentration is achieved.

Press home your attack to your precise objective with the utmost determination and resolution in the foreknowledge that, if you individually succeed, the most shattering and devastating blow will have been delivered against the very vitals of the enemy. Let him have it – right on the chin.

THE 'THOUSAND' GATHER

On the Bomber Command airfields, aircrews donned their flying gear, made final personal preparations, and were transported to their weapons. Thousands of airmen climbed into their bombers, made final checks and waited for the call to take to the air. Victor Martin recalled:

As time for take-off approaches we are ferried to the aircraft. Engines running and all checks carried out, we taxi to runway to await take-off signal, the green light flashes and with throttles opened to full power and boost the aircraft gather speed down the runway, a slight bounce and we are airborne. The lights of the flare path disappear below into the darkness and the raid begins as we trim for climb and set course.

Tom Dailey had been sitting patiently in his 158 Squadron Whitley:

A flash from an Aldis lamp, on the darkened runway, was the only signal for our five-man bomber to lumber into the air. The sound of a thousand engines would have been deafening as we passed over the east coast of England heading across the North Sea. But at 10,000 feet, it was bitterly cold. There was no formation flying at night. Each aircraft was alone. As wireless operator, I used Morse to obtain coded fixes, triangulated from ground control, for the pilot to set our course.

The atmosphere aboard was edgy. But no one was biting their nails. There was always fear of the unknown, but you didn't show it. Training bolstered your spirits and we had already been bloodied on previous sorties. Still miles from the target, the skipper called me up to the cockpit, 'Tom, come and have a look at this.' It was astounding. The night sky was a swirling fire of red, orange and yellow. Cologne was alight. We were in the second or third wave, and the bombers which had gone in ahead of us had dropped incendiaries. In our plane was a feeling of exultation. This was payback. We had suffered the Blitz for all those years and were full of venom and hate for all things German. I was 20 years old and twice, before I joined up, I was nearly killed by bombs falling on London.

But not all the crews that set out that night would reach their destination. Ian Robertson, despite using full throttle, had great difficulty achieving height:

By the Dutch coast we had only reached 9,000 feet. Shortly after crossing the coast, the starboard engine failed and as the aircraft could not maintain height on one engine, the bomb load was jettisoned. Even after this, the aircraft was losing height and some fuel was jettisoned. We hoped to be able to reach an emergency landing ground at Woodbridge, near Orfordness. On reaching the coast of England at Orfordness, at 800 feet, it was obvious that we could not make the airfield and it was decided that rather than crash-land on land we would try to land on the beach, as near to the sea as possible. In the dark at least the seashore could be seen. The landing was successfully achieved, no one was injured and there was no fire. We were rescued by coastguards from Orfordness Lighthouse, who had heard and seen us land.

Back to the raid, and those remaining continued on to the target. Vivid recollections of the raid became etched in the airmen's minds, in particular for those who approached the target after the incendiary bombing had opened the attack. Shortly after the operation, Flying Officer Friend made a recording of his experience:

> The dykes, the towns, and sometimes even the farmhouses of Holland: we could see them all clearly as we flew towards Cologne soon after midnight. The moon was to our starboard bow and straight ahead there was a rose-coloured glow in the sky. We thought it was something to do with a searchlight belt, which runs for about 200 miles along the Dutch/German frontier. As we went through this belt we saw by the light of blue searchlights some friendly aircraft going the same way as ourselves and a few coming back. But the glow was still ahead. It crossed my mind then that it might be Cologne, but we decided between us that it was too bright a light to be so far away. The navigator checked his course. It could only be Cologne.[12]

Victor Martin sat in the 'dim glow' of his cockpit:

> Silence reigns until the navigator's voice comes over the intercom with the words 'enemy coast ahead'. Shortly after crossing the coast we encounter the defensive line of searchlights and anti-aircraft guns set up to protect entry into Germany. The searchlights sweep the night sky and should an aircraft be caught, the master searchlight immediately focuses onto it, then all others follow suit. The guns begin what is called a box, they fire above, below ahead and astern and gradually reduce the box until the aircraft is hit or can take violent evasive moves to extricate itself.
> Silence once again as we enter enemy territory with its defences now on alert following earlier waves, broken only by the gunners as they quietly check with each other regarding

the sighting of a nightfighter; we do not attack to give away our position but observe in case of a sudden turn for hostile action. The first wave has now attacked and in the distance a red glow is already visible in the sky. Above the fleecy lining of the clouds hiding the enemy below all seems so peaceful; another aircraft appears ahead and travelling at the same speed we are motionless. Suddenly the heavy anti-aircraft guns open fire and the exploding shells shatter our world of peace. The aircraft ahead receives a direct hit and with a blue flash is gone. Taking the immediate evasive action of undulating and banks to port and starboard, we continue our course.

ABOVE THE CITY

As Flying Officer Friend's crew neared the target area, such was the size of the glow in front of them that they prepared to bomb somewhat prematurely:

It looked as though we would be on top of it in a minute or two and we opened our bomb doors. We flew on; the glow was as far away as ever, so we closed our bomb doors. The glare was still there like a huge cigarette-end in the German blackout. Then we flew into smoke; through it the Rhine appeared a dim silver ribbon below us. The smoke was drifting in the wind. We came in over the fires. Down in my bomb aimer's hatch I looked at the burning town below me. I remembered what had been said at the briefing, 'Don't drop your bombs on the buildings that are burning best. Go in and find another target for yourself.' Well at last I found one right in the most industrial part of the town. I let the bombs go. We had a heavy load, hundreds of incendiaries and big high explosive. The incendiaries going off were like sudden platinum-coloured flashes, which slowly turned to red. We saw there many flashes going from white to red and then our great bomb burst in the centre of them. As we crossed the town there were burning blocks to the right

of us and to the left the fires were immense. They were really
continuous. The flames were higher than I had ever seen before.
Buildings were skeletons in the midst of fires. Sometimes you
could see what appeared to be frameworks of white-hot joists.
The blast of the bombs was hurling walls themselves across
the flames. As we came away, we saw more and more of our
aircraft below us silhouetted against the flames. I identified
Wellingtons, Halifaxes, Manchesters and other Lancasters. Above
us there were still more bombers lit by the light of the moon.
They were doing exactly as we did; going according to plan and
coming out according to plan and making their way home.

Victor Martin also witnessed the conflagration below, before dropping
his explosives and turning back towards England:

Closing in on the target, the intensity of the fire became
more apparent: not the usual cluster of separate burnings, it
appeared that the complete area below was ablaze in one large
fire. A feeling of sorrow came, but with a ferocious burst of
anti-aircraft fire bouncing the aircraft about with explosions,
concentration on the purpose of the mission became uppermost.
With the most dangerous part now commencing, a level and
steady course had to be maintained for accurate aiming, the
navigator lying down over the bomb sight giving instructions
for lining up the target – 'left, left, steady, right, steady, bombs
away'. As all bombs are released at once, the aircraft, relieved of
its heavy load, rose like a lift and with so many bombers above
this could cause a serious problem unless quickly controlled.
    Course was set for home and the running of the gauntlet of
ack-ack, searchlights and nightfighters once again. Dropping
down to an altitude below the range of the heavy guns and
above light fire, we were suddenly in a ring of searchlights
giving a most eerie feeling, a ghostly light filling the darkness
of the cockpit. The tracer shells from the guns seem to be still

as you look at them, coming up and then flashing past the windscreen. A bank to starboard gave the gunners a better view to return fire, the aircraft fills with the sinister sound of machine guns firing at a rate of several thousand rounds a minute. Searchlights are hit and the tracer shells coming up, like water from a hose pipe moving around to cover an area, also cease.

Over the target, Tom Dailey recalled the buffeting of flak as his crew prepared to release their bomb load:

As we went in on our bombing run we had to observe W/T [wireless telegraphy] silence. Flak was bursting around us. Our bomb aimer, lying prone above the open hatch, was guiding the pilot. Left was always repeated twice, to avoid confusion. So it was: 'left, left, right a bit'. Then the words we all waited for: 'bombs gone!' Two tons of high explosives, and incendiaries in canisters, had been delivered to their destination.

We felt the aircraft lift, and then tilt as the pilot put on full throttle and banked to the left, heading for the North Sea and home.

With bombs gone, dropped on the target, a Bomber Command airman's main duty had been fulfilled. Now it was a matter of surviving to fight another day: getting home, increasing the return on the RAF training investment, and bringing back a valuable piece of equipment. With returning crews came stories of the night's activities: the sight of the burning city, the flak, the fighters, seeing other aircraft exploding and falling in flames. Victor Martin was one man who could relate such tales:

Dawn broke as we crossed the coast and the number of aircraft in the sky was awe inspiring. Back at base it was discovered the navigator had cuts on each side of his neck, probably caused by shrapnel during the steady bombing run in. If so, a slight waver could have proved fatal. The raid was considered an outstanding success.

Tom Dailey was also able to bring his story home:

> Apart from a few small holes in the fuselage we were unscathed. But dirty, dog-tired and sweaty. Beneath our sheepskin flying jackets we all wore three or four woollen vests to keep out the cold.
> At breakfast we had our bacon and eggs. But there were gaps around the Mess tables. Nobody mentioned them.

Geoffrey Hall, who had been learning his trade at an operational training unit, had taken a Wellington to Cologne with his fellow crew trainees. In addition, 'My son, Peter, who was now over a year old, also accompanied me on every flight via a photo that I carried inside my flight jacket.' For Geoffrey the experience over Cologne remains vivid:

> The weather that night was fine and clear. The moon was full, and over Germany the river Rhine showed up like an illuminated winding ribbon. I will always remember experiencing the spectacular view of aircraft exploding and the crowded sky of aeroplanes, shell bursts, and searchlights around Cologne as the great fires burned below. We did nearly collide with another aircraft over the target as we were running in to release our bomb load. That is a night I shall never forget and it brings tears to my eyes even now when I talk to other people about it. This was the start of a new phase in the air war and all units involved received many plaudits for this raid. [13]

One of the most conspicuously heroic actions of the raid resulted in a Victoria Cross for Flying Officer Leslie Thomas Manser, of 50 Squadron, who gave all to fulfil his commander's request to give it to the enemy, 'right on the chin'.

Flying Officer Manser was captain and first pilot of a Manchester aircraft which took part in the mass raid on Cologne on the night of 30 May 1942. As the aircraft was approaching its objective, it was caught by searchlights and subjected to intense and accurate anti-aircraft fire. Flying Officer Manser held on his dangerous course and bombed the target successfully from a height of 7,000 feet.

Then he set course for base. The Manchester had been damaged and was still under heavy fire. Flying Officer Manser took violent evasive action, turning and descending to under 1,000 feet. It was to no avail. The searchlights and flak followed him until the outskirts of the city were passed. The aircraft was hit repeatedly and the rear gunner was wounded. The front cabin filled with smoke; the port engine was overheating badly.

Pilot and crew could all have escaped safely by parachute. Nevertheless, Flying Officer Manser, disregarding the obvious hazards, persisted in his attempt to save aircraft and crew from falling into enemy hands. He took the aircraft up to 2,000 feet. Then the port engine burst into flames. It was 10 minutes before the fire was mastered, but then the engine went out of action for good, part of one wing was burnt, and the air speed of the aircraft became dangerously low.

Despite all the efforts of pilot and crew, the Manchester began to lose height. At this critical moment, Flying Officer Manser once more disdained the alternative of parachuting to safety with his crew. Instead, with grim determination, he set a new course for the nearest base, accepting for himself the prospect of almost certain death in a firm resolve to carry on to the end.

Soon the aircraft became extremely difficult to handle, and when a crash was inevitable, Flying Officer Manser ordered the crew to bale out. A sergeant handed him a parachute but he waved it away, telling the non-commissioned officer to jump at once as he could only hold the aircraft steady for a few seconds more. While the crew were descending to safety they saw the aircraft, still carrying their gallant captain, plunge to earth and burst into flames.

In pressing home his attack in the face of strong opposition; in striving, against heavy odds, to bring back his aircraft and crew; and, finally, when in extreme peril, in thinking only of the safety of his comrades, Flying Officer Manser displayed determination and valour of the highest order.[14]

EVIDENCE IN CAMERA

The eyewitness accounts above are, of course, from those who returned from the raid. In total, Bomber Command lost 41 aircraft and crews, a record high figure for the war to date. But was it all worth it? What were the results of this historic effort? Leonard Pearman was a de Havilland Mosquito pilot with 105 Squadron. Leonard and his squadron colleagues were given the task of photographing Cologne in the aftermath of the raid. The RAF hierarchy was desperate to know the extent of the damage, and to have something tangible to publicize and promote the cause:

We began to send our Mosquitoes; about eight o'clock the first one went, and didn't come back. The second one went about ten o'clock, came back and told us the smoke was up to 20,000 feet and that it was quite impossible to get any kind of evidence of what had been done. The fires were still raging. We let it go for about 2 hours and then sent another Mosquito, which didn't come back. A squadron leader went at ground level all the way to Cologne and back, and he said that there was very little he could photograph.

At four o'clock in the afternoon I went. It was a beautiful summer day and we carried four 500-pound bombs and full camera equipment. We crossed over the Dutch coast and stayed on course fairly consistently at 23,000 feet; no sign of enemy fighters. We saw a few parachutes descending just after we crossed the coast, but couldn't see any fighters and we had a fairly peaceful entrance into Germany. We flew over the Rhine about 40 miles south of Cologne and could see on our port side the smoke rising from the town. We saw a vapour trail in the distance, north of Cologne; I think that may have been another Mosquito from 105 Squadron. We continued over the Rhine, and when we were about 20 miles east of the river, we turned onto 270 degrees and came over the middle of the town, with bomb doors open and the cameras working. We were unopposed.

(Leonard Pearman's account comes from a sound recording. At this point in the interview Leonard pauses, becomes somewhat emotional, and expresses how he now feels extremely uncomfortable about the bombing of the city. The interviewer asks him, 'Did you think that at the time?' Leonard replies, 'Yes, I often did. Anyway.')

We dropped the bomb load right across the centre of the town. Up to that time we had no opposition whatsoever. As soon as the bombs began to explode – my navigator was lying in the nose watching the effect – the flak came up. They seemed to have difficulty in finding our height and speed. There was a heavy flak cloud on the starboard quarter, nowhere near us, and I put the nose down slightly to increase our speed. I turned about 20 degrees south to try and spoil the prediction of the anti-aircraft.

After we had gone about another 10 to 20 seconds another cloud of flak appeared, some of it fairly close now. Suddenly the starboard engine was taken out; in fact it began to drop off, and the port wing was very badly hit. A huge gaping hole appeared in that wing and we were set on fire. I told my navigator to bale out. The hatch is just in the middle of the cockpit, in front of his feet. He jettisoned the hatch, clipped his parachute on and began to put his legs through the hatch.

We had not practised baling out before. We thought ourselves clever and we didn't have to practise. Richard [the navigator] put his legs out and wedged himself in the hatch; his legs were taken underneath the fuselage with the slipstream. He was immovable. He shouted, 'I can't get out, I can't move!' By this time it was getting rather urgent to get out. It was getting very hot. I caught hold of the harness on his neck and pulled with all my might. With his exertions as well we managed to get him out again. He turned round, facing aft, hung on to the bottom of the aircraft and then disappeared. I had to do the same. I was sitting on my parachute so I was able to get out rather more easily.

What beautiful peace. It was so quiet. We had travelled a considerable distance from Cologne by then, mostly losing height. Richard baled out at about 12,000 feet and I was able to get out at about 6,000 feet. I waited to reach the ground and all was well, it seemed. Then an aircraft began to come towards me. I thought it was a German who was going to finish me off. In fact it was the aircraft that I had just left, which was pouring smoke, well alight. It missed me by about 100 yards, went down and blew itself up in a farmhouse.

I continued my descent and landed in a ploughed field, where about 15 to 20 Hitler Jugend were waiting for me; they had been watching my descent. They formed a rough circle and I landed in it without any harm to myself. I stood up and began to think that after all it wasn't so bad. It was a beautiful day and these delightful young men were being polite to me, made no attempt to molest me, folding my parachute and firmly refusing to allow me to move from that spot:

After a few minutes an elderly gentleman, who appeared to be a policeman, arrived on to the scene, went up to Leonard and forcefully pushed a revolver in his ribs.

He was terrified, white with fear, more frightened than I was. I was relieved to be alive. He shouted something to me in German, which I didn't understand. One of the boys said in perfect English, 'He means hands up.' I raised my hands and the policeman looked very much relieved. He searched me thoroughly to see if I had any weapons, and then relaxed. I gave him a cigarette and we became rather friendlier.[15]

Eventually three German officers came and took Leonard away and as he was passing out of the field a farm labourer threw a bike at him.

Despite 105 Squadron's initial problems, photographs of Cologne were eventually taken, showing widespread destruction. Final assessments of the raid results were most promising for Bomber Command. Harris had certainly made his statement of intent both to the doubters at home and, with equal importance, to his enemy across the sea. The Reich's Minister of Armaments, Albert Speer, recorded the disbelief in the results of the raid at the highest levels of the Nazi hierarchy:

We were given a foretaste of our coming woes . . .
By chance [Erhard] Milch [overseeing the development of the German Air Force] and I were summoned to see [Hermann] Goering [commander-in-chief of the German Air Force] on the morning after the raid . . . We found him in a bad humour, still not believing the reports of the Cologne bombing. 'Impossible, that many bombs cannot be dropped in a single night,' he snarled at his adjutant. 'Connect me with the Gauleiter of Cologne.'
There followed, in our presence, a preposterous telephone conversation. 'The report from your police commissioner is a stinking lie!' Apparently the Gauleiter begged to differ. 'I tell you as Reich Marshal that the figures cited are simply too high. How can you dare report such fantasies to the Fuehrer?' The Gauleiter at the other end of the line was evidently insisting on his figures. 'How are you going to count the fire bombs? Those are nothing but estimates. I tell you once more they're many times too high. All wrong! Send another report to the Fuehrer at once revising your figures. Or are you trying to imply that I am lying?

I have already delivered my report to the Fuehrer with the correct figures. That stands!' . . .

A few days later Speer was in Hitler's presence and the 'excitement' over the Cologne raid was still evident. Speer mentioned to Hitler the conversation between Goering and the Gauleiter, 'naturally assuming that Goering's information must be more authentic than the Gauleiter's':

> But Hitler had already formed his own opinion. He presented
> Goering with the reports in the enemy newspapers on the
> enormous numbers of planes committed to the raid and
> the quantity of bombs they had dropped. These figures were
> even higher than those of the Cologne police commissioner.
> Hitler was furious with Goering's attempt to cover up, but
> he also considered the staff of the air force command partly
> responsible.[16]

There was also one further important consequence of the Cologne raid – the effect on the morale of the population in the United Kingdom. Doctor Chave kept an extensive diary during the war and provides a suitable example of the effect. He recorded his feelings of the news of the raid:

> On that night of [the raid] I stood outside the house and
> listened to the roar of the planes passing overhead. They
> were like a great aerial armada flying over in the darkness.
> I had never heard so many before. The next day we learnt that
> a thousand bombers had been launched against Germany
> that night. This was for me a moving experience, because
> for the first time since the war began I felt certain that we
> would win. For if we could make these massive airborne
> attacks on the enemy in his homeland, then, no matter how
> long it would take, the victory must in the end be ours. [17]

Cologne was truly a historic turning point in the war. Germany had no choice but to respond; and the air defence of the Reich would draw in further war resource. Bomber Command was fighting back and the bomber crews were putting their lives on the line. Cologne was a 'new start' in the bomber war.

# 3
# DAMBUSTERS

*The Dambusters Raid of May 1943 has a special legendary status.*
*It required highly trained crews to perform a dangerous low-level*
*precision attack, using an innovative but hitherto operationally untested*
*weapon: the 'bouncing bomb'. The whole planning and execution of*
*the raid required genius, bravery, skill, dedication and determination.*
*This special operation proved a military success, and the aircrew*
*that took part were decorated abundantly. But there was a cost.*

Following the Cologne raid, Sir Arthur Harris's force carried out two
further 'thousand bomber raids' in June 1942, to Essen and Bremen.
For the remainder of that year such numbers would not be repeated,
but Harris had made his point.

Through to the end of 1942 there was one most important
development in the air battle, the introduction of a Target Finding
Force (later to be named the Pathfinders), of which more detail will be
provided later. But even more importantly, it must be noted that on
17 August 1942, 12 B-17 'Flying Fortresses' of the American Eighth
Air Force, operating from England, attacked the Rouen railyards; this
was the first American four-engine bomber mission.

Through the winter months of 1942/43, Bomber Command's
operational ability was enhanced with the addition of electronic aids
to aid navigation, target finding and marking, and the countering of
German radar. With the approach of spring, Harris now threw his
crews into what he called his 'main offensive', opening up with the
Battle of the Ruhr, an all-out concentrated attack on the German
industrial heartland. In response, the German nightfighter arm had
grown in strength, and as one historian noted, 'The levels of death and
destruction were about to mount dramatically.'

The Battle of the Ruhr opened on the night of 5/6 March 1943
with 442 aircraft: Lancasters, Halifaxes, Wellingtons, Stirlings and

Mosquitoes, going to Essen (14 aircraft failing to return). In the coming weeks, Essen would be on the target lists again, as would Dortmund, Bochum and Duisburg. Bomber Command would also venture outside the Ruhr to Berlin, Nuremberg, Kiel, Frankfurt, Stuttgart, Pilsen, Mannheim and Stettin, not allowing the Germans to concentrate their defences. But Harris was particularly focused on the destruction of the Ruhr.

Conventional bombing was not the only way that the Ruhr could be attacked, however. Another way of targeting the Ruhr had been considered for some time. Industry requires water and a series of dams formed the reservoirs that could meet the Ruhr's demands. It had long been postulated that a breach of these dams, and the release of millions of tons of water, would cause widespread flooding and disruption in the area, seriously impacting on Germany's war production. How could it be achieved? By scientific genius and outstanding airmanship.

## 617 SQUADRON

At the end of March 1943 and into April, what would become the most famous unit in the RAF was formed. Initially designated as Squadron 'X', the number '617' was soon allocated, and the squadron came under the control of Bomber Command's 5 Group. Sir Arthur Harris had told 5 Group's Air Officer Commanding Air Vice-Marshal, the Hon. R. A. Cochrane, to assemble the squadron, putting forward the name of Wing Commander Guy Gibson as the squadron's commanding officer. Indeed Gibson's destiny would be to lead one of the most daring and historic bombing raids of the entire war. Prior to joining 617 Squadron, Gibson had already completed one tour on nightfighters and two tours in the seat of a bomber. His abilities were in no doubt: he sported a Distinguished Service Order (DSO) and a Distinguished Flying Cross (DFC) and Bar. In the third week of March, Squadron 'X' came into being, then making a home at RAF Scampton; and on the evening of 21 March, Gibson arrived. He was aware that the squadron would be carrying out no ordinary operation, but he was not told the target. He knew he would only have a couple of months to prepare his crews for their task, which would involve low-level flying. Immediately he set about recruiting and training the crews to meet the demands of the 'special' operation. Edward Johnson joined the squadron, flying as a bomb aimer on Australian pilot Les Knight's crew:

> The people going there were all very experienced pilots, mostly decorated or having done one or two tours of operations. It was obviously something rather special that it should be collecting all these well-known bods if you like, to form a new squadron.[1]

Australian Dave Shannon had already completed a tour and been posted to another squadron to prepare for further duties with the Pathfinder force. But within a few days he received a phone call from Guy Gibson:

> Asking whether I would rejoin him again as he had been asked by the AOC of 5 Group to form a special squadron for a special operation. At that time we were given absolutely no details at all. We had no idea what was in the offing. But having served with Gibson for quite a long period, a full tour, I was very happy to say, 'Yes I'll drop the idea of going into the PFF [Pathfinders], and if you can pull the necessary strings, I'll come to you.'
> The necessary strings were pulled and I was flown to Scampton.
> Gibson was an absolutely fantastic character. I should think, in my own estimation, he was one of the finest leaders of men that I've ever met. He was the type of chap that would never ask anybody to do anything he couldn't do or hadn't done himself. And he was known in the RAF terms as an operational squadron commander; that is to say that he flew just as much operationally as his crews did, which was not always the case with squadron commanders because they had plenty of administrative work and other things to do. And many of them were there for quite a long period of time to get in their full tour of operations, but Gibson

was a fantastic leader. He was very strict on duty, and one of the boys off duty, and he managed to carry that off to perfection. Everybody admired him and having been with him over a year at that stage I was very happy to continue serving with him.

Through April 1943, airmen, aircrew and ground personnel joined the squadron. Most stayed. Some left, including a few not deemed up to the task. It wasn't until the last week of April 1943 that the crew lists were, with the odd exception, finalized. Nineteen crews and their Lancaster bombers would carry out the raid. But very few knew exactly what the task was going to be. At the end of March, Gibson became part of the small circle of people who were aware of what the target was, having been given the chance to study models of two dams, the Möhne and Sorpe. But this information, for the time being, was still withheld from the crews. Within days of arriving at Scampton, Gibson addressed his assembled aircrews, making clear the importance of the forthcoming task, and giving brief details of the type of flying that would be required of them:

> You're here to do a special job, you're here as a crack squadron, you're here to carry out a raid on Germany, which, I am told, will have startling results. Some say it may even cut short the duration of the war. What the target is I can't tell you. Nor can I tell you where it is. All I can tell you is that you will have to practice low-level flying all day and all night until you know how to do it with your eyes shut. If I tell you to fly to a tree in the middle of England, then I will want you to bomb that tree. If I tell you to fly through a hangar, then you will have to go through that hangar, even though your wing-tips might hit either side. Discipline is absolutely essential.

Such secrecy as to the exact target led of course to a considerable amount of speculation; Edward Johnson joined in:

It was mostly guesswork as to what the target might be. Most of them were more terrifying than it turned out to be. There was a favourite rumour that we might be going to try and blow up U-boat pens by tossing bombs into the entrance to the pens and blowing them up internally, since they hadn't succeeded in doing much damage externally. It sounded a pretty terrifying experience, since most of us had been to one or other of the Atlantic ports at some time.

The security was very close. There was no inkling floating around of anything that was in the least bit positive as it turned out. They were all rumours. We were told not to talk to people, and we didn't convey anything to our families. We were particularly not to talk about the type of training that we were doing, and I think everybody was sufficiently experienced to observe that and keep it honestly. Most of the crews were experienced at being shot at and knew what might happen if they didn't keep security.

Dave Shannon also joined in the guesswork:

We had all sorts of speculation going on. Once we were told to practise flying over water of course the first thought was that it would be U-boat pens or something like that. Never, at any moment, do I think that any of the crews ever suspected that the target eventually was going to be the German dams.

SPECIALIST TRAINING
Even though the exact target was unknown to the crews, the nature of the attack and the flying requirements were known and in the weeks preceding the raid specific training was intense, as Dave Shannon recalled:

We were told that we had to practise flying at 150 feet in formation and once we had perfected that and could navigate all round the country, we would move on and start flying at night, in moonlight periods. Well, there are not an awful lot of moonlight periods available in this country, even in the summer, so we did a lot of very early morning flying, and a lot of dusk flying to try and simulate the light. Even then we weren't getting sufficient practice . . . so the cockpit of the aircraft was covered in blue Perspex and we were to wear yellow goggles, and fly during daylight. That was as near as we could get to moonlight flying. It was quite successful; a little bit hairy to start with, taking off with these things on. On a bright day one tended to want to take off the goggles, but we very soon became accustomed to it.

The three major points which were made by Gibson were navigation, that we had to fly in formation, and to fly at low level. The latter was literally map-reading because the navigational aids which we had at that time were not frightfully effective at low level. And we were flying mostly overland, apart from crossing the North Sea into enemy territory; it was pinpoint flying from one strip to another. To reach a form of perfection in this we had to map out about eight or ten different cross-country routes, flying time about three and a half to four hours, and all the navigators made bearing strip maps of the sections.

Once the varying cross-country routes had been planned, all of the stations and patrols and anti-aircraft systems in the country at the time were warned of this, because in the early days there were nothing but complaints and confusion coming in to Bomber Command headquarters, that everybody was sighting Lancasters flashing all around the country at very low level and what the hell was going on.

Unbeknown to us at the time Gibson was having varying meetings with Group and with specialists, and particularly the research departments. He was let into the secret of what the target was to be and what the bomb load would be.

While his crews honed their skills, Gibson learned further details of the task at hand, including the type of 'bomb' his crew would be dropping.

One name forever associated with the dambusters raid is that of Barnes Wallis. Whilst the dams had indeed long been under consideration as a worthwhile target, it was the esteemed aeronautical engineer who developed the weaponry to breach the dams. But the process of developing a means of placing enough explosive in the right place to crack open walls designed to hold back millions of tons of water had been far from smooth. To drop the bombs conventionally from height at such a target required a level of precision beyond the technological abilities of the bomber force. So how could the explosive be placed against the wall? Genius was applied with the concept of skimming the bomb over the lake, 'bouncing' over any torpedo nets and on to the dam wall, where it would sink, set to explode at a certain depth. The 'upkeep mine', as it came to be called, certainly went through various stages of development, including many failures. By the date of the actual operation the mine was indeed ready, as was the means of delivery. But it is worth noting that the development stages did impact on the training of the aircrews, in one notable way increasing the perils of the operation. An example of one such failure was witnessed by Gibson in the middle of April, when he attended a trial of the mines, early one morning on the south coast of England:

Out of the sun came the two Lancasters. They were both in fine pitch and making a very hearty noise for that time of the morning. They flew in formation: one the motion picture aircraft, the other with one of our mines slung underneath. Inside the gaping bomb doors we could see it quite clearly painted black and white, looking large enough even against the massive black Lancaster itself. Down came the Lanc with Shorty Longbottom at the controls to about 150 feet, travelling at something like 270. We saw him level out for his run, and then climb a bit to get exact height over the calm water. We saw him tense at the controls, getting his horizon level on the cliffs further on. Jeff [who was in fact Barnes Wallis – his name was kept secret owing to the wartime publication of this account] stood beside Bob, crouching like a cat. The movie camera began turning. I picked up a pair of binoculars. Then the mine fell out quite slowly. It seemed to hang in the air for a long time before it hit the water with a terrific splash and a dull thud. In a minute we would know whether or not Jeff's calculations had been right or wrong, but for the moment there was nothing except that mighty wall of water, which reached up to the aircraft's tail as if to grab it. Then it all subsided and we knew. The great mine could be seen taking its last dive, smashed into six broken fragments.

'Broken,' said Jeff, and looked at the ground. I said nothing. I knew the work he had put in, the hours of sitting at the desk with slide rule and calculator. Now it had failed.

Barnes Wallis was not going to accept defeat that easily. He arranged for the strengthening of another of the test mines for a trial. Gibson again recalled the scene as the Lancasters approached for the second test drop:

Over they came again, once more the suspense and once more the mighty splash. Then Mutt, who was flying it this time, banked steeply away to have a look. But we weren't looking at him, only at the bits of our smashed-up weapon which were hurtling round the sea like flying fish. Then the foaming water settled down again and there was a long silence. Jeff suddenly said, 'Oh, my God,' and I thought he was going to have a fit. But he soon calmed down, for he was not temperamental, and as we trudged along the shingle to the car park he began his next move. Here was a man who would not be beaten.

Despite the technological setback, Gibson returned to Scampton to oversee the ongoing training of his 'crack' squadron. Meanwhile trials of the weapon continued and as Gibson recalled, 'One after another, the experiments failed.' Then one day Gibson was called to a meeting with Barnes Wallis:

> He said to me, 'The whole thing is going to be a failure unless we jiggle around with our heights and speeds.'
> 'What do you mean?'
> 'Simply this. From the slow-motion movie cameras which have taken pictures of these things dropping I have found out a few facts. I have drawn this graph here to illustrate what I mean. It's all a combination of speed and height. You see here that they will work and won't break up if we drop them from 150 feet at a certain speed. On the other hand, if we drop them from 40 feet at this speed they will also work. The best height to suit your aircraft is here – at the 60-feet level at 232 miles an hour. But that is very low, and that's what I have asked you to come down to. Can you fly at 60 feet above the water? If you can't, the whole thing will have to be called off.'
> I though for a second and wondered if it could be done. If 150 feet was low, 60 feet was very low. At that height you would only have to hiccough and you would be in the drink. But I said, 'We will have a crack tonight.'

Dave Shannon describes having a 'crack' at flying even lower:

> About half-way through our training the height of flying was dropped from 150 feet to 60 feet. And flying at 60 feet in daylight or thereabouts is a very different kettle of fish from flying at 60 feet at night. And the only way that we could fly at that sort of level without killing ourselves was with a very accurate altimeter. Now there was no altimeter sufficiently accurate designed at that stage to allow us to contour fly at 60 feet.

So again the research people came up with the idea that the only way they could overcome this was to put a spotlight in the nose of the aircraft, and a spotlight in the tail of the aircraft, and set the beams, set the angle of these lights, so that they converged into one spot at an exact height of 60 feet below the aircraft.

Having practised over the aerodrome with the spotlights, we then moved on to flying over water . . . We found that one of the problems was getting down to the right height from 150 feet or 200 feet and then getting the spotlights right. This was done by the navigator or radio operator looking through the blister in the side of the aircraft and saying, 'down, down, down, down, down' until the two beams converged, making one spot on the water. It was very successful but it was hellish low, I don't mind saying, especially in the first runs that we made with this; one thought that the chap that was calling out the 'down, down, down' was never going to stop. But once we got the feel of it, it was perfectly all right.

Harold Hobday, the navigator on Les Knight's crew, was one of those whose job it was to look at the spots and direct his pilot:

It really was first class. I looked through the bubble in the side of the aircraft onto the water and when these spots coincided it was the right height. So I had to say, 'up' or 'down' to the pilot. A lot of people didn't want us to use this method because obviously there were German gunners who could see the lamps and could take better aim on the lamps. But we had to risk that because it was essential to have the aircraft at that exact height of 60 feet when we dropped the bomb.

As a bomb aimer, Edward Johnson had to learn a new bombing technique, owing to the nature of the 'bomb' and the 'bomb-run' flying height:

There was no bomb sight of any consequence that was made to operate at the height that we were going to be required to operate at, so it did mean doing a lot of low-level bombing to try and develop some technique of dropping bombs, which was made more difficult because we didn't know the target at the time.

The height was already fixed and the speed of the aircraft had been fixed so it was a question of gauging distance really. As soon as the type of target was known, shall I say, not the real target, we were then able to think about how we were going to make these distance judgments. The official way turned out to be a T-shaped piece of wood with two pins on the end of the T and an eyepiece in the stalk of the T . . . reproducing inside the aircraft a small triangle that was identical with the triangle that you wanted to reproduce outside using the towers on the dam walls (eye – Lancaster, pins – towers). Personally I didn't use it at all. I found it clumsy and inconvenient and not very accurate. I developed my own technique of using a long piece of string fastened each side of the clear bombing panel and some marks on the panel in grease pencil. It enabled me to have two marks, one to suit the Möhne tower distances and another one to suit the Eder tower distances (which weren't the same).

It worked very well because I had a bigger triangle than the official one, and it was stationary rather than having to be held.


THE RAID IS ON

Barnes Wallis was able to sort out the problems with the mine and eventually the time came when the 617 Squadron airmen came to see the weapon they would be dropping. Edward Johnson was:

. . . absolutely staggered. It was just like a big cylinder. It just didn't seem possible that this enormous piece of machinery [could] revolve. The first thing was it had to be revolved and the thought of this thing whizzing round in the aircraft and then being released just didn't seem feasible at the time.

The Lancaster bomb bay had been removed entirely and it had been fitted with two hydraulically operated V-shaped arms, which had discs on the end at the point of the V . . . to grip the bomb. The action of pressing the bomb release opened the arms, letting the bomb fall. There was also a pulley driven by the hydraulic motor to start the bomb revolving, which had to be done in the aircraft before the attack commenced, and led to some difficulties in flying because it was like a gyro, in effect, of trying to stabilize the aircraft, making it very difficult to manoeuvre.

The night of the operation loomed ever closer. Work continued on training and preparing the aircraft, focusing on the loading of the mines. On 15 May 1943, 5 Group's AOC Cochrane came to Scampton and informed Gibson that they would be taking off the following night. The great dams raid was finally on, and Gibson began making final preparations:

> Next day, on 16 May, reconnaissance aircraft reported that the defences on the dam had remained unchanged and that the water level was just right for the attack. It was a great moment when the public address system on the station said, 'All crews of No. 617 Squadron report to the briefing room immediately.' The boys came in hushed, having waited two and a half months to hear what it was they were going to attack. There were about 133 young men in that room, rather tousled and a little scruffy, and perhaps a little old-looking in spite of their youth. But now they were experts, beautifully trained, and each one of them knew his job as well as any man had ever known any job he was to do.

Barnes Wallis took the stage, informing the expectant airmen of the task that lay in front of them. The 617 Squadron aircrews came to learn of why the dams were there and what they were constructed of.

Barnes Wallis explained the theory behind how they were going to break the seemingly impenetrable constructions. To Harold Hobday, Barnes Wallis's presentation certainly made an impact:

> Barnes Wallis was a very kindly man, very dedicated, frightfully clever obviously, but a fatherly type. We were impressed with him and thought he was marvellous. He described all about the action of the bomb, skipping along and dropping down just at the parapet, exploding at 30 feet and hopefully cracking the actual parapet of the dam itself. He was very enthusiastic and explained it in minute detail. We trusted him implicitly. We didn't dream that it wouldn't work. We were absolutely astounded that Barnes Wallis could have invented something which was quite unknown before. There had been nothing like it. It was just one of those innovations which one wouldn't expect; a 6,000-pound bomb to bounce on water? I wouldn't. The aircrews were confident. This wasa marvellous thing to be on.

Now that the target was finally known, the crews could focus on the job in hand. Dave Shannon recalls his feelings:

> There was elation, excitement, and to a certain extent, relief that the training we'd been doing was coming to an end. Here we could see that the actual operation was about to take place and we were to strike a blow against the Hun. At last we were going to do something, because we had done nothing but practise. We were on an operational station which was home to another bomber squadron; and there was a certain amount of talk about 617, 'The squadron that does nothing but practise – when are they going to do something?' We were all very keen to get on and do it.

Gibson described the rest of the day at Scampton as being 'a **terrific flap**' as aircrews prepared, aircraft were tested and tractors transported the mines (bouncing bombs) to the Lancasters. Some of the crews were also given the opportunity to further study the task in hand: pilots and navigators, including Dave Shannon, were called in for a special viewing:

> Scale contour models of the Möhne, Eder and Sorpe dams had been made and sent up to us. We were called to the briefing room and they were uncovered. We were told to study them and get as much from the models as we possibly could. Gibson and the navigation officer together with some of the pilots with experience of Germany had mapped out the routes; [ours was] from Scampton, across the North Sea to some islands just off the Dutch coast, both heavily defended, then cross the Dutch coast, down into Germany, keeping over the Rhine, north of the Ruhr, as well as we could, which was a very heavily defended area, and then turning on down firstly to the Möhne dam. We spent 2 to 3 hours discussing the models and the route.

The afternoon wore on and beneath a hot sun final adjustments and repairs were made to the aircraft. Gibson prepared for the final pre-operational gathering of his crews.

> As the day cooled down we had our briefing. I will never forget that briefing. Two service policemen stood outside on guard. The doors were locked. No one was allowed in except the boys who were going to do the job and four other men.

Gibson initially allowed Barnes Wallis to reiterate his words of that morning and go on to describe the difficulties in the weapon's development. Gibson recalled then talking to Barnes Wallis in an aside:

> He [Barnes Wallis] was very worried, I knew, because he felt responsible for sending these boys off to this target and personally responsible for each and every one of their lives.

He said to me, 'I hope they all come back.'
I said, 'It won't be your fault if they don't.'

Meanwhile 5 Group's AOC Cochrane was 'giving the boys a pep talk':

> Now you are off on a raid which will do a tremendous amount
> of damage. It will become historic. Everyone will want to know
> how you did it, and it will be very difficult not to tell them.
> You must not do so because we have other uses for the weapon.
> I am giving you this warning now because, having watched your
> training from the beginning, I know that the attack will succeed.[2]

Gibson then once more took the stand to detail the final plan. In summary, the attacking force was to be split into three formations.

First formation: Three sections of three aircraft to fly by a southern route, over the Scheldt Estuary, to the Möhne dam and to attack until the dam was breached. Then the remaining aircraft of this wave were to proceed on to the Eder. Then when the Eder was breached any aircraft that had not dropped their mines were to proceed on to the Sorpe.

Second formation: Five aircraft to fly a northern route over the North Sea, to the island of Vlieland, then south-east to the route of the first formation, close to the German border, and then go on to attack the Sorpe.

Third formation: Five aircraft (although six were initially detailed) to act as an 'airborne reserve' controlled from England by 5 Group, flying the southern route.

In addition to the Möhne, Eder and Sorpe, three further 'last resort' targets, the Lister, Ennepe and Diemal, were also detailed.

The task was now clear to the crews, Gibson recalled:

> So the briefing came to an end. Everyone knew
> exactly what to do; everyone knew the plan. We went
> up to the Mess and had some bacon and eggs.

The scene was set. Nothing more could be done in terms of preparations. The 617 Squadron diarist recorded:

> This was Der Tag for 617 Squadron. Hardly a soul with the exception of the crews knew the target. Very few people outside the squadron knew we were operating – not even the WAAFs. From eight o'clock onwards the scenes outside the crew rooms were something to be remembered. It was not like an ordinary operational scene, all the crews on this occasion being aware of the terrific task confronting them. Most of them wore expressions varying from the 'don't care a damn' to grim and determined. On the whole I think it appeared rather reminiscent of a crusade.[3]

THE ATTACK

The crews, 133 airmen, went to their 'pregnant ducks', as Gibson called them, and settled into the pre-flight checks. Although aircraft were allocated to specific formations, as detailed above, the sequence of take-offs did not follow this order. The aircraft took off in the three formations and, in the first, Guy Gibson, John Hopgood and Harold Martin took off at 21.39 hours. Then Henry Young, David Maltby and David Shannon at 21.47 hours. Henry Maudslay, William Astell and Leslie Knight took off at 21.59 hours. These had been preceded by four of the five crews in the second formation: Robert Barlow, John Munro, Vernon Byers and Geoffrey Rice took off at 1 minute intervals between 21.28 and 21.31 hours and at 22.01 hours the fifth Lancaster of the second formation, flown by Joseph McCarthy, left the Scampton runway (as a result of having to switch to a reserve aircraft). In the third formation, the 'airborne reserve', Warner Ottley, Lewis Burpee, Kenneth Brown, William Townsend and Cyril Anderson took off at 00.09, 00.11, 00.12, 00.14 and 00.15 hours respectively.

As the Lancasters became airborne the station personnel looked on. For those left behind the scene was unforgettable. The 617 Squadron diarist scribed his thoughts in the squadron's operational records book:

The great machines with their loads trundled off in formation
and left the grass surface whilst onlookers held their breath.
All went well, however, but they all seemed to get airborne
after extremely long runs. After they had gone and Lincoln
was silent once more and the evening mist began to settle on
the aerodrome, the squadron personnel sat around talking in
groups for a short time and then dispersed to their respective
quarters with the object of returning when the machines
were due to land. It all seemed very quiet and we wished
the boys over there good luck and a successful mission.

Seventy-six Packard Merlin engines hauled the Lancasters up and
onwards towards the sea. Harold Hobday, in Les Knight's aircraft, was
flying in the first formation:

We took off and formatted into threes; we were the last
three taking off on the main force. I was navigating all the
time and I had my head bowed down over maps whilst over
the North Sea, to make absolutely sure we were going to hit
the coast at the right place. Once over to the other side, in
threes, we started crossing Holland on these dog-legs. After a
couple of these I noticed that one of our three was too much
to the right so we broke off. The next thing was he [Astell]
got shot down. I had seen plenty of planes shot down, but
you wouldn't know who they were, but I knew this crew.
It brought it home too, but one had to press on. We went
from dog-leg to dog-leg until we reached the Möhne dam.

Dave Shannon was flying in the second wave of the first formation:

We formed up into our three Vics and flew across the North
Sea, quite uneventful until we hit the coast of Holland.
The main hazard was light flak. Flying at that level, although
the searchlights would come up, we were too low for

them to catch and hold us in the beams for any length of time. Recollection of the route is of the tracer that you could see, from the light flak and the searchlights waving. I believe there were plenty of fighter aircraft about but we were down on the deck and the fighters didn't really know whether we were enemy aircraft or their own. And it was too low for the fighters to operate.

Once we got to the dams, silhouetted in the moonlight, Gibson said that he would do a reconnoitre, and we were told to hold off back in the hills, 3 or 4 miles back from the dam itself. Gibson made his attack and then we found out that the Möhne dam was very heavily defended.

Gibson had preceded his first attack with a dummy run. Then as he prepared to open the raid, he warned the other crews to come in on their individual runs when ordered, also telling Hopgood that he was to take command should anything go wrong. The brilliant 617 Squadron commander lined up his aircraft, and flew head-on into the hot metal spitting from the dam's defences:

The gunners had seen us coming. They could see us coming with our spotlights on for over 2 miles away. Now they opened up and their tracers began swirling towards us; some were even bouncing off the smooth surface of the lake. This was a horrible moment: we were being dragged along at 4 miles a minute, almost against our will, towards the things we were going to destroy. I think at that moment the boys did not want to go. I know I did not want to go. I thought to myself, 'In another minute we shall all be dead – so what?' I thought again, 'This is terrible – this feeling of fear – if it is fear.' By now we were a few hundred yards away, and I said quickly to Pulford, under my breath, 'Better leave the throttles open now and stand by to pull me out of the seat if I get hit.' As I glanced at him I thought he looked a little glum on hearing this.

The Lancaster was really moving and I began looking through the special sight on my windscreen. Spam had his eyes glued to the bomb sight in front, his hand on his button; a special mechanism on board had already begun to work so that the mine would drop (we hoped) in the right spot. Terry was still checking the height. Joe and Trev began to raise their guns. The flak could see us quite clearly now. It was not exactly inferno. I have been through far worse flak fire than that; but we were very low. There was something sinister and slightly unnerving about the whole operation. My aircraft was so small and the dam was so large; it was thick and solid, and now it was angry. My aircraft was very small. We skimmed along the surface of the lake, and as we went my gunner was firing into the defences, and the defences were firing back with vigour, their shells whistling past us. For some reason, we were not being hit.

Spam said, 'Left – little more left – steady – steady – steady – coming up.' Of the next few seconds I remember only a series of kaleidoscopic incidents.

The chatter from Joe's front guns pushing out tracers, which bounced off the left-hand flak tower.

Pulford crouching beside me.

The smell of burnt cordite.

The cold sweat underneath my oxygen mask.

The tracers flashing past the windows – they all seemed the same colour now – and the inaccuracy of the gun positions near the power station; they were firing in the wrong direction.

The closeness of the dam wall.

Spam's exultant, 'Mine gone.'

Hutch's red Verey lights to blind the flak gunners.

The speed of the whole thing.

Someone saying over the R/T, 'Good show, leader. Nice work.'

Then it was all over, and at last we were out of range, and there came over us all, I think, an immense feeling of relief and confidence.[4]

The crews of the waiting Lancasters had looked on as Gibson opened the attack, as recalled by Edward Johnson:

> We watched Gibson attack. We were perhaps a little bit shattered at the amount of flak, a bit more than anybody had anticipated. They were very active and kept it up quite stoically after the bombs had started going off, which I thought was quite heroic really. It must have been quite terrifying on the dam wall or in the vicinity.

Gibson called in Hopgood to attack next. Dave Shannon watched as his colleague took his turn to try and break the dam:

> Hopgood's run in attracted tremendous flak and he was hit. His wing on the starboard side caught fire. I think his bomb aimer must have been hit because the bomb was released late and bounced over the wall. There was a tremendous explosion. Hopgood did his best to gain height, I suppose 400 to 500 hundred feet, then the entire aircraft exploded in mid-air, beyond the dam wall in a steep climb. Goodness alone knows how it happened, but one survivor from that terrible smash was his rear gunner. That was the second bomb against the Möhne dam – the wall was still standing.

The loss of Hopgood sent a wave of doubt through the waiting crews. Edward Johnson:

> We were distressed when we saw Hopgood. After a few drops we began to wonder if this thing was going to work.

Dave Shannon, still orbiting, looked on as further attempts were made:

> Next to go in was Mickey Martin. He was hit several times going in. But to try and draw off some of the flak Gibson

was flying down one side of the lake just out of range of the flak, but with his navigation lights on and his spotlights on under the aircraft, to try and fool the gunners, which was a bit of a spoof but it did work. Martin's bomb was released, as far as we could tell, exactly on target. Again there was this tremendous, vast explosion of water up into the air, and then when the whole thing subsided again, the wall was still there.

So the next Vic was called; the leader of that was Dinghy Young. This time Martin was also flying down one side and Gibson on the other, trying to draw the fire to get some of the flak away, giving the flak gunners three aircraft to shoot at instead of one. Young dropped his mine, again, as far as could be assessed, in the right place. Again there was a tremendous explosion of water. Young called up and said that he thought the wall would go. As far as he could tell, it had been a perfect run. But when it subsided the wall was still standing.

Next to go in was Maltby, flying his number two. The same procedure was carried out again. Maltby, as far as he could tell, had dropped his mine in exactly the right place. Again we had this tremendous explosion of water. It settled down and still the dam wall was there.

I was then called in by Gibson to start my run. I was just starting the run, with Gibson flying down one side and Martin flying down the other when there were sort of excited yells over the R/T. 'It's gone, it's gone, it's gone.' The whole wall had collapsed and the water had started spewing out down the valley. Gibson rapidly said to me, 'L-Love steer off the run, stand by, I think it's gone.' Then he came back and confirmed it had gone.

Young's mine had damaged the dam. Maltby's mine had finished it off. A gaping breach in the dam opened up and millions of tons of water belched out. Gibson would later recall it as 'a tremendous sight, a sight which probably no man will ever see again'. The R/T buzzed with excitement but Gibson brought the crews back to reality. The job was not over. Maltby and Martin set course for England. Gibson, Shannon, Maudslay, Knight and Young (who would act as Gibson's deputy) set course for the Eder. Dave Shannon recalled:

By this time it was getting on and the mists were starting to form across the hills and down in the valleys. The route was 60-odd miles; we had to fly towards Kassel to find the Eder dam. It was a huge dam; there was a tremendous amount of water. It was difficult to see what was what. Gibson called 'Where are you?' I called up and said I was in the vicinity. In fact I was making a dummy run on what I thought was the dam; it was another arm of the Eder which looked very similar in the night.

Gibson said, 'Stand by; I'll fire a Verey light.' When he did I said, 'Ah yes, I see now' and all the aircraft responded. We moved across and found the Eder.

The Eder was not protected by anti-aircraft defences at all. I think the Germans had thought that it was so difficult for anybody to deal with owing to its natural surroundings. It was way down in a very steep valley. We were flying above the hills, about a 1,000 to 1,500 feet above the water. There was a castle at one end of the lake over which we had to drop down, immediately over the side of the hill. Then level out over the water, fly over a spit of sand jutting out into the lake with the dam wall beyond that. I tried, I think, four times to get down but each time I was not satisfied with the run and I told the bomb aimer not to release. To get out of this predicament we had to immediately pull on full throttle and do a steep climbing turn to the right to avoid a vast rock face up in front. The approach to the Eder dam – it was fairly hairy.

Gibson told me to have a rest, and called in Maudslay.

Maudslay tried a couple of times but ran into similar problems.

Dave Shannon then tried again:

Gibson told me to have another go. I got what I thought
was an excellent run and we released the mine. As far as I
could tell there was a small breach made on the left-hand
side of the wall. But there was nothing significant.

Maudslay came in again. Edward Johnson looked on:

Maudslay did get down and attack but it seemed obvious to
us that he was a bit too high to release his bomb. But they
did, and the bomb was too close to the target, or they were too
high. The bomb bounced too much and it actually hit the top
of the dam rather than sinking into the water. It went off on
impact with a terrifying flash; we could see Maudslay's aircraft
silhouetted against the light. Gibson of course could see the
same and he called up almost immediately after the explosion,
'Are you all right Henry?' It was quite a time before something
was said. We were sure that we heard Maudslay reply that he
thought he was all right, in a very weak voice, a bit shaky, and
not at all like himself. His aircraft went on and we thought
it had crashed into the mountain facing the dam. We saw a
second explosion, which we felt sure was Henry Maudslay.

Now there was only one more chance: Les Knight still had his mine.
Edward Johnson recalled:

We were then instructed to bomb. We made a trial run before
we made our final attack. Les Knight was very good and
got us down quickly to a low level.

Knight's navigator Harold Hobday felt the air of expectancy.

I wasn't tense. I was excited, it was a great thrill. My job
was to make sure the height of the aircraft was all right.
The wireless operator had his job to do to make sure that the

bomb was spun in the right direction at the right speed. The flight engineer had to make sure that the speed of the aircraft was exactly right: he worked the throttles. The pilot, of course, had to steer the aircraft to make sure it was going in the right direction. And the bomb aimer had to use the triangulation business, which made sure he released the bomb at the exact moment. So each had a job to do. And the gunners, of course, they were just waiting for any activity to open up fire.

Edward Johnson could clearly see the towers:

. . . and I was quite happy with my bomb sight, position and everything. I released the bomb. I forgot all about the bomb from that moment on because we were flying directly into this large piece of land, which was only just across the river from the dam. Being in the front of the aircraft it's quite a terrifying experience to see this looming up at high speed. I was very anxious that he should get pulling the stick back and get over the top. He did, pushing the throttle right through the emergency gate to get the maximum power. We skimmed over the top of this hill, into which we felt sure we'd seen Maudslay crash shortly before. I didn't actually see the dam burst because I was out of sight, being in the front of the aircraft. But it was obvious what had happened by the noise on the intercom from the rear gunner and the mid-upper gunner. And everybody else who could see anything was going mad on the intercom. The centre had fallen out of the dam and the water was absolutely pouring out down this narrow river, causing a veritable tidal wave. We forgot all about safety and going home, we were trying to follow the water down the river to see what happened. It was a terrifying sight really – we could see cars engulfed. Gibson called up and said, 'Well it's all right boys, you're having a good time, but we've still got to get back to base, let's go.'

THE OTHER DAMS

The Möhne was breached, as was the Eder, but the night's activities were far from over. The second formation was looking for the Sorpe, and matters were not going well. Nothing further was heard of Barlow's Lancaster. Munro had to return early owing to flak damage. Byers would not return from the raid. Rice's Lancaster struck water en route to the target and lost the mine, forcing an early return. With four of the five out of the picture, this only left one Lancaster to attack the Sorpe from the second formation, piloted by Joe McCarthy. George Johnson was a bomb aimer on Joe McCarthy's crew and described his experiences that night:

> We were briefed for the Sorpe dam. The Sorpe was different in that it couldn't be attacked in the way that we had been practising. The geography of its situation was such that it had to be attacked by flying along the length of the dam. It still had to be at 60 feet. In the first place we had a problem with our aeroplane [at base]. It misbehaved on run-up and we had to transfer to the reserve. This aircraft had only arrived that morning. It had been fuelled, it had been bombed up, it had had a compass swing, it had been armed. The fact that we had to transfer meant that we were late off. We therefore went out on the reverse route because that way we felt that we would be able to catch up with the others. The inward route was more distant than the homeward route. Just south of Hamm we saw this goods train stooging along very comfortably. The mid-upper gunner had been transferred to the front turret and he said to the captain, 'Can I have a go?' He said all right and the gunner opened up. What we didn't realize but very soon found out was that it was an armoured goods train, and it replied in far more than we could give it. We felt a hit but nothing seemed to be wrong, nothing upset the aircraft.
>
> We eventually got to the Sorpe. We had a little difficulty in finding it because it was quite misty. But then we found there

was an additional hazard – on the line of attack. The Sorpe was right in the valley, so it was a question of going down the hillside, then up and out the other side. The hazard on the line of approach was a church steeple. We had to avoid that, lifting the wing slightly to get over it and then down to height.

On the first bombing run George was not happy so they went round again. He also wasn't happy on the second run, and around they went again. The third, fourth and fifth runs were also unsuccessful, as were the sixth, seventh, eighth and ninth. As George would recall, the crew had come thus far and were going to ensure the attack was carried out to the best of their abilities:

We actually made ten attacks before we released the bomb. The dam wasn't defended and we weren't having any real trouble with the flying. There seemed no point in making the journey if we couldn't do the job that we had been sent to do. The mines were set with a depth device, which gave the aircraft time to get out of the way before the plume of water was shot into the air. We dropped and when we came back to have a look the crown of the dam had crumbled but there was no sign of any actual breakage. . . . Barnes Wallis had said that it would need at least six mines to crack it and then the water would do the rest. It had such a thick earth core, far thicker than either of the others. Unfortunately we didn't have six, we had just one. Until later when a second aircraft, a reserve, made it and again had great difficulty in finding the dam, and made the attack with no positive result.

As we came back home we flew over the Möhne, or what had been the Möhne dam. It was just like an inland sea, nothing but water was visible for literally miles. Quite a sight.

We came back, and as we landed the right wing was very low. In fact that hit that had occurred was a piece of shrapnel going through the undercarriage nacelle and bursting the tyre. This we didn't find out until we landed. We also found a second piece lodged in the fuselage underneath the navigator's feet. So we had been hit although not severely damaged. It could easily have been much more serious, for the navigator particularly.

That leaves the final 'airborne reserve' to account for. Ottley, who had been diverted to the Lister dam, failed to return, shot down over Germany. Burpee also would not be making it back to Scampton that night, shot down over Holland. Townsend managed to reach a dam, the Ennepe, and drop his mine but without success. Anderson did not attack a target and returned with his mine intact. Ken Brown had similar difficulties to McCarthy, but similarly did manage to attack the Sorpe, without success.

Nineteen aircraft had set out on the raid. Eight aircraft were lost from which only three men survived. In addition to the losses mentioned already, Young's Lancaster had been shot down on the return to England. Eleven aircraft returned, and for the men who landed back at Scampton the celebrations began. Harold Hobday recalled:

We didn't have any trouble on the way back. We were allowed to use full power on the aircraft engines, which was not good for them, but was very good for us because we got home very smartly, no trouble at all. We crossed the coast at the right place and at low level, then gained height across the North Sea, landed, and had a very nice reception.

We were debriefed and then started having drinks. My goodness it was quite a night. I went to sleep in the Mess, and woke up in the morning in an armchair. After that we were fêted all over the place, and had a marvellous time for a week or two. Barnes Wallis was shattered because so many planes were missing. We were used to it of course, although it was rather more than average.

Edward Johnson celebrated in a time-honoured fashion:

There was a good deal of boozing through the night. I haven't the faintest idea what time I went to bed but I know it was quite a while after breakfast time.

We were a bit shattered at the losses, but I think somehow we'd expected they would be fairly high. When we got back Barnes Wallis was there, but he didn't stay very long because he was very upset at the losses. He was a very sensitive man, and a gentleman. He couldn't, I don't think, face the fact that we lost so many.

Dave Shannon recalled the 'sense of elation':

. . . in that it had been so successful, and depression to a certain extent that we had lost about 50 per cent of the squadron, 50 per cent of the people that took off. It was very expensive in crews but again with hindsight, I would say it was in every way worth it, even if we had lost everybody. It was a tremendous blow.

Despite the initial wide-scale disruption in the Ruhr, the long-term material effect of the dams raid on German industry, is questioned by modern historians. But what is not in question is the bravery of the men who flew the raid, and the propaganda opportunity to bolster British and undermine German morale. The breaching of the Möhne and Eder dams was another in a growing list of setbacks to the German war machine. And in the months to come the Allied bomber forces would extend the list further.

# 4
# SECOND SCHWEINFURT: ATTRITION OVER THE REICH

*Any mechanized armed force is dependent on certain fundamental components to keep it moving. One such is ball-bearings. In 1943 the American Eighth Air Force set out to target this perceived bottleneck in German war production; notably attacking the factories at Schweinfurt. A special mission in August only met with partial success and the 'Mighty Eighth' would need to go back. The Americans put great faith in the defensive power of unescorted bomber formations, but the special raids to Schweinfurt were instrumental in forcing a change of policy – a war-winning change.*

In August 1942, aircrews that manned the bombers of the American Eighth Air Force made their debut flight over enemy territory; 12 four-engined Boeing B-17s, 'Flying Fortresses', delivered their bomb loads to the marshalling yards at Rouen. Six further bombers carried out a diversionary attack. There were no losses but the bombers had the reassurance of Spitfire escorts both in and out of the target. One participant in this momentous mission recalled almost a sense of anti-climax:

> When I was a little kid, I had a cousin and I used to hear him tell about the last war and how, when a bunch of men were asked to volunteer for a dangerous job, the whole damn line stepped forward, just like one person. I used to think that sure was fine, but I thought that if it was me I'd have been scared. And so on this show I expected to be scared, too.
>
> Well, sir, it was a funny thing. When we got over the Channel and sighted the French coast I kept thinking, 'Well, here it starts.' But nothing happened, just a little flak that never even touched us. Then, as we got to the target and went into the bombing run, I thought, 'All right, there is where it starts.'

But it didn't start there either, because we just dropped our load and turned around and headed back without being bothered by a single fighter. Some of the ships were, but ours wasn't.[1]

Following this first cautious entry into the European air battle, RAF Bomber Command's Air Chief Marshal Sir Arthur Harris congratulated his new American partners, 'Yankee Doodle certainly went to town, and can stick yet another well-deserved feather in his cap.' Although the reply came back that one swallow did not make a summer, in the ensuing months the Eighth Air Force built up strength and made further tentative flights over enemy territory. The North African Campaign, and the opening of Operation Torch in November 1942, would result in a tapping of the Eighth's men and aircraft and therefore a delay in the expansion of its operational capacity. Nevertheless, those American heavy bomber crews still in the UK would continue to engage the enemy, notably attacking U-boat bases in France. During this period the aircrews of the Eighth had to come to terms with the rigours of aerial combat, be it from flak or the hostility of enemy fighters. Stories steadily filtered through of the risk and dangers of operational flying, the hostile conditions and the extraordinary sights, and the sheer bravery of some of the airmen. The stories concerning two American airmen, who went to war in their four-engine bombers, provide graphic examples:

I was radio gunner in a Fort called the Jersey Bounce. We were getting along all right until the flak caught up with us and a fragment sliced through the fuselage into the ankle of our navigator. The pilot called me on the interphone to come and administer first aid to the navigator, but I was too busy fighting off enemy planes that were attacking from the rear. As soon as I had a chance, I crawled forward to the nose and found the navigator sitting on an ammunition box cheerfully spotting fighters for the bombardier, who was leaping from one side of the nose to the other, manning both guns.

I applied a tourniquet to the navigator's leg, gave him some sulfa pills, and sprinkled the wound with sulfa powder. Three times I had to stop to take a gun and help the bombardier ward off attacks from dead ahead.

Then the lead ship of our element was hit in the number one engine and began to fall back. We dropped back too, holding our position on our leader's wing. Just then a Focke-Wulf [190] flashed in like a barracuda, came right between the two Fortresses, and raked our ship with cannon fire. I could feel the hits slamming into us. Word came through that the tail gunner was hit, and then just afterward the interphone went dead.

The wounded navigator seemed all right, so I crawled back to the tail gunner. He was intact, but he told me that the ball turret had received a direct hit. I went back to take a look and found it completely wrecked. The gunner was crumpled in the wreckage. I tried to do what I could for him, but it was no use. I don't think he ever knew what hit him. I reached into the turret and fixed the broken connection of the interphone, then I went back to the nose and gave the navigator a shot of morphine to ease his pain. Then I went back to the radio compartment to man my own gun again. That's all there was to it.[2]

On 3 January, 68 aircraft dropped their explosives on St Nazaire, 'Flak City' as it came to be known. This was the day that one top turret gunner, Sergeant Arizona Harris, won the Distinguished Service Cross: his military's second-highest decoration. An officer in his squadron told the story:

His name was really Arizona – they christened him that way – and he came from Tempe, which is a little desert town not far from Phoenix. He had a big leonine head and tawny hair and steady eyes and thick strong wrists, and he was one of the best top turret gunners you ever did see. He usually fired in short, quick bursts, to keep his guns from overheating, and he didn't miss, not often. He already had two FW190s to his credit, and he had an Air Medal, too, that he was going to show to his father and his two brothers and his married sister when he got home.

He went out that day with Charlie Cramner, one of the most popular pilots in the whole group, and I think Arizona was proud to ride with him because he knew that if anybody could bring the ship back, Charlie would. Even when two engines were knocked out and the whole bottom was blown clean out of the nose, so that the bombardier and navigator simply disappeared and nobody knew what became of them; even then it looked as if Charlie would bring her back, because when the formation finally pulled away from the enemy fighters, there was his ship staggering along with us.

Not quite with us, though. The formation came down to 'zero' feet for protection against possible attacks from below. But Cramner didn't dare lose altitude that he couldn't regain, so he kept his ship as high as he could – 1,500 feet, maybe – and the rest of us thought he was safe up there. As safe as you can be in a riddled ship with two engines out and most of the nose shot away. So we didn't join him.

But all of a sudden, about 40 miles north-west of Brest, six Focke-Wulf 190s and a Messerschmitt 109 came hurtling out of nowhere. They spotted the limping Fortress, and one after another they made a pass at it from behind. The other bombers were too far away to help. We saw two parachutes from the Fort flare open after the first attack, and two more after the second attack – although there was barely time for the chutes to open before the men hit the water.

We saw the Germans circle the drifting chutes, and whether or not they machine-gunned the fliers is something that can't be proved, so why think too much about it? But when the Fortress settled into the sea – and Charlie Cramner, who had stayed with his ship as a captain should, set her down as gracefully and gently as if he had four engines and a 6,000-foot concrete runway under him – then the Germans did strafe her, and you could see the steel-gray sea boiling under the rain of bullets. But there was something else you could see, and that was the guns in the upper turret still blazing, even as she settled. She settled fast; she lasted only about half a minute. But the top turret was still spitting as the waves closed over it. And that was the end of Arizona T. Harris, American fighting man.[3]

BY DAYLIGHT AND UNESCORTED
Despite engagements such as those mentioned above, the early months of the Eighth Air Force's campaigns are now noted for the small number of losses sustained. In October 1942 General Ira Eaker, who was overseeing the organization of the American heavy bomber force presence in the UK, expressed his opinion to General Carl 'Tooey' Spaatz, who was in command of all American air forces in Europe, that B-17s could 'cope with the German day fighter'. Eaker also made clear his future plans:

> The second phase, which we are about to enter, is the demonstration that day bombing can be economically executed using general fighter support . . . in getting through the German defensive fighter belt and to help our cripples home through this same belt; the third phase will include deeper penetrations into enemy territory, using long-range fighter accompaniment of the P-38 [Lightnings] type in general support only and continuing the use of short-range fighters at critical points on a time schedule; the fourth phase will be a demonstration that bombardment in force – a minimum of 300 bombers – can effectively attack any German target and return without excessive or uneconomical losses. This later phase relies upon mass and the great firepower of the large bombardment formations.[4]

But still, at this stage, the B-17's defensive capabilities had yet to be genuinely tested beyond the help of 'little friends', i.e. escort fighters.

Following the diversion of resources to support the Mediterranean campaigns in November 1942, markedly delaying the growth of the Eighth Air Force, it was not until the spring of 1943 that Eaker really began to trial the theory of daylight precision by unescorted bombers. But early indications were that the Luftwaffe did have the means to defend German airspace – to engage, oppose and shoot their American counterparts from the sky. On 17 April, 16 bombers were lost from a mission carried out by 115 American heavies to the Focke-Wulf factory near Bremen; 46 further aircraft were damaged. On 13 June, 26 bombers were lost from 228 aircraft sent to target Bremen and Kiel.

Yet still great faith was placed in the defensive capabilities of a close formation of aircraft bristling with guns. The B-17s and the B-24s flying in bomb group, combat wing and air division formation were weighed down with firepower, to such an extent that the bomb loads would often approximate half that of the RAF's Lancasters and Halifaxes. But of course RAF Bomber Command operated with the protection of darkness. The Eighth Air Force believed in accuracy through daylight. This aspiration was now to be tested to the full as the Eighth Air Force planned deeper flights into Germany, beyond the range of fighter cover.

In mid-1943 Eaker had more than 300 aircraft at his disposal. But this would be quickly worn down: in the last week of July 1943 penetrations into Germany cost 87 bombers, and it was not until 12 August that the Eighth returned once more, in strength, to Germany, when 25 bombers out of the 330 sent were lost. Five days later and Eaker would send his aircrews on what became one of the most famous air raids of the entire war: the Messerschmitt works at Regensburg and the ball-bearing factories at Schweinfurt. The defensive bomber force theory was again under scrutiny; the Luftwaffe would oblige this day and once more test that theory.

Lieutenant Colonel Beirne Lay Jr, flying with the 100th Bomb Group, wrote a vivid personal report concerning the 17 August 1943 mission to Regensburg:

When the 100th Group crossed the coast of Holland south of the
Hague at 10.08 hours at our base altitude of 17,000 feet, I was
well situated to watch the proceedings, being co-pilot in the lead
ship of the last element of the high squadron. The Group had all
of its 21 B-17s tucked in tightly and was within handy supporting
distance of the 95th Group, ahead of us at 18,000 feet. We were
the last and lowest of the seven groups of the 4th Air Division
that were visible ahead on a south-east course, forming a long,
loose-linked chain in the bright sunlight – too long, it seemed.
Wide gaps separated the three combat wings. As I sat there
in the tail-end element of that many miles long procession,
gauging the distance to the lead group, I had the lonesome
foreboding that might come to the last man to run a gauntlet
lined with spiked clubs. The premonition was well-founded . . .

It was indeed well-founded, because shortly afterward, German fighter
pilots lined their sights up on the American bombers and tore into
the formations. Beirne put into words the plight of other aircraft and
aircrew, from both sides:

. . . two B-17s from our low squadron and one from the 95th
Group falling out of formation on fire with crews baling out,
and several fighters heading for the deck in flames or with
their pilots lingering behind under dirty yellow parachutes.
. . . a B-17 turned gradually out of the formation to
the right, maintaining altitude. In a split second the
B-17 disappeared in brilliant explosion, from which the
only remains were four small balls of fire, the fuel tanks,
which were quickly consumed as they fell earthward.
. . . I watched two fighters explode not far beneath,
disappearing in sheets of orange flame, B-17s dropping out
in every stage of distress, from engines on fire to control
surfaces shot away, friendly and enemy parachutes floating
down, and, on the green carpet far behind us, numerous

funeral pyres of smoke from fallen fighters marking our trail.

... On we flew through the strewn wake of a desperate air battle, where disintegrating aircraft were commonplace and 60 chutes in the air at one time were hardly worth a second look.

... I watched a B-17 turn slowly to the right with its cockpit a mass of flames. The co-pilot crawled out of his window, held on with one hand, reached back for his chute, buckled it on, let go and was whisked back into the horizontal stabilizer. I believe the impact killed him. His chute didn't open.

... A B-17 of the 95th Group, with its right Tokyo tanks on fire, dropped back about 200 feet above our right wing and stayed there while seven of the crew successively baled out. Four went out the bomb bay and executed delayed jumps, one baled out from the nose, opened his chute prematurely and nearly fouled the tail. Another went out the left waist gun opening, delaying his chute opening for a safe interval. The tail gunner dropped out of his hatch, apparently pulling the ripcord before he was clear of the ship. His chute opened instantaneously, barely missing the tail, and jerked him so hard that both his shoes came off. He hung limp in the harness, whereas the others had showed immediate signs of life after their chutes opened, shifting around in the harness. The B-17 then dropped back in a medium spiral and I did not see the pilots leave. I saw it just before it passed from view, several thousand feet below us, with its right wing a solid sheet of yellow flame.

... One B-17 dropped out on fire and put its wheels down while the crew baled out. Three Me109s circled it closely, but held their fire, apparently ensuring that no one stayed in the ship to try for home. I saw Hun fighters hold their fire even when being shot at by a B-17 from which the crew were baling out.[5]

Pilot Bob Wolff also flew with the 100th Bomb Group that day, and described his experiences on the mission:

[After flying for approximately an hour over enemy territory] we took what appeared to be a 20-millimeter shell in the leading edge of the vertical stabilizer. The rudder was vibrating so badly that it was difficult to keep my feet on the rudder pedals. Shortly after that, something, flak or machine gun fire, hit the latch on the port life raft door and out came the raft. It hit the horizontal stabilizer and we started into a dive. We were able to pull out and regain formation.

Fighter and flak attacks continued until we were about 5 minutes from the target, and when they quit, it was so quiet . . . The target, an aircraft plant, was successfully plastered and our group, following the other groups, made a right turn and headed for the Alps. Because so many of the planes were shot up, the formation leader, Col. (later he was a four-star general) Curtis LeMay circled the formation over Lake Como in Switzerland, to let the stragglers catch up. Once more together, only diminished in numbers – our group had lost half of the original 21 planes – we headed for Africa. As we flew over the Alps, Italy and Sicily, things were relatively calm. Except for the vibration in the tail, it could have been another training mission.

Over the Mediterranean, the red lights began to blink on our fuel gauges. The extra drag caused by the tail damage was using too much of our fuel. Our plane was so badly damaged we could not make the designated field and we had to land at an emergency field at a place called Bone, on the North African coast, in Tunisia. The field was made of metal mats laid on the desert sand, and as we made our approach, the tower advised that another plane had cracked up on landing and to 'please go around'. With the damage to our tail, the plane would not respond, so with all the fuel lights blinking, we landed anyway and avoided the damaged aircraft. We taxied off to one side and the engines stopped. I don't remember kissing the ground, but they tell me my face was sure dirty.[6]

Many others brought back similar stories of combat, not just from the Regensburg force, but from the Schweinfurt force as well. But many airmen were not able to return with their stories: 24 bombers were lost on the Regensburg attack, and 36 bombers failed to return from Schweinfurt. Although some of the aircrews may not have appreciated it at the time, they had forced the Luftwaffe to take to the sky and fight, and become involved, in the truest sense, in a battle of attrition.

HARD LESSONS
Following the high losses experienced on the August Schweinfurt/Regensburg attack, the Eighth Air Force needed time to regroup and build strength once more. Only once in September were the aircrews on the Eighth asked to fly deep into the skies of the Reich, and they paid the price: 45 bombers – 450 airmen – missing from the 338 bombers sent to targets near Stuttgart. Into October 1943 and the air battle escalated once more: the 7 days between 8 and 14 October are remembered in Eighth Air Force circles as Black Week. On the first day an attack on Bremen and Vegesack resulted in the loss of 30 bombers; the next day 28 bombers fell. On 10 October Münster was targeted; 12 aircraft from the 100th Bomb Group were reported missing at the end of the day and the Eighth Air Force lost 30 bombers in total. They had 3 days' respite before the next major attack, a return to a target that had already cost the Eighth Air Force dearly, and was still fresh in the memory. Unsurprisingly, when the aircrews heard the word 'Schweinfurt' at briefing, shoulders dropped, sighs escaped, foreheads creased and stomachs churned.

The day of the mission to Schweinfurt on the last day of Black Week was given the name 'Black Thursday'. But before we hear some of the first-hand experiences that led to such a name, it is worth noting the effect these loss rates were having on the crews. One good source of such information is the medical diary of the 381st Bomb Group. On 10 October the diarist recorded, '**The mental attitude and morale of the crews is the lowest that has been yet observed.**' Hardly surprising, considering the losses suffered by the bomb group in recent missions.

Below are a few more examples of entries in the medical diary, starting with the effect that combat stress was having on one particular man:

17 September – There was a briefing of crews at 10.00 hours but the mission was scrubbed at 12.00 hours.

Capt. AB (who shall be nameless) reported to Capt. Bland and stated that he did not wish to go on the mission. He further stated that he had ideas of homicide and suicide. Since the Schweinfurt mission of 17 August, Capt. AB says he has not slept well and feels the odds are overwhelmingly against the individual in raids over German territory. He was interviewed by me, he was quite introspective and downcast, quiet and stated he had no desire whatsoever to get near a B-17 and that he was not equal to go on this raid. It is rather hard to decide whether it was feeling for personal safety or the weight of the responsibility of leading the group into combat that was responsible for his attitude. It was pointed out to him that he was one of the leaders in the group and that the personnel looked to him for direction and guidance, and further that personal failure on his part would have a disastrous effect upon the squadron and very likely on the group as a whole.

He finally agreed somewhat reluctantly to go to the briefing. The group surgeon spoke to Col. Nazzaro and gave him the gist of the conversation outlined above and the colonel put the issue of going on the mission squarely to Capt. AB, who agreed to go much easier than would have been anticipated. It is the feeling of myself and Capt. Bland that another mission is indicated to restore confidence (Capt. AB has led seven missions to date since Schweinfurt) and that following the mission a period of rest is indicated. It is also our feeling that unless this procedure is carried out Capt. AB will be lost to us as a combat flier. In the meantime we are going to use our utmost to incur adequate sleep.

On 8 October 1943 seven of the 21 aircraft sent out by the 381st on the mission to Bremen failed to return. And on some of those aircraft that did return there were casualties, which the medical diarist recorded in graphic and unpleasant detail:

Of those ships returning, several were badly damaged and 'Tinkertoy' ground looped just off the runway. It had the nose shot out and the pilot, 1st Lt William J. Minerich, had his head blown off by a 20-millimeter cannon shell. There was hardly a square inch of the entire cockpit that was not covered in blood and brain tissue. One half of his face and a portion of his cervical vertebrae was found in the front of the bomb bay. The decapitation was complete. The co-pilot, Lt Thomas D. Sellers, is certainly deserving of any award that may be given him for his heroic work in bringing this ship back to base. The bombardier and navigator, 2nd Lt Henry G. Palas and 2nd Lt James K. Stickel, were also slightly wounded and frostbitten.

The tail gunner on Lt Miller's crew, Staff Sergeant Stephen J. Klinger, 534th BS, was KIA [killed in action]. His diagnosis was as follows: 1. Wound, perforating, sideline of neck, about 2 inches diameter involving the brachea and great vessels of the left side of the neck. 2. Compound fracture of the upper one-third right forearm, wound of entrance about 1 inch diameter, incurred by low velocity missile.

After this mission, in visiting the many crews right after they hit the ground, the tense excitement of many was apparent and in many cases were borderline hysteria. An effort was made to massively sedate a large number of the crew members and it seemed to work quite satisfactorily.

The next day another mission was scheduled to the Focke-Wulf factory at Anklam. Three of the 16 381st Bomb Group aircraft sent failed to return and the medical diary recorded:

9 October 1943 – In the last 2 days this group has lost
ten aircraft and many old crews and the effect has been
demoralizing to the staff and the combat crews. We all
feel these losses very keenly and smiles and apparently
cheerfulness are forced and everyone is quite well aware of
the others' feelings. The loss of two squadron commanders,
Majors Ingenhutt and Hendricks, has especially affected us,
both from the standpoint of morale and administration.

So with morale seemingly at a low the news that greeted the crews on
the morning of 14 October 1943 was certainly not welcome, as noted
again in the 381st's medical diary:

14 October – Crews were briefed at 07.00 hours and the
target was the ball-bearing works at Schweinfurt, Germany.
The mention of the word 'Schweinfurt' shocked the crews
completely. It will be recalled on 17 August this group lost so
heavily at this same target. Also conspicuous by its omission
was the estimated number of enemy fighters based along
this route. Upon checking with S-2 [the intelligence officer]
later, it was found that this omission was intentional and
that the entire German fighter force of 1,100 aircraft were
based within 80 miles of the course. The implications are
obvious. As I went round to the crews to check our equipment,
sandwiches, coffee, etc., the crews were scared, and it was
obvious that many doubted that they would return.[7]

For 60 of the 320 crews that took off on the Schweinfurt mission, any
doubts and fears they had would become reality.

BACK TO HELL

The Schweinfurt force was split into two 'task forces': the 1st Bomb
Division in the lead, with the 3rd Bomb Division following on a
parallel course. In addition, a small force of B-24s carried out a

diversion. Escort was provided by P-47s, Thunderbolts, of the Eighth's Fighter Command. Robert Hughes served as a pilot with the 100th Bomb Group (3rd Bomb Division) and recalled, '**14 October 1943 dawned like many other English countryside mornings, cold, damp and hazy. The call came for the 100th to mount maximum effort.**'[8] David Hutchens served as a pilot with the 532nd Bomb Squadron, part of the 381st Bomb Group of the 1st Bomb Division:

> As usual Doug Winter, the 532nd Operation Officer, woke me up in the middle of the night with a loud yell, 'Get your butt out of bed you're flying today.' I stumbled up to the Mess Hall for breakfast. The menu was good old American bacon and eggs. This was a mixed blessing because it meant that we would be flying a deep penetration into Germany. If the target were to be into occupied Europe which meant less fighters and flak, we got fed powdered eggs and Spam.[9]

Robert Hughes recalled that his respective Mess Hall seemed virtually empty at breakfast, which included:

> . . . toast and good old 'orange marmalade'. Oh, yes! We had vast amounts of good American butter to go on that wonderful English dark bread. Even now when I think of those cool nights when we would go by and pick up a loaf or two of bread and a pound of butter and return to our huts, stoke up the coke fire in our little stove, toast and butter bread, my mouth waters. I ate it then and I will do it often now.

Twenty-year-old Robert 'Bob' Slane flew as a pilot with the 91st Bomb Group, 1st Bomb Division:

> It was an early wake-up call. My navigator, Lieutenant Foster, had returned from pass and my crew, without substitute, was scheduled to fly this mission. We discovered, just prior to the mission briefing, that our flight position would be tail-end

Charlie. The Group leader would be my roommate, Captain Harry Lay. This was to be his thirtieth and last mission with the 91st Bomb Group. Lieutenant Colonel Milton would accompany him as co-pilot and mission commander.[10]

Following his 'mixed blessing' for breakfast David Hutchens went to the mission briefing room 'to get the bad news':

The curtain was pulled back by the briefing officer and we saw a long red target line going into the heart of Germany with the target labelled Schweinfurt. We let out a loud moan. Our Group had been to this target on 17 August '43 and the losses from German fighters had been so high that the Group had been labelled non-operational. Now, to make matters worse, I was told that I would have two substitute crew members in the nose to man the guns and to drop the bombs. It seems that both my regular navigator and bombardier had ruptured their eardrums during a rapid descent from altitude to escape the fighters on a recent mission so they were grounded by the flight surgeon. This was really bad news because it broke up an experienced crew who had flown together and completed 14 missions toward the magic 25 [the number of missions set as a 'tour' for Eighth Air Force aircrew].

Robert Hughes of the depleted 100th Bomb Group recalled that his briefing was like no other he had ever attended:

There were only eight crews available and they had to be substituted from other Bomb Groups for certain key positions on the crew, such as Bill Allen being loaned to fly bombardier for one of the crews in my unit. The low number of crews was brought about by the extremely heavy losses suffered by our group on 8 October 1943 (seven crews), and on 10 October 1943 (12 crews), the latter being known as 'Bloody Münster', a complete story in itself. Thus only eight crews.

The eight crews had been broken into flights. Four aircraft to be led by Lt Owen 'Cowboy' Roane, flying with the 390th Bomb Group, and four being led by Lt Robert 'Bob' Hughes, flying with the 95th Bomb Group.

Lt Richard E. Elliott, our bombardier, and I attended a special briefing on the target even though we were scheduled to drop on the lead bombardier's release. Intense target study before take-off paid off handsomely in allowing us to distinguish the target under most unfavorable conditions, like cringing from pink bursts of flak and uncontrolled aircraft.

With breakfasts in stomachs and briefings over, the crews were taken to their bombers. Bob Slane recalled:

It was still dark and very foggy after the briefing as we were being trucked to our aircraft. We were the last crew out of the truck – arriving at an aircraft from another squadron (aircraft 42-5714 of the 323rd Squadron). When we arrived at the aircraft I was met by the aircraft crew chief. He was distraught and excited when he informed me that there must be a mistake because his aircraft was not 'combat ready' and it had never, ever, been scheduled for combat. In response to my question concerning its use, he informed me that it was an older aircraft used only for local flying and primarily for instrument flying. While this discussion was taking place the bomb-loading crew arrived and began loading the bombs. I had no time to discuss this situation further with the crew chief, as it was obvious the aircraft was on the schedule if bombs were to be loaded.

We discovered the aircraft had the old-style bladder-type oxygen system and that meant we needed extra masks as the bladder types would clog up with ice at high altitude. My crew had flown with this equipment when flying older model B-17s during training missions prior to our overseas assignment. The demand-type oxygen system on the later model aircraft corrected this problem. The crew chief – once reconciled that his aircraft was going into combat – did everything possible to assist my crew in obtaining additional oxygen masks and additional ammunition. He advised me that the engines on the aircraft were 'high-timers' and that particular problem was his main concern. The extra weight from the additional ammunition was one of my concerns and both the flight crew and ground crew monitored the distribution of the additional ammo.

The weather remained wet and foggy and we would not have been surprised if the mission was scrubbed, but after a long wait the green 'go' flare appeared and we were on our way.

Once on the runway, the only visible directional mark was the white center stripe. It was a full instrument take-off and climb-out using air speed, climb rate and timing procedures.

David Hutchens gathered his crew at their aircraft:

. . . and gave them my usual pep talk. Then we all had our last-minute nervous pee and climbed aboard. We started engines and went through our checklist and on the time signal taxied out for take-off.

As I recall, I made a low visibility, heavy loaded instrument take-off, which meant that I held the brakes on while my flight engineer advanced the four throttles; at near max power I took control and released the brakes. At full power and a bit of a lurch we were under way. With a full load of bombs and full fuel load the next few seconds were very critical so I didn't allow any interphone chatter. As we started our climb out to altitude I got a call from the waist-gun compartment. It was reported that when I released the brakes both 50-caliber waist guns had snapped off their pivoting post and had tumbled back into the waist compartment and were lying useless on the floor. Considering the mission this was really bad news. My flight engineer and senior enlisted man stated that two guns out would be equivalent to having a gun turret out, which was a legitimate reason to abort the mission. We talked this over as a crew. We didn't really want to abort. We all wanted to get another mission in toward that magic 25. When my waist gunners said that they thought that between them they could jury-rig one gun and be able to fire the gun, we decided to go for it.

At Thorpe Abbots, Norfolk, the B-17s of the 100th Bomb Group prepared to take off, including that flown by Robert Hughes. Robert was one of over 3,000 bomber airmen taking part in the mission:

The flight line was no more crowded than the chow hall was. There was no crowding up for take-off. Cowboy's unit went first and in a couple of minutes, at 10.15, we followed. We climbed through scattered clouds making one full circuit of the base and rendezvoused with the 95th Bomb Group at 2,000 feet. The time was 10.27. They were four ships short on the high squadron. We moved our left wingman up into a left-wing position on the element leader and moved our slotman to our left-wing position and we had a square group.

Above England the bombers gathered into bomb groups, combat wings, and bomb divisions. Bob Slane recalled:

We were the third aircraft to locate Capt. Lay's lead aircraft, and after waiting for some time for other aircraft to join up, I pulled into formation on the right wing of the high element leader. It became increasingly obvious as we started on course that several aircraft assigned to our formation had either aborted or for some reason were having difficulty in locating the formation. The left wing position in Capt. Lay's lead element remained vacant for a considerable period of time and I debated whether or not to fill that slot; however another B-17 finally pulled up into that position.

In the vanguard of the bomber formation were the bomb groups of the 1st Bomb Division. They were escorted by P-47s of the 353rd Fighter Group. At Walcheren Island, on the Dutch coast, 20 Me109s had mixed it with the fighters, but by the time the 1st Bomb Division reached Duren, the P-47s had to turn for home. The Luftwaffe pilots seized their chance and, as an official Eighth Air Force report put it, '1st Bomb Division had the strongest opposition yet encountered.' David Hutchens recalled:

After getting into formation, climbing out, crossing the English Channel, and picking up our fighter support, we were under way. In a short time our fighter support had run out of their range and had to turn back. This was when the German fighters came in like a swarm of angry bees. We tightened up our formation for mutual protection. We weren't exactly defenseless. Each B-17 had at least ten 50-caliber machine guns which the Germans learned to respect. The Germans would usually pick on a Group that was flying a loose formation and gang up on a B-17 that was disabled and not able to stay in formation. Our group was staying pretty much intact when we turned at the IP [initial point] and started our run into the target. Here the sky became black with flak bursts from the ground defenses of 88-millimeter guns. Their best gunners were at this target. But there was at least some relief from those fighter attacks.

At this time my ball turret operator reported oil leaking off the left wing trailing edge. Since I was busy flying I asked my co-pilot to watch the oil pressure gauges. In a short while he reported that the oil pressure on number one engine was dropping. This meant that we would have to shut that engine down, but with a feathered prop we should still be able to stay in formation. We shut the engine down and tried to feather the prop. We had lost so much oil the prop would not feather. This was really bad news. This meant the prop would windmill, causing a large drag on the airplane, causing a big loss in airspeed so that

SILVER BAY PUBLIC LIBRARY

we could not maintain our position in formation. We had to drop out of formation and the fighters came in for the kill.

As we left formation the tail gunner reported four or five fighters were closing in from the rear. I looked down and saw that there was a thick cloud cover at about 5,000 feet. We were flying at about 20,000 feet. Our best chance to survive was to get into that lower cloud cover. I told my crew to hang on. I pulled all the power off and put the airplane into a steep dive. My tail gunner reported a kill on one of the fighters. Airspeed was approaching red-line max and to make matters worse the left wing was in a violent vibration caused by the stress of the spinning prop on number 1 engine. I had to slow down. My top turret gunner reported a kill on another fighter. I pulled the nose up into a steep climb and slowed the airspeed down to near stall. My ball turret gunner reported that the attacking fighters zoomed under us as we pulled up into the climb. At this point I did a wing-over manoeuvre and continued the dive for the cloud cover. For some reason the fighters did not continue the attack and we were in the clouds.

As we resumed flying airspeed the left wing again went into violent vibrations. I now became concerned about losing the left wing. In previous missions we had witnessed B-17s in a dive with the wings coming off. The airplane tumbles, and we did not count any chutes of escaping airmen. I decided that we should bale the crew while we still had control of the airplane. I told my co-pilot to hit the bale-out alarm and get ready to leave. Tex looked at me with those cold blue steel Texan eyes and said, 'Hutch let's give it 2 more minutes.' By some miracle the wing vibrations ceased. (I found out later that the prop shaft had sheared from the engine and was now spinning free of the engine.) We had a new lease on life. I told the crew we had two options. We could head for Switzerland and be interned. In my escape kit I had Swiss maps and the telephone number of our embassy. If we couldn't land we could probably ditch near the shore in Lake Geneva. One caution: during the escape briefing we were told that it had been reported that there were cases where Nazi sympathizers were selling escaping airmen back to the Germans. To a man, my crew said, 'Let's go home.'

Whilst David was throwing his aircraft around the sky to avoid the enemy, Bob Slane's crew pressed on to the target:

Me109s and FW190s were the principal attack aircraft – coming in from all directions – while Ju88s, Me110s and Heinkel 111s were observed flying parallel to our formation, just out of range of our gunner's 50-caliber guns. These aircraft were reporting our position and firing rockets into the formation. Any aircraft in our formation that was crippled or fell behind could expect to be singled out for mass attack by the enemy. On the way to the target, FW190s were lining up ahead of the formation and then making head-on attacks; doing a 'split-s' manoeuvre after passing under the B-17 formation. It was during these attacks that the navigator, bombardier and lower turret gunner were most effective in providing defensive fire from our aircraft.
    At the initial point, the fighter attacks lessened and intense enemy flak was encountered. Just after bomb release over the target our aircraft received what appeared to be a direct hit by a burst of flak and the number 4 engine caught fire. We were able to feather the propeller, the fire was extinguished and we remained in formation with three operating engines.

OVER THE TARGET
The 56th Fighter Group had been able to escort the 3rd Bomb Division as far as Dison. The opposition from the Luftwaffe was not as intense as that experienced by the 1st Bomb Division crew. Nevertheless the skies remained hostile in other ways. Robert Hughes described his flight to the target and his somewhat unique bomb run:

Rendezvous was made with the 390th Bomb Group at 12.18 and this formed the 13th Combat Wing. Our climb to departure altitude was made and we departed the English coast. We met our American fighter escort at the enemy coast. We were flying over an undercast but as we penetrated inland we began to come out. We were a little south of course and about 4 minutes late. We could hear chatter on the radio from units and their escorts ahead of us. They seemed to be drawing enemy fighters. We seemed to be getting much less action than the units ahead of us. In fact, it seemed to me that the 390th was getting more action than the 95th Bomb Group. Please do not misunderstand me, although I did not see many enemy aircraft making direct attacks on our Group, the gunners on the eight 100th Bomb Group ships were credited with destroying seven enemy aircraft.

After we had flown over the undercast, we were able to see gas and oil fires dotting the countryside attesting to the furious defense and the determination of the bomber crews to place bombs squarely on the target and not be denied. From time to time, we had seen flak from a distance, but as we neared the target it took on a more personal feeling. Periodically, we could see the red hearts of the bursts of 'Big Stuff'. We could now see the target area, and as we had been briefed about the smudge pots which mark the dummy target area, Lt Elliott, our bombardier, and I recognized them for the dummies they were. Smoking like the whole town was on fire. Suddenly, our attention was diverted. The leader of the 95th was struck by flak just as we approached the initial point for final turn to the target at 14.47. He was descending rapidly from formation. Flak was intense. Our co-pilot, Lt Donald S. Davis, yelled, 'Move Bob!' I had felt the 'WHUMP' from the burst of flak which had lifted our wingman's plane, and was sending it directly into us. Lt Howard Keel temporarilly had no control over the craft. The Good Lord kicked left rudder, down stick, left aileron, then back stick and rolled out of a well-executed diving 'split-b' which allowed Lt Keel to pass through the space which we had occupied and execute a coordinated recovery. He also placed our ship on a direct course to the primary target upon which Lt Elliott and I had been carefully briefed just a few hours before.

Robert's crew were now out of formation and somewhat isolated:

Elliott picked up the target immediately and called,
'Skipper, target dead ahead, set up and follow
PDI [pilot direction instrument].'
I replied, 'Dick, I do not have the right to commit a man to this course of action against his will. It would have to be a 100 per cent volunteer.'
Dick called for a vote starting with the lowest-ranking man, and quicker than it takes to tell about it, the answers read:
'Come in tail guns.'
'Tail gunner – Go.'
'Left waist – Go.'
'Right waist – Go.'
'Ball – Go.'
'Radio – Go.'
'Top turret – Go.'
'Nav – Go.'
'Dick, I have your vote,' I added quickly.
'Co-pilot, who are we waiting for?'
'Gentlemen, we go! Elliott, do you not have a bombsight?'
Dick replied, 'Yes, I do. I caged it just before you made that wild peel-off. I also reset the altitude to 1,000 feet lower.'
'Dick you have it. We will maintain altitude and airspeed.'
We talked about the fact that we had the element of surprise on our side, and that we would maintain the appearance of a crippled aircraft by not opening our doors until just before bombs away. We informed the crew that we were flying in a

gun-defended area, and that best info had it that the German planes would not penetrate the area. We also conjectured that the flak guns would not fire upon the one ship, but would allow us to leave the area and become fighter bait. It was our best guess that they did not want to draw attention to the steam plant and allied ball-bearing shops by firing on one ship. If we couldn't find it, they were not going to disclose it. Lt Elliott opened the doors just long enough to release the bombs, and we already had our strike camera running . . . bombs were away at 14.54, thus, all bombs in MPI [mean point of impact]. The roar on the intercom was 'pickle barrel'.

Ahead of Robert Hughes, Bob Slane had also managed to release his bombs, his formation then leaving the target area. The fighters now reappeared and Bob's gunners fought back. Bob's ears filled with the sound of his gunners calling out kills:

However there was no time for discussion – everybody was too busy fighting off the enemy. Approximately 45 minutes after departing the target area we were still in formation and for the first time on this mission I turned over control of the aircraft to Lt Johnson, the co-pilot. We were holding our own and the three operating engines were also holding steady, despite higher than normal power settings. At this time FW190s were observed flying above our formation and they were releasing what appeared to be bombs, down, into and through our formation. I was busy looking up and trying to help Staff Sergeant Sly, the top turret gunner, in locating the enemy fighters flying overhead. Our aircraft was suddenly struck by heavy enemy gunfire. The right inboard engine (number 3) was hit, severing fuel and oil lines. The main oxygen tank – located in the passageway below the pilot – exploded with a loud 'bang'. Concurrent with the explosion, Lt Johnson let go of the control wheel and 'hunched' down and forward,

covering his head and face with his arms. His shoulders
shoved the control wheel forward and the aircraft immediately
started a severe descending dive out of the formation.
From my seated position I could not force Johnson to release
the control wheel. I unbuckled my seat belt and standing in the
aisle used all my strength to finally force him back upright.

Bob wrestled back control of his bomber, but they had lost 1,500 feet
and were out of the 'protection' of other bombers:

Regardless of the cause, our aircraft was now out of formation
and severely crippled with two engines inoperative.
I was unable to feather the propeller on number 3 engine.
There was no fire despite an obvious fuel leak in the inboard
section of the right wing. We continued to drift further behind
our formation and in fact we found ourselves, for a short period
of time, in the middle of another group of B-17s that were
at a lower altitude but following the route of the 91st Bomb
Group leader. That formation, also, soon left us behind.
It was a battle trying to keep the aircraft airborne
without exceeding the engine operating limits on the
two remaining engines. Main system oxygen had been
destroyed and the emergency oxygen was near depletion.
The bladder-type masks were a major problem. I descended
to 18,000 feet, the maximum altitude where we could
operate for a time without oxygen. There was no cloud
cover below us that might help in evading the enemy.

For the next half hour Bob Slane's B-17 was under constant enemy
attack:

. . . and it was a life or death struggle to survive. We were
no longer being attacked head-on, but we had enemy
fighter and fighter-bombers attacking us from side angles.

The last words I received from the tail gunner, Sgt Smith, were, 'Skipper, there are seven Me109s trailing us with their gear down. They are making single passes – gear up – then attack.' I told Sgt Smith to 'get one for me'.

We still had a limited supply of ammunition and we retained the hope that we could fend off the attackers and return to England with the two remaining operating engines. I wanted to maintain altitude until we were closer to the enemy coastline before starting a descent with two engines inoperative on the right wing. A descent too early could result in having to ditch in the North Sea. During this period of struggle for survival, I heard several crew members announce hits and possible destruction of enemy aircraft. I remain convinced that Staff Sergeant Brown, the ball turret gunner, and other members of my crew destroyed as many as four enemy aircraft during the unrelenting attacks by German aircraft.

Suddenly, and without warning, number 1 engine lost power. It appeared from my position that the two top cylinders had blown, with smoke pouring out. Flames were also coming from the lower part of the engine. My attempts to feather the propeller were futile.

Bob hit the bale-out warning bell and gave the verbal order for the crew to exit the crippled aircraft. All the crew members acknowledged with the exception of the tail gunner, Sgt Smith. Bob noted that Johnson and Sly were assisting each other with their chutes and with the bomb bay doors opened, both men jumped out:

As the crew members were departing the aircraft, I received word from Staff Sergeant Kuhlman, the radio operator, that Sgt Smith was unconscious – no apparent wounds. Kuhlman had been to the rear of the aircraft to obtain additional emergency oxygen bottles. After this report I received no response from any crew members in the rear of the aircraft. All forward members of the crew, with the exception of the navigator, Glen Foster, had departed the aircraft. Foster had not yet baled out, but had assisted Runner, the bombardier, in evacuating the aircraft. Runner was suffering from mild anoxia and appeared to be confused; however, thanks to Foster's valiant efforts his bale out was successful.

Foster came to the cockpit area wanting to know if I was going to crash-land or bale out. He wanted to do whatever I was going to do. I told him that I was going to parachute out, but that I had received word that Sgt Smith was unconscious in the rear of the aircraft and I wanted him to check on Smith and if he was in the aircraft but unconscious to attempt to get Smith to an exit and if possible throw him from the plane concurrent with pulling the parachute ripcord. That accomplished, he should notify me and immediately bale out. If Smith was not in the aircraft, Foster was to notify me and then bale out without further delay. Foster acknowledged and headed for the bomb bay.

Within moments of Foster entering the bomb bay, on the way to the rear of the aircraft, a Ju88, coming in from the right rear, strafed Bob's B-17. Gunfire tore into the fuselage and the cockpit area just to the right of the pilot's control column. The co-pilot's windshield and the right cockpit window were shattered, along with the co-pilot's instrument panel. Bob escaped injury, although his left leg felt numb from the shock of the explosion in the cockpit:

All crew members with the exception of Foster and possibly Smith, should have been out of the aircraft before the initial hits from the Ju88. The landing gear on the B-17 had been placed down after the bale-out order was given in the mistaken belief that the aircraft would not be fired on. With the wheels down, it signalled, and became obvious, that the crew was abandoning the aircraft. My first action was now to retract the gear. I glanced to the left and saw the Ju88 pulling up into position just above and behind the left wing of our aircraft, possibly positioning for gunfire into the left cockpit. I immediately made a sharp left turn directly toward the Ju88 and kept the B-17 in a tight spiral turn to the left. I maintained maximum air speed while in this circling dive.

Bob received no news from Foster, so made the assumption that Smith, and possibly Foster, were still aboard, unable to bale out:

I was flying at 18,000 feet when the Ju88 struck and the spiral dive was started. I could see a small postage-sized clearing of land in the middle of what appeared to be a dense forest. I decided on a forced crash landing. Number 1 engine was still on fire, but I could only see white smoke – no flames. I kept the airspeed above 300 mph until level-off about 200 feet above the ground. The descent had been so rapid the windshield and pilot's side window were frosted over. I opened the side window as I flew over the small clearing. The airspeed was still high, 240 mph. I saw Bill Runner on the ground, at the edge of the clearing, wildly waving his arms as the aircraft went by.

I made a tight circle to the right, as I had full visibility from the shattered windshield and co-pilot side window. I could not maintain airspeed on one engine for any extended period and I completed the low-level circling manoeuvre, levelling off for the final approach. The airspeed had slowed to 150. I slapped the flap lever down and flew flat for a fairly high-speed, gear-up landing. I went through a small wire fence, stopping just short of a larger wooden wire fence and a ditch. I had 'unbuckled' to take control of the aircraft from Johnson and from that period on had been so occupied with the recovery and control of the aircraft that I had no opportunity to get strapped back in. I had made the crash-landing without benefit of the seat belt and shoulder harness.

With the bomb bay doors open, all of the sounds of an aircraft making a belly landing were amplified. The first sound I became aware of after the aircraft came to a stop

was the pounding of my own heart. I glanced out to the left
wing – the fire in number 1 engine had been in the lower
part of the nacelle. There was some smoke, but no visible
fire. The landing had evidently smothered the flames.
I had cut the ignition switches just before touchdown.
I glanced around the cockpit and remembered to push in the
IFF [identification friend or foe equipment] destroyer buttons.

I called out Foster's and Smith's names as I scrambled through
the aircraft to the rear entrance. There was no response; and
there was no one in the area of the main fuselage. Once outside
the aircraft I checked the tail gunner's position and it was also
vacant; I then assumed that all crew members had baled out.
I initially departed the immediate vicinity of the B-17, fearing
the Ju88 might strafe the downed aircraft. Seeking cover, I ran
across the field to a hedge at the edge of the clearing. A few
minutes after taking cover, the Ju88 flew directly overhead,
low, and then started a climb to altitude. With the departure
of the Ju88 from the area and no one in sight, I returned to
the aircraft, intending to destroy the B-17 by firing a flare into
the number 3 engine nacelle where fuel was still flowing down
the wing root. I found the flares but could not find the flare
pistol. I found the canister designed to destroy an aircraft,
but I could not get the firing mechanism to work. While thus
engaged I was then startled to hear voices outside the aircraft.
I immediately leaped out of the rear exit and began to run.

Hearing a sharp order to 'Halt', I glanced over my
shoulder and saw a man holding a rifle, pointed right at
me. I stopped running, raised my arms and walked back to
the aircraft. Two Me109s flew over, dipping their wings.
Two Germans in civilian clothes had driven directly on
the field, apparently coming from a small village located
at the south edge of the clearing, providing me with only
10 or 15 minutes of freedom after the crash landing.

I was held at the aircraft for a short period and during that time one of the Germans discovered Smith's body behind the bulkhead located aft of the main entrance door. This area is not visible from the main fuselage interior and was an area that, in my haste, I had not searched. Smith had evidently left his gun position and crawled forward toward the main fuselage interior. The Germans would not let me view his body. I was told he had been killed by massive wounds in his chest. He could have been wounded during the fighter attacks, but more than likely, in my opinion, he was killed by gunfire from the Ju88. The radio operator, Kuhlman, reported that Smith was unconscious during the time frame that crew members were complying with my bale-out order and he, Kuhlman, stated he saw no wounds or other indications that Smith had been hit by gunfire. I will always believe he was initially suffering from anoxia and would have survived had it not been for our last encounter with the Ju88. I was taken from the vicinity of the aircraft before Claud Smith's body was removed.

With the exception of Foster, all the other surviving members of the crew were captured and imprisoned. Foster was initially captured but managed to escape, and with the assistance of the Resistance, made his way to neutral Switzerland. Arthur Glenn Foster gives his account of the events in the back of the stricken bomber:

Bob via intercom sent me back to the waist to determine the condition of our tail gunner who had been reported by the waist gunners as badly wounded. He was dead from very serious wounds. I was supposed to intercom this info back to Bob who was in good control of the plane but it was losing altitude rapidly while still under heavy fire from Luftwaffe aircraft. Some pieces of either flak or metal chips from 20-millimeter enemy fire skimmed my forehead and back left shoulder about that time, although I didn't know that until later. Apparently I was somewhat dazed by those minor injuries,

but probably more because of having no bale-out oxygen
bottle. I was beginning to pass out as I staggered forward.
We were still at about what I guessed as 18 or 19,000 feet.

I never managed to get Bob on the intercom. Somehow
I managed to fall out of the plane, unconscious or semi-
conscious, leaving Bob with the thought that maybe both
the tail gunner and myself were laying wounded in the rear.
So he, I found out much later, decided to take the plane
down and crash-land it instead of baling out himself.

I have no recollection of pulling the ripcord on the British Irwin-
type chest-pack chute. But the shock of it opening, causing me
to kick myself in the back of the head, crushed a couple of lower
vertebrae and brought me to full consciousness. Strangely,
I looked at my wristwatch (navigator habit) and it was 3.43 pm.
I hit the ground 17 minutes later, at 4.00 pm. (The watch stuck
at 4.00 pm, because it was damaged by the landing, and had to be
repaired later.) So that also told me that the chute had opened at
about 17,000 feet.[11]

Foster was quickly captured by two German soldiers, who began to
march him away through some woods. 'I won't go into the details,
but I managed to "subdue them," leaving them unconscious on the
trail, and took off.'

STAGGERING HOME
To return to the 14 October mission, and the battle in the sky: when
we left David Hutchens he was preparing to fly his crippled aircraft
back home:

I wasn't sure of my present location. Now I really missed my
navigator. I knew we were in southern Europe so decided to pick
up a north-west heading and hoped to have enough fuel to get
back to England. The cloud cover held and we flew and we flew.
Suddenly the clouds turned black with flak bursts. There was a

break in the clouds and I knew exactly where we were – there was the Eiffel Tower – we were over the heart of occupied Paris and were being shot at by the top German gunners. We got back in the cloud cover and survived. We flew and we flew. Now I saw that we were over water. I was afraid we would miss England and head out over the Atlantic. I corrected to a more northerly heading. We flew and we flew and we flew. Suddenly I saw land ahead. By now I am completely confused on our location. I had visions of turning too far north and with a strong wind from the west we could be back over occupied Europe. Then I saw some odd-looking small twin-engine aircraft with engine nacelles over the landing gear. I was low on fuel with red lights blinking. I saw an airfield, I had to land and I headed for the nearest runway. My radio had been shot out but the tower gave me a green blinking light. Then I saw some familiar aircraft in the pattern, the beautiful British Spitfire. After landing, an armed jeep met the airplane and guided us to a parking spot. We shut the engines down. On opening the nose hatch to leave the airplane, empty 50-caliber shells poured out. I heard the comment, 'These blokes have been in a fight,' and we had!

When we left Robert Hughes, his B-17 had just released destruction on to Schweinfurt:

'Nine Little Yanks and A Jerk' had just opened up the north segment of the target area and there were more bombs to follow. Our aircraft was strike photo aircraft for the 100th Bomb Group and we had picked up a fine set of pictures. We made a left turn from the target, and picked up the 95th Bomb Group, which was still struggling, trying to get into formation.

My wingman joined me and we asked the new leader if we could be of assistance in re-forming the group, explaining that we had an experienced formation controller riding tail guns. The offer was graciously accepted and in a very short time

the 95th was formed and the 100th flight took its position
in the high squadron. Sergeant Robert L. McKimmy, our tail
gunner, was one of the finest formation critics in the business.
He lined them up for us in a hurry this day, because we were
running out of the gun-defended area. We joined the 390th
Bomb Group and were once again the 13th Combat Wing.
Our return trip was no cakewalk, but it was not spiced with the
vast number of oil and gas fires we had en route to the target.

After our strike photographs had been developed and
the damage assessed by our local intelligence people, the
results were called into Division. Elliott and I had been called
down to observe the strike photos. Later in the evening
word was received that General LeMay wanted me to attend
the critique the next day. This was to be an experience for
me; I had never seen so many 'Eagles' in one room.
I had never been out of formation over a target before.

When all of the representatives from all of the groups were
assembled, the critique was called to order and we had just
been seated when General LeMay asked, 'Will Lt Hughes
from the 100th Bomb Group come forward.' When I stepped
upon the stage he said, 'Will you tell this group what you did
yesterday.' I related how we had been forced to dive for our
lives and that when we recovered, the target upon which we had
been briefed, lay dead ahead. How all the men volunteered.
The fact that we had a perfect bomb run and that Lt Elliott
pickle-barrelled the target. General LeMay asked how I knew
that we had pickle-barrelled the target. I informed him that
I had studied the strike photos and the fact that our aircraft,
'Nine Little Yanks and A Jerk', was designated strike photo
aircraft for the 100th, to which he responded, 'That is right
gentlemen, ten bombs MPI.' Stepping up to the strike map, he
pulled the butcher paper away to reveal an enlarged strike photo,
showing the strike. His next comment was, 'The lieutenant
should have a commendation.' To which the reply came from

the back of the room in clearly enunciated words, 'The SOB should be court-martialed for breaking formation.' Those words were spoken by my 'now' good friend, Colonel Bud Peasley, who was the airborne commander for mission 115. . .

Thus ended 'Second Schweinfurt'. Sixty American bombers and 60 American aircrews had been shot from the sky. Five men could be listed immediately as killed in action, 40 as wounded, 594 as missing. The 381st Bomb Group medical diary recorded the injuries to the men that returned to Ridgewell that day. Crews that were 'missing' had not, of course, returned, and those at airbases in England were not going to witness at first-hand their fate. But aircraft returning often brought the air war home. The medical diary listed the concerns facing the 381st Bomb Group's medical crews:

> The wounded were as follows:
> 532nd BS [bomb squadron]: Staff Sergeant Ernest
> E. Smith; 1. Wound, penetrating of right thigh,
> junction of lower and middle third, anterior surface
> – caused by exploding 20 mm cannon shell.
> 533rd BS: 2nd Lt Turner I. Jones; 1. Wound, lacerated, nose, left side of bridge, severe. 2. Fracture, compound, comminuted, nose, severe. 3. Contusion right infra-orbital, moderate severe (flak).
> 534th BS: Staff Sergeant LeRoy C. Weaver; 1. Contusion, moderate severity, left leg, distal one third, accidentally incurred by catching leg in ball turret of ship. 2. Abrasion, mild, left ankle, anterior surface, accidentally incurred in plane.
> 535th BS: 2nd Lt Carl W. Dittus; 1. Wound, lacerated 2 inches in length, moderate severity inner aspect, lower one-third forearm, left. Caused by 20 mm cannon shell.
> 413th BS (96th BG): Staff Sergeant Alan W. White; 1. Wound, penetrating mild, posterior aspect, right thigh, midline 2.5 inches above popiticel, caused by flak, low velocity.
> 413th BS (96th BG): Staff Sergeant James L. Berry; 1. Wound,

penetrating scalp, frontal portion, 1 inch long, moderate severity, caused by flak. 2. Frost bite, moderate severe, second degree, involving all terminal phalanges, both feet and both small fingers. Caused by failure of heated suit.

Two ships ground looped on their return, but there were no casualties . . . Colonel Nazarro was more visibly effected by this mission than by any I have observed, and he stated last night that he was more tired than when he, himself, had flown long missions. He seems to embody the personal feelings for his men that is sometimes lacking in commanders, and yet does not hesitate to do what is necessary to accomplish the mission.

Had the cost in men and material been worth it, from a military perspective? Albert Speer commented on the attacks on the ball-bearings factories at Schweinfurt in his book *Inside the Third Reich*. After the August attack, Speer noted that the production of ball-bearings had dropped by 38 per cent. 'Despite the peril to Schweinfurt we had to patch up our facilities there, for to attempt to relocate our ball-bearing industry would have held up production entirely for three or four months.' Stocks met demand in the short term, but, 'they lasted for six to eight weeks – the sparse production was carried daily from the factories to the assembly plants, often in knapsacks'.

In those days we anxiously asked ourselves how soon the enemy would realize that he could paralyze the production of thousands of armaments plants merely by destroying five or six relatively small targets. The second serious blow, however, did not come until two months later.

On 14 October 1943 Speer was discussing armaments with Hitler when they were interrupted with 'pleasant news' from Goering. The Reich Marshal informed Hitler that '. . . a new daylight raid on Schweinfurt had ended with a great victory for our defences. The countryside was strewn with downed American bombers.' Speer asked for a brief break in his meeting and contacted Schweinfurt direct.

> But all communications were shattered, I could not reach any of the factories. Finally by enlisting the police, I managed to talk to the foreman of a ball-bearing factory. All the factories had been hard hit, he informed me. The oil baths for the bearings had caused serious fires in the machinery workshops; the damage was far worse than after the first attack.
> This time we had lost 67 percent of our ball bearing production.

Thus the raids were a success in terms of the material damage resulting, but the loss of American life was high indeed. As one notable historian recorded, 'The disaster at Schweinfurt ended the nonsense about unescorted bomber formations.' Long-range fighter escorts, with drop tanks, were now of paramount importance. But the lives of the airmen had not been sacrificed in vain. The mere fact of their presence had forced their adversaries into the air and they too had suffered. In September and October 1943, 560 German fighters exited the air battle in the west. Historian Williamson Murray summarized the position in his book, *The Luftwaffe 1933–1945: Strategy for Defeat*.[12]

> The level of attrition for both Germany's fighter forces as well as Eighth Air Force during September and October bordered on the point where both were close to losing cohesion and effectiveness as combat forces. In the long run, considering the massive influx of bombers, fighters, and crews already swelling American bases in England, Eighth held the strategic advantage. It was, of course, difficult for the crews who flew to Schweinfurt to recognize that advantage.

# 5
# THE PEENEMÜNDE RAID: THE SECRET WEAPON RESEARCH STATION

*By 1943, a new and most serious threat to the Allies had materialized. German scientists were nearing the final stages in the development of secret 'reprisal' weapons, that some believed could swing the war back into Germany's favour (following the setbacks at Stalingrad and in North Africa). The weapons research station had to be taken out and RAF Bomber Command was called upon to carry out this special operation to critically disrupt German plans.*

On the night of 29/30 May 1943, as part of Sir Arthur Harris's Main Offensive, RAF Bomber Command sent 719 bombers to the German town of Wuppertal. Bomber Command historians Martin Middlebrook and Chris Everitt called the results of the attack:

The outstanding success of the Battle of the Ruhr. Large fires developed, and somewhere in the region of 1,000 acres of the town was destroyed. All but one of the six large factories in the town succumbed to the flames and 211 other industrial properties and 4,000 houses became rubble and dust. One estimate places the number of dead as 3,400.[1]

On 18 June 1943 the Nazi master of propaganda, Joseph Goebbels, attended a memorial service in Wuppertal. In his speech he heavily criticized Allied bombing policy and warned of future retribution:

They intentionally and cynically carry the war to civilian areas, turn them into a battleground, and force women, the aged and children to live and fight like soldiers. The fate and the future of our people is being decided not only at the Front, but also in the Homeland. The children who fall to enemy terror prepare the way for millions of other children in the future. The women who lose their lives to enemy bombing terror prepare the way for millions of women to give birth in the coming decades and centuries. As I speak to you in deepest sorrow and proudest memory of those who have fallen in this city and throughout the Reich, I know that I express the deepest feelings of the people of this province. The sacrifice of life that so many of your fellow citizens have made for the freedom and future of the Fatherland is but a reason and obligation for you to continue your bitter resistance to enemy air terror. It is not customary to speak of hatred at a grave side. Death usually brings not only sorrow, but also a kind of reconciliation. But in this case, it cries for revenge. The dead whose memory we honour today are the victims of the enemy's cold, calculating cynicism. The cynicism will end only when it is beaten down by painful, repeated counter-blows. Through me, the German people praise our dead. We understand their deaths in this sense, and know they did not die in vain. The hour is coming when we will defeat terror with counter-terror. The enemy is committing one bloody deed after another. He will have to pay the bill one day. Countless engineers, workers and builders are at work to speed that day. I know that the German people are waiting impatiently. I know the thoughts that fill our hearts as we remember those who have fallen in the air war. The name of the enemy has been written deep into our hearts during the past sorrowful weeks. That will be the basis for our coming actions.[2]

This was not mere rhetoric either. Goebbels knew that German scientists were, as he spoke, developing the means to exact that revenge. But what he perhaps did not know was that the Allies had been monitoring these developments and the time was fast approaching when something had to be done.

## THE NEST OF REPRISAL

The name Peenemünde had featured in Allied intelligence reports from the early days of the war; not that it had received too much attention. It was not really until the early months of 1943 that the developments at the Baltic German secret weapon research station came under closer scrutiny. Aerial reconnaissance and agent reports fuelled speculation, all of which had to be sorted and processed. To this effect, a certain Mr Duncan Sandys, MP, was appointed in April 1943 to investigate the full potential of this threat. Sandys was soon able to report that this was more than a potential danger, it was a real one: the Germans had developed a rocket which could be used against the United Kingdom in the very near future. Sandys presented his findings to the Defence Committee (Operations) with Winston Churchill as Chairman. Something had to be done, and it had to be done quickly. A number of decisions were made; most importantly that as soon as was feasible, the Royal Air Force was to attack the research station.

Bomber Command planners soon began work on the detail of the raid. It would be carried out in moonlight, overseen by a 'master bomber', with three targets: the housing estate, the production works and the experimental works. Bomber Command's 3 and 4 Group aircraft would attack the housing of the scientists and their families, then 1 Group would follow with a bombardment of the production works, and 5 and 6 Groups would close out the raid with an attack on the experimental works. The target area would be marked by Pathfinder aircraft tasked with 'shifting' the aiming points as the raid progressed. In addition, 5 Group would use a time-and-distance bombing method to attack its allotted target. Bomber Command also planned a ruse to deceive the German defences: a small force of Mosquitoes would attack Berlin, mimicking the opening of a large raid, in the hope that they would draw the German nightfighters away from the actual main attack to the north. The RAF bombers would leave the English coast, cross the North Sea towards Denmark, then over enemy-occupied territory to Peenemünde. The return route was an almost reciprocal of the approach. However, much of the aforementioned detail of the target, and its nature, would not be passed on to the RAF airmen who would carry out the attack. Bomber Command Operation order number 176 details the deception of the aircrews:

Heavy and successful bombing of Germany has forced the enemy to concentrate his energies on increasing the production of countermeasures against our night bombers. It is known that among these countermeasures is a new form of highly specialized RDF [radio direction finding] equipment, which promises to improve greatly the German night air defence organization, [which] is being developed and made at Peenemünde.

The experimental establishment at Peenemünde is situated on a tongue of land on the Baltic coast, about 60 miles north-west of Stettin. The whole complex, which covers an area of some 8,000 yards by 2,000 yards, includes the experimental station, assembly plant and living quarters housing the scientific and technical experts. The destruction of this experimental station, the large factory workshops and the killing of the scientific and technical experts would retard the production of this new equipment and contribute largely to increasing the effectiveness of the bomber offensive.

The order went on to emphasize the importance of the attack:

*Bombing tactics:* The extreme importance of this target and the necessity of achieving its destruction with one attack is to be impressed on all crews at briefing. If the attack fails to achieve the object it will have to be repeated the next night and on ensuing nights regardless, within practicable limits, of casualties.[3]

One interesting aspect of this operation was the use of a 'master bomber' controlling the raid over the target. This task was designated to the commanding officer of 83 Squadron, Group Captain John Searby, who had experience of approximately 50 bombing operations to his name. Despite being designated to lead the raid, John would still be kept in the dark as to the exact nature of the target he was to attack on the night of 17/18 August 1943:

> On the previous day, together with my crew, I had studied a model of the target together with Don Bennett (Commanding Officer of 8 Group, Pathfinders) and his staff. This model, beautifully constructed, was the result of taking photographs from our reconnaissance aircraft some time earlier. We endeavoured to memorize certain features which lay near the three aiming points and discussed with Bennett the essential features. We did not know any more than that this was an experimental station.[4]

On the day of the raid the crews of 596 aircraft prepared for the operation that night. John Searby recalled the scene at 83 Squadron, and the emphasizing of the importance of the airmen's task:

> 'If you don't knock out this important target tonight it will be laid on again tomorrow and every night until the job is done.' The significance of these words were not lost on the Pathfinder crews assembled in the 83 Squadron briefing room on the afternoon of 17 August 1943. To return to a target on successive nights might mean stiffer defences and heavier casualties. Once the element of surprise was gone no one could say how much effort and how many lives might be required to take out Peenemünde . . . Having shown our hands with a first abortive attempt, the Nazis would take steps to move out much vital equipment together with the scientists and technicians. In short, the moment would have passed and might never occur again.
>   From the low dais in front of the large map of Europe with its coloured tapes and pins which marked the heavily defended areas of occupied territory, I watched the faces of my crews. They were impressed by the urgency, but not worried, for the job would be done to the best of their ability. I caught the eye of

Brian Slade, veteran Pathfinder captain at 21 years of age, and he grinned; he was all for it. Against the background of Essen, Berlin, Hamburg, Munich, Cologne and similar bloodbaths Peenemünde did not, at this stage, make much impression. In fact, the reactions of the crews was one of relief at the prospect of a sortie to northern Germany. The only real hazard lay in the long penetration under conditions of full moonlight with the possible increased fighter activity. No one had heard of this insignificant pimple sticking out of Pomerania and there was nothing humdrum about the operation. Hence Brian's smile. Alas, he would be lost over the Big City (Berlin) in 5 short days.

The plan for the night's operations was well-conceived and in the course of the briefing I acquainted the crews with the fact that Mosquitoes of 139 Squadron would make a 'spoof' attack on Berlin with the object of holding the German nightfighters in that region, or at least a proportion of them. By the time the ruse was discovered many fighters would require refuelling before proceeding to the scene of the actual attack. Clearly we could not hope for this plan to do more than delay the opposition but if it worked long enough to enable the Pathfinders and following waves of heavy bombers to make an effective start on the destruction of the target much would have been accomplished. The full moon was at once a friend and an enemy. It would help the bombers initially but on balance it would serve the cause of the German nightfighters even more: with so much light there would be scope for the freelance or 'catseye' fighter and this would greatly increase the strength of the opposition.

At the bomber bases that stretched along the east of England, from East Anglia to North Yorkshire, crews came to learn of their responsibilities that night. It was clear to them that this was something out of the ordinary, as the following aircrew accounts testify. Wilkie Wanless was a rear gunner with 4 Group's 76 Squadron:

When we were briefed for Peenemünde we were told, 'This is top secret, can't tell you anything about it.' It's the only briefing I ever went to where the briefing hut was surrounded by service police. You had to go to the door with your crew and show your identification with your pilot. We were told that if a word leaks out about the target you don't go tonight, and the source will be summarily executed. So we paid attention, we said this has got to be a biggie.[5]

Reginald Fayers was a navigator with 76 Squadron:

We weren't told the absolute truth. We were told some story by a very senior officer that the Germans had developed some new radar station or anti-navigational device of some sort or other, and it was absolutely vital that we knocked out this Peenemünde place.[6]

Dennis Slack served with 4 Group's 158 Squadron:

We did not know what was there . . . When we were given this briefing we knew this was a new target and the squadron were speechless. The CO did not even know what was there but we were told that this area needed destroying ASAP. If we did not succeed this night we were told we had to keep going until we had destroyed it.[7]

Flying Officer Tommy Treadwell was the bomb aimer on a 4 Group 77 Squadron Halifax, and also recalled:

If we did not succeed in doing it properly, it would be repeated on consecutive nights. We were also given a strong hint that we would be destroying something that could affect our operations in the future. This was to increase our keenness, if that was necessary.[8]

David Balme served with 5 Group's 207 Squadron:

When the actual operation was put on, we were amazed to
find that the target was not the 'Big City' but this tiny research
station on the Baltic. Its importance was not explained, but
since the bombing height was to be 5,000 feet in full moon,
and since we were kindly told that if we missed it tonight we
would go again every subsequent night regardless of casualties,
we got the message. Other groups were to go in first on
separate aiming points, while 5 Group had the place of honour
– last – and our target was the workshops. To overcome the
Peenemünde smokescreen we were to make a timed run down
a north-south coast . . . and then the run-in from a second
pinpoint after finding the wind. 'Z' hour was soon after
midnight, so take off was about 20.00 hours; still daylight.[9]

INTO THE UNKNOWN
So somewhat oblivious to the true nature of the target, the bomber
crews went through standard pre-raid routine. John Searby recalled
the scene at RAF Wyton, home of 83 Squadron:

The briefing over, all crews returned to their Messes for a meal
and at eight o'clock were dressed and ready to go out to the
dispersal points where the Lancasters stood ready. This was the
final moment in the long programme of preparation. This was
a time for something to go wrong – an aircraft unserviceable
perhaps; ground crews had toiled to haul the bombs from the
fusing points to load them in the long bomb bays; radio, radar
and electrical circuits had been checked and rechecked. Petrol,
oil and oxygen had been fed into the wings and fuselages;
magnesium flares placed in the flare chutes; hydraulic systems,
release mechanisms and safety devices examined; guns
loaded and turrets swung; bombsights and controls checked,
flight rations put aboard and many more essential services

performed. It was a matter of personal pride with our ground
airmen that the Lancasters were supremely fit to go into battle
and as spotless as time and circumstances would permit.

I saw my crews away and then climbed into the vehicle with
my own crew to go out to Lancaster William. I can remember
Chick and his merry men departing, laughing as usual because
with Chick around nothing could be serious for long.
They were clutching the odds and ends of their various trades,
the two gunners huge in their padded suits. I waved to Chick
and set out. 'W' William stood on the far side of 'B' flight
dispersal area. It was a fine evening, warm and pleasant, the
sun about to set and the long twilight beginning, a time for the
river pub down at the Ferry where 83 Squadron foregathered. I
suppose there will never again be gatherings quite like that and
to recapture the atmosphere is impossible. All was warmth and
friendliness with much laughter . . . 'W' William was ready – we
were ready. Our part [was] to control the bombing over the full
45 minutes of the Bomber Command attack and stay with it.

At the prearranged hour Frank Forster pressed the starter
buttons and the four Merlins came to life. We would set out 5
minutes ahead of the others in order to have time to make a run
across the targets and verify the landmarks we had noted the day
previously.

We taxied past the squadron dispersals and got a wave from the
crews, then turned into wind at the runway threshold. A quick
brake check, flaps to take-off setting, and Frank moved the four
throttle levers slowly forward. The Merlins thundered out their
full power and Lancaster William moved easily at increasing
speed up the wide runway. This was the moment, when one forgot
the worry, the anxieties and stress of the day's pressing sequence
– keep her straight – tail coming up – airspeed building up and
suddenly the jarring and roughness ceases. Easily, beautifully, the
great Lancaster leaves the ground with her burden of men, bombs
and equipment. 'Wheels up.' 'Wheels up skipper,' and the flight

engineer moves the undercarriage level. Now the drag is less and she gathers speed, being held in level flight for a few seconds until the far runway lights flash past and we fly out into the twilight.

At Langar, Nottinghamshire, 207 Squadron put nine aircraft into the sky, one piloted by David Balme:

There was radio silence as usual, and a green Verey summoned us to trundle along the peritrack like dinosaurs and queue up until a green Aldis invited us on to the flare path as the previous aircraft began to move. When his tail came up we opened full throttles on the brakes then gently let her go. As always, a little group stands there to see us off: the station commander salutes (the only occasion when a group captain salutes a sergeant first), the WAAFs wave, and off we go with that never forgotten roar. The engineer's left hand supports the pilot's right hand on the throttles; keep her straight, ease her off, wheels up as soon as you think you won't bounce back, flaps in bit by bit, gain speed before height, and now there is half an hour to fly around making as much height as possible before setting course.

From the ground they seem like angry wasps circling aimlessly, until suddenly they all vanish in the same direction; then an anxious wait begins down there, with wondering whether all the equipment was checked, and what the weather will do at the target, and how soon will the German fighters cotton on to our route (there is a diversion on Berlin, hoping to cause them to re-fuel).

The bombers individually set out across the vast expanse of the North Sea, to a point where they converged, forming the bomber stream. Whilst they were over the water, night fell. David Balme continued:

Over the North Sea we waddle along under full bomb and fuel load, with luck making 20,000 feet at 160 knots indicated.

The light fades, but up comes that unloved moon.
Near the Danish coast we start letting down, then turn north
to find our first pinpoint. A sea mist makes it difficult, and
as we fly around we stir up the shore batteries. At 5,000 feet
now, the light flak seems to spiral lazily towards you and
then whizzes past; we tend to prefer the heavy, which can be
outwitted, whereas this stuff is hosed up all over the place.

The vanguard of the bomber force approached Peenemünde, having
had little trouble over Denmark and the Baltic. Meanwhile the
Mosquitoes of 139 Squadron were fulfilling their role, dropping
target indicators on Berlin, as if a large raid were about to open. The
German nightfighter controllers responded, sending their pilots to
the dark skies above the city. Although two Mosquitoes were lost in
this role, and two men lost their lives, the spoof was a success; the
Peenemünde aircrews had breathing space.

On approach to the research station, John Searby's navigator
informed his skipper to prepare for a course change:

'Five minutes to Rugen Island when we alter course to one seven
oh degrees.' To my disappointment I observe a sheet of cloud
ahead but on closer inspection it proves to be higher than at
first estimated and I can fly beneath it easily, keeping the island
in sight. Shortly after this we are over the tip of Usedom on
which Peenemünde is located. In the bright moonlight we fly
close to the objective, and Ross, Forster, Scrivener and I take a
close look at that which so far we have only seen as a model.
It is all there – the airfield at the tip and the development station
spreading along the coast on the east side. We run directly down
the line of the buildings and check off one by one the important
features. Hundreds of smoke canisters are commencing to belch
out fumes and the wind from off the sea is carrying the smoke
across the target area. This could be serious. In succession we
pass over the three aiming points: the development factory, the

rocket assembly plant and the large living site where the German workers and technical staffs are housed. 'Light flak opening up skipper,' from Ross. The green and red shells shoot past the aircraft and we turn out to sea where in the moonlight I observe two ships anchored. As we near them they open up with both light and heavy flak but the shooting is poor and the aircraft is in no danger at present. We pull away to the north and stand off a short distance from the coast. Within 2 minutes to go before 'H' hour, when the heavy bombing would commence, we waited for the preliminary marking of the target to begin.

Behind Searby the main force bomber stream edged closer. Tommy Treadwell of 77 Squadron recalled:

We flew across Jutland and the islands in the Baltic, finding it a real joy to be able to map-read all the way, partly because of the unusually low height at which we were flying, 5,000 feet, and because of the moonlight; but as we neared the target, a haze developed.

We had been warned not to be in advance of our bombing time so that early Pathfinders could do their job properly and, for this reason, the early waves were not carrying incendiaries. The Met winds were a bit out and despite corrections made en route, many planes, including our own, were ahead of time. To lose this we did a dog-leg to port and immediately found ourselves mixed up with numerous other Halifaxes who were either still on course or doing the same as we were. There were many near misses for several minutes before all was sorted out.

But before long the Pathfinders opened the raid. John Searby looked on:

Suddenly, the area was lit up by brilliant light from the flares as the first wave of Pathfinders passed over and red target indicators dropped in dazzling cascade to the ground. Ross, my bomb aimer, had his eyes glued to the aiming point and startled us all with a shout that their first markers had fallen to the south by more than a mile, but in the same instant another clutch of red markers fell almost an equal distance to the north and a yellow marker, most important of all, fell between the two, virtually on the mark . . . backed up at once by the green target indicators. Immediately, I broadcast to the bombers approaching the target and instructed them to bomb the green markers which we judged to be accurate. We made another turn out to sea and the flak ships had another go at us but it was not their night and we passed round in a circle for another run across the aiming point.

By now the area was beginning to assume the familiar spectacle of a target under massive attack: bursting bombs, masses of billowing smoke through which the sliding beams of the searchlights crossed and re-crossed. The red bursts from heavy anti-aircraft mingled with it all and yet we could not say that the defences were anything but light in character. This happy situation continued for some 20 minutes until the second aiming point, the actual rocket factory, was under heavy bombardment.

Because the target area was rapidly becoming a veritable inferno in which it became increasingly difficult to identify the various features, we flew lower on our next orbit and to my horror the gunners informed me that they had seen large 4,000-pound bombs falling past our aircraft. This was most alarming but was to be expected since many bombers were flying well above the height at which we were orbiting. Curiously enough, this simple fact had quite escaped notice when considering how best to do our job and yet it was the most obvious one. The possibility of our being walloped by a passing 'blockbuster' was more frightening than anything the enemy could do.

Wilkie Wanless took part in the initial stages of the attack, although there was a requirement for his crew to stay over the target for longer than was usually necessary:

> Before we had been bombing at 16,000 feet with the Halifax, but Peenemünde was 4,000 feet. It was the only low level I was ever on, and we were in the first wave. We were there before there were any markers. Our navigator had a movie camera and we were taking pictures that night for the RAF Film Unit. We kept flying back and forth over this target and the navigator kept saying, 'I think the damn thing's working now, do another run.' This was just terribly nerve-racking. The fighters had all been decoyed to Berlin, which was fine for the first wave or two.

John Martin flew as a pilot on the raid, with 3 Group's 620 Squadron, part of the first wave. He did recall an engagement with an enemy fighter. He also recalled one other 'engagement', brought on by the fog of war:

> During the attack we had a master bomber directing the dropping of the bombs. His call sign to us was 'Raven', and as soon as we were getting ready to do our run in to drop the bombs, he would call, 'Raven aircraft, Raven aircraft, don't drop the bombs, the TIs [target indicators] are falling into the sea.' Because of this we had to go around and start our bomb run again. The next number of crews had had the TI problem rectified; by the time it came our turn the target indicators were again falling into the sea so we had to abort our bomb run and again go around to start our bomb run again. On our next approach I was in the astrodome looking out, when suddenly this fighter came up dead astern. I shouted, 'Rear gunner, fighter, dead astern' The rear gunner fired at the fighter and shot it down. I was still in the astrodome and saw the glow of engines coming towards us and shouted, 'Rear gunner there is another one coming in.' The rear gunner started shooting. We then heard,

on the radio, 'Saint, saint'. It was a Halifax that we were shooting at. We dived and got away from it. We dropped our bombs on target and returned back to base. We had a second pilot with us that night, Bunse was his name. I was sitting in the Mess the next morning when Bunse came over to me and said, 'Would you read that there, Paddy.' The report was of a Halifax crew, being attacked from below and the flight engineer lost his foot in the incident. It seemed like the incident we had been involved in.

That was an awful night, the night of that Peenemünde raid. Can you visualize 600 aircraft going round and round, aircraft here and aircraft there, TI going off in the middle of it. During the bomb runs there was radio silence, apart from the master bomber. The master bomber shouted over the radio, 'Raven aircraft, Raven aircraft, don't bomb now the TIs are falling into the sea.' A wee voice from somewhere came up on the radio, 'Raven, Raven, we're Raven mad, would you drop those TIs.'[10]

Tommy Treadwell of 77 Squadron was also in the first wave of the attack:

Peenemünde appeared to be on a ridge running north to south on the coastline . . . The ridge has on its northern end a small island [Rugen] and it was this which the Pathfinders were using as a pointer to the target by placing on it a red spot fire . . . It was burning nicely as we passed over but we could in any case see the ground detail quite well. The target was progressively advanced with each scheduled wave of bombers . . . I found a convenient red upon which I dropped our load.

As we turned north from the target the fighters from Berlin were now in evidence, but they were not our immediate concern as we were paying more attention to the flak which could be just a little dangerous at the altitude we were flying. As the bomb doors were closing we felt sharp raps on the bottom of the aircraft and we thought we had been hit. A strong smell of burning permeated though the aircraft and a fire amidships was suspected. The rear gunner was the first to spot this as he turned in his turret to look forward. He reported a glow which he suggested was getting brighter. Having completed my own job as bomb aimer, and was then a 'spare bod', John Daffey asked me to go back to make an on-the-spot assessment of the situation. I did so and to my considerable relief I found that the red glow was coming from one of the red lamps in the fuselage . . . The cause of the raps was still not evident but it was a loose shutter which was causing the red glow to vary in intensity.

Tommy's crew, still on edge, prepared to land in Sweden if necessary, but John Daffey managed to bring the Halifax back to the UK, where they discovered the cause of the burning and the raps:

The raps were caused by a wire protruding from the bomb bays, having been trapped outside when the bomb doors were closed and whanging against the fuselage. There had in fact been a fire, and we were fortunate that this was only the motor of the F24 camera, which had jammed as it tried to take pictures of the target below when the bombs dropped. We had seen a number of aircraft shot down at the target, and everyone, including ourselves, was obviously in mortal danger but this dangling wire shows that the mind can create false dangers from circumstantial evidence, but is just as real at the time.

THE FOG OF WAR

The first wave of bombers had opened up the attack and dropped their bombs with little opposition; 500 tons of high explosive and 100 tons of incendiaries. The attack was not completely unopposed and flak would claim two aircraft. Unfortunately the initial marking at the target was not accurate; many of the first markers came down 2 miles south of the housing estate, with only a few in the correct position. Follow-up markers were able to initiate a correction of this error, and

Searby informed the main force crews that the initial marking should be ignored. Tragically, however, some crews in the early part of the raid did bomb the misplaced markers; these had dropped in a camp for foreign workers at nearby Trassenheide. Carnage ensued and there was a heavy loss of life. But with the marking corrected and with little aerial opposition at that stage, the RAF bombers of the first wave brought the war directly to the inhabitants of the research station's housing estate.

Next to attack were the Lancasters of 1 Group, but before they could bomb the production works it had to be marked by the 'shifters' of the Pathfinders. This too, did not go according to plan: only one set of markers was placed on the aiming point. But John Searby directed the incoming Lancasters to concentrate on the correct markers. The production works would be blasted but the bombing spread, owing to difficulties caused by a cross wind, smoke from previous bombing and a smokescreen. Some loads were dropped into nearby woods, or even into the sea. But at least there was still little opposition in the air.

Sam Hall was a navigator with a Pathfinder squadron and provides a good account of the importance of timing as a Pathfinder, and on this raid he would experience at first hand the arrival of nightfighters:

For me it was one of the most memorable raids. In the Pathfinder force you had to be accurate. Your target indicators had to go down on time because the rest of Bomber Command, the main force, was waiting to see those target indicators at the time that they'd been told. Now in order to achieve your timing, you had to keep time in hand in case the winds were such that you couldn't get there at the time you expected. When you got near the target you had to get rid of that time, and one way of doing it was to do dog-legs. You would go 60 degrees to the left, say, for 2 minutes and then come back 120 degrees, and by doing that you'd have an equilateral triangle for every 2 minutes. For every 2-minute leg you lost 2 minutes along the main track. That wasn't the best way of losing, but most people did it. But in our aircraft I had an arrangement with my pilot whereby I'd say a 1-minute turn or a 2-minute turn, and he would do a 360-degree turn and then go back on track. That would get rid of the time in one fell swoop. We did this in front of the thundering herd of Bomber Command behind us, but we reckoned it was worth it. We did that manoeuvre that night and it saved our lives. When we straightened up I decided to have a look at the war, pulled the navigator's curtain back, and immediately a German fighter came across our nose so close I could see the crosses under the wings and the wheels in place. The fighter had committed himself to a curve of pursuit against us in such a way that he'd expected us to be 4 miles further on and he couldn't reorganize his curves to get behind us. After we'd bombed, the mid-upper gunner said, 'There's a fighter coming in! It's got a Lanc, it's got another, it's got another!' Three Lancasters were going down in flames. You didn't waste too much time thinking about it. So many things were going on – all sorts of lights in the sky, flashes on the ground.[11]

To move the aiming point for the third wave, Pathfinder 'shifters' once more came in, but had similar success to those preceding the second wave. Under Searby's direction, the 6 Group crews bombed the markers conventionally. The time-and-distance method of 5 Group was now to be tested. The crews focused on their task, made even more difficult by the German nightfighters that had been released from Berlin, to head north to what was now, clearly, the main RAF target that night. John Searby recalled:

The second mark, aiming point 'B', was well and truly covered, and a mass of fire and smoke. [The marking of the third aiming point was problematic], since little could now be identified ... We were hard put to it to discern anything at this stage but continued as before to orbit out to sea and return back along the line of targets.

It was about this time that Ross called me over the intercom, 'Bomb aimer to captain – look out for fighters – a Lanc

has just blown up over the target.' I saw it almost at the
same moment. So the fighters had arrived, and from now
on things were likely to be difficult. Silhouetted against
the flame and smoke of the burning research station, the
bombers presented a clear mark and in the next 20 minutes
we were able to see many of our aircraft destroyed. The moon
was high and in short the odds were now against us . . .

The German fighters were now right in amongst the bombers
and one after another was shot down around us, exploding
before our eyes and falling in burning fragments. Twin and
single-engined fighters flew through the bomber stream and
the bright tracer shells were all too plain to see. This was
our seventh orbit of the target and the final scene in one
of the most impressive bombing attacks we had witnessed.
Enormous destruction lay below us. It is not possible to find
words which will convey accurately the true picture. Only a
bomber crew can appreciate the truth of these words and the
awful fascination in watching an assault of this magnitude
taken to a wide target area. It was one o'clock in the morning;
nothing more remained to be done at Peenemünde. These
50 minutes of time would remain long after other and similar
experiences had been forgotten. We turned for home.

David Balme had flown in the last wave of the attack. We join him as
he prepares to bring his Lancaster in on the timed run-in:

At last we are ready for the timed run-in, the navigator has
made his wizardlike calculations, and we suddenly hear
the 'Master of Ceremonies' [i.e. Searby] telling us to avoid
certain target indicators which are falling towards the sea.
Some crew is bombing too early, and he is peeved: 'Please
remember that I'm down here, you stupid prune.'

Our run is nearly finished, and in a moment we must decide
whether to bomb on markers or on time; but now we are in

luck, for the bomb aimer says, 'Target sighted dead ahead.'
So both Cocky [5 Group's AOC – Cochrane] and our navigator
are vindicated, and finally everything is up to the bomb
aimer and gunners: if they can't get us accurately and safely
to the target, the whole enterprise will go up in smoke only
too literally. So here we come, full boost and revs, '. . . steady,
steady – right a bit – steady – bombs going – steady'.

Bombing runs are our least favourite moment, and last forever.
This time the bomb aimer is moved to uncharacteristic eloquence:
'Cor, look at that,' he says. Then 'bombs all away, flash gone
off' and a climbing turn west to get the hell out of here. As the
bombs left, the aeroplane lifted like a young horse and is now
beautifully responsive. A quick glance shows roofless burning
buildings below and a runway to the right, but this is no time
for sightseeing: all eyes are watching for fighters, of which there
is no shortage. But nothing hits us, though we see other aircraft
burning on the ground and one poor devil blows up in the air.

HOMEWARD BOUND
With Peenemünde burning in their wake, the RAF bombers set course
for the long journey home. Not that they were out of danger. John
Searby's Lancaster was at the tail end of the bomber stream:

> . . . all heading back over the Baltic and our best chance of
> survival lay in losing our identity amongst them. After our last
> pass across the target we turned starboard instead of port and
> said farewell to the persevering gunners on the flak ships off
> the coast. We did not feel cocky, only thankful, and if we could
> survive the attentions of the nightfighters during the next hour
> or so all would be well. Alas, our hopes were short-lived, for
> within a matter of minutes of leaving Peenemünde the battle was
> on again. 'Rear gunner to captain. Fighter attacking from astern
> and below,' and I heard the rattle of the four machine guns in the
> same instant. Heaving on the controls violently, I brought the

Lancaster in a sharp turn to starboard 'nose down', a manoeuvre which strained every rivet in her frame, and red tracers streamed past without finding us. The fighter was attacking in a climb and the nose down attitude proved more effective than the turn, though the combination made the evasive action complete. 'Captain to gunners. Watch for him returning,' and there was complete silence amongst the crew. Every man took a point of vantage from which he could observe the night sky. Classically, I expected the enemy to attack from the dark side, with the Lancaster silhouetted against the moon, and the rear turret was watching this flank, the dorsal gunner taking the starboard side. Suddenly, 'Mid-upper gunner to captain, fighter coming in starboard quarter down,' and the Lancaster heaved over in a smart turn towards the attacking fighter. Both turrets opened fire and I saw the enemy's tracer bullets pass a little behind the tail. An excited shout from Flight Lieutenant Coley: our mid-upper informed me that he had got in a burst and hit the fighter and we claimed this German as damaged since we did not see him crash. Certainly, this was no time in which to stay and look for him. We sped on into the night. The fires of Peenemünde made an impressive glow behind us as we left Stralsund on our right and lost height over the Baltic Sea. Any elation we may have felt over the apparent success of the operation was tempered by the knowledge that the German nightfighters were taking a fearful toll of our returning bomber stream.

My crew were tired but for the next hour and a half unremitting vigilance would be needed. Fighter aircraft from all over northern Germany were concentrating on the Lancasters and Halifaxes and in the bright moonlight, conditions were perfect for interception. By flying at a low altitude over the sea we might hope to escape attention for a while, since the majority of the combats we witnessed were taking place around 8,000 to 10,000 feet. The chief danger for us lay in the distribution of light flak guns along the coast and on the many small islands in the Little Belt.

'Mid-upper to captain . . . Lancaster on fire to port.' I looked to
the left of the aircraft and watched a small point of bright light
grow rapidly until the aircraft was entirely visible – illuminated
by its own burning fuselage. The fighter struck again and his
tracer bullets ploughed through the flaming mass, which quickly
broke apart and plunged into the sea below. In a moment or
two we observed another bomber shot down a few miles ahead
of us and this one exploded in mid-air. Combats took place
the whole way across the sea to the Danish mainland, where
the leading wave of the bomber stream was now located.

John took his crew across Denmark and approached the North Sea
coast:

'Crossing the coast skipper,' from the bomb aimer, and
immediately one felt relieved. How many times had one heard
this simple but significant phrase; the feeling of escape from
danger and things which go bang in the night . . . Ahead of us the
bomber stream wound its way home. We were certainly the last.
Sharp eyes continued to search the sky and the surface below.
A convoy of German ships making its way down the coast could
strike us down in a moment at the low height we were flying.
The full moon cast cloud shadows on the sea below – our faithful
Rolls Merlins drummed on a fine even note as we continued our
course to the west. I eased my straps a little to take some of the
ache away. I felt grubby, and the rubber lining of my face mask
was sticky against my cheeks, the familiar stench of the aircraft
– oil, body odours and the strange indefinable smell given off
by the heated radar and electrical equipment – all combined
to make one think of getting clean again. I thought about the
gunners, Coley and Preece, cramped in their turrets, staring into
the dark hour after hour, hands always on the gun controls,
flung madly against their straps when the aircraft took evasive
action. 'Captain to mid-upper, can you see anything?' 'Mid-

upper to captain, all quiet.' 'Rear gunner to captain, nothing to report.' Nothing to report and the likelihood of interception was decreasing every second as we flew towards England.

Once out over the sea, crews often felt they could relax to some extent. German nightfighter crews were not going to risk a long pursuit over water at night. David Balme recalled:

As we get clear out to sea, we reach what is really the favourite moment. Everything has gone quiet. I look out along the wing where the two port engines crouch like tigers, purring now under reduced boost and revs, but nursing their power if it should be needed. Soon the W/Op will bring that disgusting coffee which is pure nectar. But not before he performs one vital task. Having had to listen out in silence all night, he is now permitted one call to base. He comes up with information about the airfield state and the barometric pressure there. We set the altimeter for home.

There comes the English coast, dark, dangerous, precious, containing everything that this whole exercise is about. Two searchlights stand like crossed swords, marking an emergency landing strip for those in trouble, but we are not in trouble tonight, touch wood. At base the flare path is already lit up and aircraft are plentiful so that we deem it prudent to put on nav lights though we dislike them, having regard to intruders [enemy aircraft patrolling British bases]. Flying control even want to stack us up to 11,000 feet if you please; what an absurd notion. We all go round the circuit together, and since the people in front look a bit close we make a tight orbit in the funnel, a manoeuvre which displeases the station commander, as we later discover.

All safely down, quick chat with the ground crew to tell them how marvellously their aircraft performed, debriefing and pint of alleged cocoa (containing, so it is said, bromide for the protection of WAAFs), our operational eggs, sausages, beans and fried bread without which we should unquestionably mutiny, and then to get our heads down. Presently a WAAF orderly comes quietly round the quarters and pulls down the sheet from each sleeping face. Somebody wakes and asks what she is doing. 'Just checking that my family are all back,' she says.

Master bomber John Searby had also managed to return to friendly airspace without further trouble:

After seven and a half hours in the air we picked up the Wyton flashing beacon and landed, to be driven immediately to the interrogation room. Mr Sandys was waiting. He had already gathered much information from the crew reports but wanted final confirmation from me. I could only say that from what I had seen this had been a successful operation but I could not confirm the destruction of Peenemünde. We must await the photo reconnaissance aircraft with its detailed survey of the area. Mr Sandys was very pressing and this was understandable but he appreciated the necessity for caution, and, in any event, he had heard enough to convince him that the job was well done . . . even had we known what lay behind it all I don't think it would have made the slightest difference; the determination and 'press on' spirit of the bomber crews never varied regardless of the character of defences of the target.

The optimism in the immediate aftermath of the raid was well-founded. History now assesses that the attack delayed the development of the V-2 by at least two months and certainly diminished the scale of the rocket attack, unleashed on England the following year. In addition to the extensive material damage, historians claim that between 120 and 178 Germans were killed, including a Dr Thiel, a propulsion specialist. Tragically, between 500 and 600 foreign workers were killed in the workers' camp. The cost to Bomber Command was 40 bombers and crews. Was it worth it? Certainly many Londoners would be seeing the end of the war because of the bomber crews' sacrifice.

# 6
# 'BIG WEEK': BOMBING THE LUFTWAFFE, GOTHA

*The Eighth Air Force raid on the Messerschmitt works at Gotha on 24 February 1944 takes its place as one of the most accurate and effective attacks during 'Big Week' – the crucial all-out attack on the German aircraft industry – but at a price. The factory was described as 'the most valuable single target in the enemy's twin-engined fighter complex'. Even more special was the fact that the opposition in the air was some of the most intense of the whole war, and rendezvous with part of the fighter escort was missed, yet the American bomber boys pressed on to the target regardless. And they suffered the consequences.*

In the months following the Eighth Air Force's 'Black Week', and the crippling losses suffered, the England-based American heavy bomber force rebuilt, bringing in new crew, new aircraft, and indeed whole new bomb groups. Missions continued into German airspace, but not outside the range of fighter escort: from the P-38 Lightnings, P-47 Thunderbolts, and bolstered by the introduction of the P-51 Mustangs.

The Eighth was still a formidable force; for example, 560 bombers and 378 fighters were involved in a mission to Wilhelmshaven on 3 November, but there would be no deeper penetrations over the Reich beyond the support of the 'little friends'. Into the new year, and General 'Hap' Arnold, Commanding General of the US Army Air Forces, set the tone for forthcoming action: '**Destroy the enemy air force wherever you find them, in the air, on the ground and in the factories.**' There were command changes, mainly in preparation for operation *Overlord*. General Spaatz took command of the United States Strategic Air Forces (which shortly after became the USSTAFE, having had 'in Europe' added), and the Eighth had a new commander, Lieutenant General James H. 'Jimmy' Doolittle. Myron Keilman, who flew with the 392nd Bomb Group, certainly recalled the impression Doolittle made:

> At group and squadron level we were quite impressed. We all felt we knew the famous aviator, if not from his airplane racing days, from his leading the famous Tokyo bombing raid.
> We didn't realize that at that moment his orders were: 'Win the air war and isolate the battlefield.' In other words – destroy the Luftwaffe and cut off the beaches of Normandy for the Invasion.[1]

The men of the Eighth now set about enacting the wishes of General Arnold and the attrition rates would once more escalate. Doolittle's bombers would target the enemy aircraft in production and at the airfields; his fighters would not just escort the bombers, they would also look to hunt out and destroy their adversaries. But, as always, the execution of the offensive was dependent upon European weather, and in the early months of 1944 there was frustration. Myron Keilman recalled:

> By 20 February our group had been alerted, briefed, and taxied for take-off nearly every morning since General Doolittle took command. There we waited for hours in the dense fog before the red flare signal of 'mission cancelled' was fired from the control tower.
> Then back to the airplane's dispersal pad, back to the dank Nissen huts, back to the damp ice-cold cots for needed sleep and tomorrow's alert. 'Damn the foggy weather, damn the war, and damn General Doolittle, too.' After those early hour breakfasts, the Mess sergeant had to pick up the General's portrait from a face-down position in the middle of the floor and rehang it in its respected place. Disrespect? Yes, but who wants to be rousted out at 03.00 hours day in and day out just to sit in the fog? We couldn't win the war doing this, and you didn't have to be a general to see that the weather was

unfit to fly a bombing mission – were our glum thoughts. The weather had been so adverse during January and to the 20 February, our group had flown only 16 missions; most of them were Noball strikes against the buzz-bomb (V1, flying bombs) launching sites. Then came a streak of decent weather and an all-out air offensive against the German Luftwaffe factories.

A HEATED ARGUMENT
Codenamed 'Argument' at the time, the series of attacks against the German aircraft industry between 20 and 25 February 1944 is now remembered as 'Big Week'. During the week, both RAF Bomber Command and the USAAF Fifteenth Air Force would also be in action against German aircraft production. And the Eighth Air Force bombers supported with massive fighter support: Thunderbolts, Lightnings and Mustangs also sought to cut off the lifeblood of the Luftwaffe.

On 20 February, 1,003 Eighth Air Force bombers, formed up into 16 combat wings, were despatched to open Big Week. Accompanying the bomber crews in the skies were 835 fighters. The next day, the Eighth despatched 861 bombers, supported by 679 fighters, and on 22 February, 799 B-17s and B-24s, and 659 Lightnings, Thunderbolts and Mustangs.

The air battle was often ferocious and intense. Lieutenant Ackerson serving as a bombardier with the 384th Bomb Group, and described a 'common' experience for crews during one mission:

On 22 February we went to Aschersleben on a scheduled visual mission. This one was the worst by far that we ever had, a long ride of more than 8 hours of hell. Not much flak, but more fighters than I've ever seen or want to see. The mission started off wrong. We (our group) had a mid-air collision on the assembly and lost two ships, and crews. Almost a half-hour inside the German border about 20 Me109s hit our squadron. They attacked for about 5 minutes and then left.

The attack was taken up by more than 30 FW190s, who kept on us for about 30 minutes, just going around and around our squadron. We lost three of our squadron, Kew, Defries and McDonald. Evasive action and accurate shooting saved our necks. We fired about 2,000 rounds in all. Tom, Red and I claimed one apiece. From there to the target we had no more opposition and no more trouble until 3 minutes from the coast on the way out, when two more FW190s made a pass. One was shot down by Red with no damage to us.[2]

There was a welcome pause the next day. Then, on the morning of 24 February, 809 bomber crews and 767 fighter pilots of the Eighth Air Force prepared once more to penetrate German airspace and keep up the pressure. Three targets were scheduled: Rostock, Schweinfurt and Gotha, to be attacked by 13 combat wings, escorted by 19 USAAF Fighter Groups and eight RAF Squadrons.

Staff Sergeant Theodore A. Rausch of the 392nd Bomb Group recorded in his diary his impression of the mission as one that, 'I will never forget till my dying day, which I thought it was.'

John Cihon also served with the 392nd Bomb Group, 2nd Bomb Division, and he too recalled the mission as, 'A day that I shall never forget.'

I credit my being alive now to unusual good luck, and a damn good parachute. Our target that day was an aircraft factory in the town of Gotha, deep in Germany. We weren't too worried about the mission, although our position of 'tail-end Charlie' in the group didn't exactly make us feel happy either. However, we were flying the good ship 'Poco Loco', the plane our crew brought over from the States, so we felt fairly confident.

Hal Turell served as a navigator with the 703rd Bomb Squadron, 445th Bomb Group, 2nd Bomb Division.

On 24 February 1944, we were briefed to attack an aircraft
factory located in Gotha, Germany, that produced twin-engine
fighters. This was to be mission number 13 for the crew.
We had been scheduled for this same target 2 days prior but it
had been scrubbed due to weather. It was a deep penetration
of enemy territory and we all had very bad premonitions about
this mission. The attrition rate on experienced crews had
been quite heavy. Our chances then of surviving to complete a
tour were one in three. In order to gain some extra crews, the
Eighth Air Force had extended the mission tour from 25 to 30
and moreover told us to fly with a nine-man crew. This meant
leaving one gunner behind. Ray Davis, who manned the ball
turret underneath the ship, was selected not to fly that day.[3]

Sam Mastrogiacomo of the 445th Bomb Group would also fly to
Gotha on that day. Sam began his active service life as a waist gunner.
Then on one occasion, he got the opportunity to defend his aircraft
from the rear, because the tail gunner was sick:

. . . and I got to like it. The tail gunner said, 'I'll tell you
what. Before we go on the missions, we'll flip a coin and if
you get what you want, you can take the tail position.'
It seemed like whenever I got the tail, we got a lot of action.
    In gunnery school they told us about these German fighter
planes that are going to be coming after us and we had better
be on our toes. On our first couple of missions I was sitting
there, (still as waist gunner) looking for any planes coming in.
I could see them coming in on the bomb groups alongside of
us, but they didn't come in on us. After our second mission, I
told our navigator, the old man of the crew – wise old man, I
think he was 27 or 28 – 'Wow, these Germans are afraid to come
in on us. I'll knock 'em right out of the air if they come closer.'
    He says, 'Don't be too anxious. Just hope they don't come

in on you.'

'Oh,' I said. 'We're trained to get 'em.'

'Take it easy,' he said. 'You'll see enough.' Sure enough, later on, we did.

PREPARATIONS

Sam Mastrogiacomo recalled the briefing the morning of 24 February:

They usually had a map that was covered with a shade.
When the doors were closed they let the shade go up.
We could see by the red string where we were gonna go. When we saw that long string to Gotha, pretty far into Germany, there were a few beads of sweat.

The 392nd Bomb Group's Myron Keilman had also seen that long string stretching across Germany:

The 2nd Air Division's target was the big airplane plant at Gotha, 420 miles due east of the white cliffs of Dover. Our briefing for the attack on Gotha was at 06.30 hours. It was our group's fortieth mission, so we took it all in stride. To most of us it meant another mission to be accomplished against our total, then back home to the safety of the ZI [zone of interior]. The intelligence officer briefed [us] on the importance of the big plant to German's ability to carry on the air war, and on the fact that it was heavily defended by big 88- and 110-millimeter anti-aircraft artillery like we faced over Bremen, Kiel, and Wilhelmshaven. We were certain to encounter heavy fighter attacks all across enemy territory: 400 miles in and 400 miles out.

Crews were transported to their laden bombers. Hal Turell climbed aboard and inhaled, 'the familiar smell of hydraulic and gasoline':

After securing my briefcase and laying out my charts, I
preflighted the navigator's compartment. The drift meter
was OK, as was the instrument panel. The only readings I
could get on the ground were the altimeter and temperature.
I checked the intervolameter on the bomb controls and saw
that the lights were working. Someone had started the putt-
putt – the auxiliary generator – so we had electric power.
I could hear the chattering of the little gasoline motor and feel
the vibrations through the thin sheet metal of the airplane's
skin. After checking to see that the windows and astraldome
were clean, I thumbtacked my chart to the plywood board that
served as the navigator's desk. I left my other instruments in
the case, as take-off usually sent them scattering. I then joined
the crew outside the airplane for a smoke and chit chat.

Because all of us were quite apprehensive about this mission,
we so loaded the ship with extra ammunition that it barely
could take off. After all, 1,000 rounds of ammunition could
be fired by each gun in 2 minutes. Our plane that day was
Dixie Dudrop. Someone else had named her but we had flown
her several times before. She was a good bird. Finally it was
time for start engines so we all took our places on board.
As the nose turret was kept empty during take-off and landings,
I positioned myself against the radio-room bulkhead, on the
flight deck behind the pilots. We watched as each engine whined
in protest and then finally caught with a burst of smoke and
loud coughs. After all four were running and the pilots had
completed their checks, there was a wait. Then the green flare
was fired from the tower and each ungainly beast waddled off
the hardstands onto the taxi way. The B-24 is graceful, beautiful
and deadly looking in the air. On the ground it looks like a
slab-sided prehistoric monster wading through swamps.

Myron Keilman's crew having gathered their escape and evasion kits,
donned heated flying suits, collected oxygen masks, flak helmets, Mae

Wests (life jackets) and parachutes, and climbed aboard trucks , 'for a cold ride to our airplane's dispersal pad':

It was still very dark as we made our airplane inspection, checking all the engine cowling for loose Dzus fasteners; the turbines of the super-chargers; the propeller blades and pushing them through to release any piston hydraulic lock; the fuel cells for being 'topped-off' and their caps for security; the guns and turrets, ammunition quantity of 500 rounds for each of the ten 50-caliber machine guns; the Sperry bombsight; the twelve 500-pound bombs, their shackles, fuses and safety wires; the oxygen supply and regulators; signal flares; camera; and many other things. At 08.10 we started engines. At 08.15 the lead ship taxied to take-off position. At 08.30 the green flare from the control tower signalled 'take off!' It was breaking dawn.

Lead crew pilot Jim McGregor 'revved-up' his engines, checked the instruments, released the brakes and rolled. Thirty-one B-24 Hs followed at 30-second intervals.

Hal Turell had followed a similar procedure to Myron:

The metal shrieks [in] protest as we rumble along and the hydraulic motors whine in chorus with it. Overall there is the growling of the engines and the steady chatter of the putt-putt. Tires squeal as engines rev up to put us into a turn and we take our place in the line of huge gray beasts in the gloom of the morning haze. In front and behind are row after row of these Liberators, waiting, poised like racehorses at the starting gate. The throaty rumble of the engines, the propellers turning and the noses bobbing up and down as the pilots apply their brakes to keep from over-running the plane in front. Each time the hydraulic pumps add their high-pitched protests to the cacophony of noise. Nose to tail they wait in a tight line, the end of the queue lost in the mist.

The take-off flare arches into the sky and before it
touches the ground, the first Liberator is hurtling down
the runway. Thirty seconds later, before the first plane
has cleared the runway, the next plane in line pushes
their throttles forward and roars toward the sky.

John Cihon recalled:

We took off at nine o'clock in the morning, formed our groups
east of the 'Wash' and then headed for Germany. Over the
English Channel I ordered the gunners to test fire their guns;
they all worked OK, except the engineer's. In a few minutes' time
he called me over the interphone. He had remedied the trouble,
we were all set. At approximately eleven o'clock we crossed the
Dutch coast, the atmosphere was sparkling clear, there wasn't
a cloud in sight. We were flying at an altitude of 20,000 feet
and I could distinguish ground objects with ease. Above us I
saw the contrails of friendly fighters, they must have been up
at about 35,000 feet, there were five or six of them. Little did I
know then, that was the last I was to see of our escort that day.

After climbing, Myron Keilman found himself in the clear at 12,000
feet:

The lead ship fired red-yellow identification flares. Flying deputy
lead, I pulled into position on his left wing, and the group
formed over radio beacon '21' into three squadrons. Then it flew
the wing triangular assembly pattern to Kings Lynn. Leading
the 14th Combat Wing, we fell into number two position of
the 2nd Air Division's bomber stream over Great Yarmouth.
Heading east over the Channel and climbing to 18,000 feet, our
gunners test-fired their guns. We penetrated enemy territory
just north of Amsterdam. At 235 miles per hour true airspeed
over the Zuider Zee, our streaming vapor trails signalled our

presence and our intent. It was a thrilling moment. Onward over Dümmer Lake, past our future Osnabrück target, south-east past Hanover's bombed-out airfields, our big formations hurried.

WHERE'S THE ESCORT?
Hal Turell had hauled his bomber up to 12,000 feet, where the 445th Bomb Group crews gathered in formation, then flying on to assemble with other groups, forming their combat wing.

The wings also formed up by flying in huge circles, allowing stragglers to catch up, and then headed out over the North Sea. By this point, five planes had turned back because of various malfunctions. We were 15 minutes ahead of schedule at this point. This was to cost us dearly in the hours ahead.

We missed our rendezvous with our fighter cover. Crossing the North Sea, the sky was icy blue, with not a single cloud in sight. We left no vapor trails as the air was much too cold. The silver formations sparkled like a ballroom's mirror globe as they promenaded their stately ballet through the European sky. The music of Ravel's 'Pavanne For A Dead Princess' glided through my mind. I thought, 'Here comes the death parade.' The sea was wild from the recent winter storms and almost white with foam. I had a vision of the sea receding as it did for Moses and the bottom exposed. What a wilderness of sunken ships and planes might lie on this narrow floor. These waters, the battle arena of so many wars, some remembered and more forgotten. Broken ships and broken bones would carpet all the sea bed. From red-bearded Vikings, the Spanish Armada, the Battle of Jutland: the remnants were now covered by a forest of Lancasters, Heinkels, Fortresses, Wellingtons and Liberators. Fresh bones from the New World come to an alien shore.

Sergeant Billie McClellan, so far from his Oklahoma farm, was flying in the ball turret that day. We had to leave Ray Davis behind as result of the new nine-man crew rule. As the formation crossed the North Sea, he could see enemy fighters picking off some B-17s that had aborted their formation and turned back to England. Mac saw eight of these Flying Fortresses go down into the icy waters. No parachutes could save them from the freezing depths. A man would live just 2 minutes at those temperatures. Mac tried to shoot at the Nazis going after the stragglers, twisting the turret through 365 degrees. He then heard a pounding on the turret. It was Sergeant Roland Woods, waist gunner, trying to get his attention. To open the ball turret, the guns have to be first pointed to the rear and then straight down. Mac opened the turret and asked Woody what the hell he wanted and couldn't Woody see that he was busy shooting!

Sergeant Woods did not say anything, he just pointed to what he was trying to hold. Then Mac saw that the main oxygen tube, that supplied the ball turret's air tanks, had broken off. Woody had folded it double but could not hold it and the tube was snaking around, bleeding the ship's oxygen supplies. The male filler plug was broken. Because Sergeant Raymond Davis had been left behind, Billie was not used to this turret and he did not spot the problem before take-off. They could not just hold the hose doubled as it was to be a long mission. We were just starting and were short one gunner. So the ball turret could not be used for the remainder of the mission. This left us no defense to attacks from below. There was no question of abandoning the mission, as the enemy was all around. Group leader kept calling for the high fighter cover to come down. They did. They were Germans!

Sam Mastrogiacomo, also of the 445th Bomb Group, was sitting pensively in the rear of his bomber:

We were about an hour into the mission and had test fired our guns, just a few rounds from each gun. When we saw our fighters turn back, we kept our eyes open because we knew they were gonna come in. Sure enough, about an hour and 15 minutes into the mission, we saw, all at once, these little dots that became bigger and bigger: enemy fighter planes. They usually worked from the back, at that time, to get the rear planes; they'd get a longer shot at you, and could angle on your tail. In a nose attack or waist attack they would have to break off, whereas from the tail they could hang on and see where the vulnerable spots were. During the thick of the battle, bullets were flying around and planes were going down. I saw a plane right alongside of us get hit, and all at once he was climbing. I kept my eye on him; he was almost right behind us to the right side. He climbed like a fighter plane, and all at once he looped. When he came out he flew level again. 'Ohhh, he's OK,' I thought. 'He's all right now.' Ten seconds later, the whole plane blew up. I didn't see anybody get out.

The bombers held course as best they could. The Luftwaffe pilots attempted to break up the formations and shoot their adversaries from the sky. Hall Turell remembered:

The Germans used a variety of attacks. First, they came in waves of fighters, line abreast, then they would form a queue and come roaring in one after the other. Other fighters stood off at a distance and fired rockets into the formation. Dive-bombers came through with a large ball hanging on the end of a cable about 100 feet long. We heard the tail gunner, Sergeant Bill Adair, say some enemy fighters, after their frontal pass, were blowing up after they were a mile or so past the group. It looked as though 300 or 400 fighters were working over our combat wing with special emphasis on our group. Mac was overjoyed to see two German fighters collide on two occasions.

Our lead plane was hit and did a slow roll towards us. At the same time, about five Germans came right at us as we were now outside the formation. Our pilot, Lieutenant Ralph Stimmel, was able to side slip our plane when the frontal pass came. This threw their aim off considerably. One of our lead ships caught a direct hit. It exploded, sending airplane and body parts through the formation, doing considerable damage to other ships. One Me109 came head-on into one of our group and blew off the Liberator's nose. As the ship went spinning down, the 109 pulled up into a steep climb. The top turret gunner of the following B-24 put a long burst into him. The 109 fell off on its back and went down through the formation, crashed into another Liberator in the low element and took off its whole tail section. This ship headed up into the bomb bay of another Lib and the two planes collided. One of them went sailing through the formation, scattering it. Breaking a formation is the German fighter pilot's dream. The 445th fortunately had their most experienced crews out that day and the formation quickly recovered, each ship taking its place as though it was a drill every time an incident like that occurred.

John Cihon of the 392nd Bomb Group, having crossed the Dutch Coast and into Reich airspace, felt the atmosphere of anxious anticipation:

We proceeded on course; all the gunners were on the alert, tense at their stations, scanning the skies for enemy fighters. The bomber formation seemed to tighten up as if they sensed that all was not well. We were only about 50 miles inland when justification for any uneasiness was realized; the scream of 'enemy fighters' was heard over the interphone in our plane, and in others too, I'll wager.

Yes, the Luftwaffe was out in force, ready to give us a rousing welcome. There were 50 to 75 FW190s and Me109s attacking, hitting us mostly from beneath which made it hard for us to spot them, as they blended with the ground in that position of attack. However, there were several wings of bombers, and we were more than holding our own with our concentrated fire power. An occasional Liberator went down in flames, but the Jerries were paying dearly for each one.

I was in the nose turret, but my chances for shots were far and few between as most of the attacks were from the lower rear. Our tail and ball gunners, Jan Brown and Tracy Kelly respectively, were doing an excellent job in staving off attacks from that quarter. I could feel 'Poco Loco' shudder each time one of them let go a volley with his twin fifties. More than one Jerry went down in smoke and was sorry he doubted their marksmanship. Our real trouble began when the different wings of bombers split up to bomb their respective targets. Our wing continued on course, while the others veered northward. Unfortunately, the German interceptors stayed with us.

We were well inside of Germany now, and knew that we were in for a bad time; the situation was desperate. Our bomber force was gradually dwindling while the number of German fighters increased steadily, more and more of them taking off from German soil. We estimated that there were about 200 enemy aircraft in the group attacking us. They queued up in fives and sixes, on all sides, striking simultaneously, hammering us from every direction. Hits were scored in every attack. We fired green flares in hope that some friendly fighters might be in the vicinity and see our pleas for help, but none came. Where was our escort? That was the foremost question in every crew member's mind. Later on, we found out what had happened: through some miscalculation we were 15 minutes ahead of schedule and were missing connections with our escort at rendezvous points all along the route. A very costly mistake, I'd say.

As we approached Kassel, the Jerries suddenly left us. We were puzzled. The answer to the situation came soon enough: over the town of Kassel we encountered the most terrific flak barrage I've ever seen. My opinion is voiced by others also. Plane after plane had engines hit, or some other damage which forced them to lag behind. (Why S-2 routed us over that town is something I never will understand.) Leaving Kassel, we were a sorry-looking formation: ships were straggling everywhere. The fighters, who had left us momentarily, sized up the situation, saw our plight and came in for the kill.

From there to the IP was a horrible nightmare. A burning ship was to be seen almost anytime. Many were German but too many were ours. 'Poco Loco' wasn't faring too well either. Our tail turret had jammed and was all but useless, our top turret was put completely out of action by 20-millimeter shells, and our ball turret was about out of ammunition.

Sam Mastrogiacomo was perfectly aware that the formation he was flying in was becoming smaller and smaller as bombers fell all around him:

Pretty soon we were tail-end Charlie; they were coming in on us. I had to really be on my toes. An Me110, a twin-engine plane, was behind us, about 2,000 yards away, and as he came in close, I give him a blast. Even though it was out of range a little bit, I'd give him a blast and he would hold off. All at once he did come a little closer, and released rockets. I'd never seen a rocket before. His two rockets came right for our airplane. And it seemed like I was the target. I thought, 'Oh no, this is gonna be the end.' Then when the rockets came real close, they were spent, went right under our airplane. 'Ohhhh,' I exclaimed. Then right after that more fighter planes were coming in at us. All at once there was a splash of machine gun fire right through my turret, and an explosion. It knocked my oxygen mask off. I was in shock. My navigator would call, about every 10 minutes, 'Everybody OK?' He would go by position, 'Waist gunner, right gunner, how ya doing? Left waist gunner, how ya doing?' And the reply normally came back 'Fine, everything all right.' This time he called, 'Tail gunner, how ya doing?' I didn't answer. 'Tail gunner, how ya doing?' I heard it over the interphone but I couldn't answer. I was thinking of my mother getting a telegram that I'd been killed. I thought of so many things, in about 5 seconds. Why did I ask for this? Why? When I went in the Air Force I said, 'Oh, I want to go in the toughest part of the Air Force.' 'Oh, you want to be a gunner . . .'

One of the waist gunners came running back to see if I was all right. I felt something on the back of my neck, hot. I said, 'Wow, I got hit but it don't hurt that bad.' I looked at my collar and it was red. The waist gunner said, 'Sam, are you all right?' I pointed at my neck. He looked and he said, 'That's only hydraulic fluid. You're all right.' What a relief.

I tried to operate my turret, but it wasn't working. I guess the hydraulic got shot out in the turret. My glass was all shattered, like spider webs, and I couldn't see out. I had to get rid of the glass. I remembered from gunnery school that there were four pins that you pulled out to jettison the glass, if it became damaged or shattered. So I pulled the pins out, and I tried to push it out, but it wouldn't go. I went back in the seat and pushed, real hard, but it wouldn't go. About the third time I tried it, I prayed, 'God, give me the strength.' When I pushed it the fourth time, it came out, and fell right between my guns, which were elevated. So I've still got to get rid of it. I used my hand cranks, elevation and azimuth, and I put my guns down so that the glass would slide from the two guns. About that time a fighter plane approached. About 200 feet away I was able to see his face and he looked like he was ready to press the trigger on me. I quickly hit the foot firing, as the one my thumbs were on wouldn't work because of the hydraulic failure and the electrical failure. I hit the manual foot firing, the guns went off, I hit him and blew him apart just like a fireball.

Now I got ready for the other planes coming in. I fired at another one and saw a piece of the plane come apart, it spun out of control. I did see the pilot, or something come out like a body; he must have baled out. You can't watch him all the time because other planes are coming in. To get a confirmation of shooting a fighter plane, you had to see the pilot bale out or you had to see the plane blow apart or you had to see the plane hit the ground and explode. Well you're not going to be watching until it hits the ground because you're like 20, 25,000 feet up in the air.

It was a running battle. I'd heard of guys that had got trigger happy. Pressing the triggers until the guns got so hot that the barrels could warp. You've got to give it maybe eight to 12 round bursts, just a short burst each time. And conserve your ammunition too; you can't use it that fast. Get trigger happy and that's your doom.

We were still flying to the target, and I was told that we had a camera on the bottom hatch. I was supposed to turn that on at the IP, 7 minutes before the target. I got out of the turret real fast, turned the camera on at the IP and jumped back in the turret because we were still under attack.

We had one engine shot up and the oil was leaking out, and our landing gear was shot up. I looked around the airplane and saw sunlight coming through the holes that had hit the airplane. One rudder had holes in it, the canvas flapping.

PRESSING ON

With the air fight ongoing, the depleted bomber formations approached their target. Myron Keilman recalled:

Bending south-eastward toward Gotha, the white, snowy earth looked cold and lifeless; only the large communities, rail lines, and an autobahn stood out in relief. Fighter attacks became more persistent. By the time we reached our initial point (IP) to start our bomb run, the sky about our three squadrons was full of busy P-38s and P-51s fending off the Germans. I remember how they dove past the lead ship in pursuit of Messerschmitt and Focke-Wulf fighters making head-on attacks. Our gunners got in a lot of shooting, too. The staccato of the turrets' twin fifties vibrated throughout the airplane. It was real scary.

The weather was 'clear as a bell' as we turned to the target. Red flares from the lead ship signalled 'bomb bay doors open'. The bombardier removed the heated cover blanket from the bombsight. He checked his gyroscope's stabilization, and all bombing switches ON. Our high and low squadrons fell in trail and all seemed great. Then pilotage navigator Kennedy in the nose turret observed the lead wing formations veering from the target heading. A fast and anxious cross-check with Lead Crew Navigator Swangren and with a recheck of compass heading and reference points, they assured Command Pilot Lorin Johnson that the target was 'dead ahead'. I don't know where the 2nd Air Division leader wound up, and I've forgotten which group and wing it was, but at that moment the 392nd, leading the 14th Combat Wing, was 'on course – on target'. Within minutes, Lead Bombardier Good called over the interphone, 'I've got the target!' Lead Pilot McGregor checked his flight instruments for precise 18,000 feet altitude and 160 miles per hour indicated airspeed, and carefully levelled the airplane on autopilot. Then he called back: 'On airspeed, on altitude. You've got the airplane.' Making a final level of his bombsight, Good took over control of steering the airplane with the bombsight.

The bombardier's target folder didn't contain a snowy, winter view of the Messerschmitt Aircraft Works. He had to use his keen judgment and trained skills in discerning the briefed aiming point. Only his one eye peering through the bombsight optics could determine where to place the cross-hair. He could and did give a commentary to the command pilot and crew of what he saw and what he was doing in steering the lead airplane and formation of bombers to the bomb release point, but only he, the lead bombardier, 'knew for sure' what was viewed through that bombsight.

At 18,000 feet, it was 40 degrees below zero, but the bombardier never felt the cold as his fingers delicately operated the azimuth and range controls. He cross-checked all the bomb and camera switches to the ON position, especially the radio bomb release (RBR) signal switch that would release all the bombs of the other airplanes in the formation simultaneously. There wasn't a cloud in the sky.

When the flak started bursting near the formation, Lieutenant Good had already attained a synchronized bombing run with the wind drift 'killed' and the cross-hair holding steady on the aiming point of the great manufacturing complex. The bombsight indices crossed and 'bombs away!' Beautiful!

While the camera was recording the impact of the bombs, Lieutenant McGregor took over and swung the formation to the outbound heading and the rally point.

In spite of the new accurate flak from the 88- and 110-millimeter anti-aircraft artillery, the second and third squadron bombardiers, Lt Ziccarrilli and Lt Jackson, steered their squadrons to the precise bomb delivery points. Of 32 B-24s that took off that morning, 29 delivered 348 500-pound bombs, precisely on the Gotha factory as briefed. Outstanding! The bombs were smack 'on target', but the battle wasn't over.

In John Cihon's aircraft the radio operator opened the bomb bay doors at the IP, 'But I had to get out of the nose turret to manipulate a stubborn bomb-release lever which was giving the navigator trouble.'

I had just gotten back into the nose when the climax to our worries was reached. A rocket tore through our flight deck, leaving a gaping hole about a foot and a half in diameter on each side of the ship. The plane started burning immediately, our electric power was out, the control cables were gone and our radio operator lay mortally wounded among the shambles of wrecked radio equipment. In the turret, being rather isolated, I was unaware of the terrific damage done by the rocket. However, when, during a head-on attack by several FW190s, my turret failed to operate, I knew something was amiss.

John tried the interphone but found it silent. Then his aircraft began to slip to the left and his navigator began pounding on his turret door, 'a signal for me to get out'.

Getting out of the nose turret, unassisted, was a problem to be reckoned with. Rigged in full flying equipment, it's a difficult task even when one is in complete possession of his faculties and has time. I had to get out in a hurry – the ship was starting a slow spin to the left. How I managed such a quick exit that day remains a mystery to me.

Once out, I wasted no time. The navigator had the escape hatch open and was preparing to jump. He had just left when I reached for my chute. In my haste I put it on backwards (it was the chest variety and this puts an opposite strain on the hooks from what was intended) but there was no time for lingering decisions; the ship was burning from nose wheel to tail turret, the acid smoke was nauseating. I plunged headlong out of the escape hatch and looking up, I saw the blazing fuselage of 'Poco Loco' pass over me. The opening of the chute blacked me out for a few seconds. When I looked in the direction where 'Poco Loco' should have been, I saw a huge black pall of smoke. 'Poco Loco' had exploded in mid-air just seconds after I had gotten out. With it, four members of our crew were blown to eternity. They died as many fliers do, may they rest in peace.

As I drifted earthward I had grim satisfaction in seeing the blazing factory in the distance. The price was high, but the boys had hit the target. Hanging in space, I was awed by the silence, broken only by the rippling of silk. I looked upward, my chute had held, God had spared me, and I thanked Him.

As I neared the earth, I was surprised at my rapid rate of descent. The ground appeared to be rushing toward me. From high altitude it hardly seemed that I was falling. Below me, a group of Germans lay in wait. I side slipped my chute to miss some buildings and buckled my knees slightly to avoid broken bones upon impact. I landed less than 50 feet from the Jerries with a hard thud, felt something snap in my back and fell forward on my chest. There was no wind and the chute covered me completely. As I clambered out from under the silk, the Germans were at my side.

I was ordered by gestures to put my hands up. I raised them without hesitation; my back ached terribly. I must have sprained a vertebra in landing. The German party consisted of several civilian home guards, armed with pistols, and two regular Wehrmacht soldiers. One of the civilians proceeded to give me a verbal lashing. He raised his voice until I thought his lungs would burst, and ended up in a series of frenzied gesticulations. My feelings weren't hurt a bit: I didn't understand a word he said. As a matter of fact I laughed quietly to myself. He must have seen through my outer complacence for he struck me full in the mouth several times with his fist. I was in no position to fight back: the muzzles of three guns were staring me in the face. One of the Wehrmacht soldiers brought this to a halt and rebuked the civilian severely, which gave me inner satisfaction. The soldier knew that some day he might be a prisoner and probably imagined himself in my shoes.

Back to the battle in the sky. Hal Turell was on the bomb run when he saw the demise of an aircraft:

Another fighter came within 100 yards of the lead plane and released a parachute bomb that the B-24 ran head-on into. The explosion tore the entire top section of the plane off back to the wing. It then caught fire and slid tail first to the ground. The deputy lead took over and continued the bomb run. Then the plane on our right wing got hit and went into a loop, heading right for us. Ralph had some frantic jockeying to clear him and get back in formation.

The action was fast, furious and enveloped in the fog of battle. At one point someone in a parachute came floating through our formation. He was close enough that I could see that he was unconscious. He seemed to be an American and was lightly dressed in green fatigues, which was surprising. I still wonder if he was alive and did he survive? Another crewman baled out and opened his chute too soon. It was caught by the tail of one of the low element and his parachute shredded. One more enemy fighter came in close and shot off the tail of another Lib. As the fighter turned, the Lib's gunners got him and he baled out. At the same time two men from the stricken plane parachuted out and the three descended together with much arm waving and gestures. We wondered if the discussion was continued on the ground.

On the way in, the right-hand nose gun jammed. When the bombardier, in the nose turret, asked Hal to check his ammunition supply, Hal saw to his horror that the last round was about to enter the ammunition chute:

Once the end of the ammunition belt is inside the feeder chute, it can not be reloaded in the air. I told Francis not to shoot. I then pulled a round from the right ammo box, lifted the remaining cartridges out, turned and placed it in the left-hand box. I then inserted the extracted round. Opening the turret door, I pounded Hugh on the back and said, 'Start shooting now.' This is a feat that cannot be done. No one can manually pull a 50-caliber round out of a metal belt by hand, much less reinsert it. I tried to duplicate this feat on the ground without the adrenaline and could not move it. I called out the fighters coming in and the gunners told me later it was quite useful as they knew which side they would come. Although Bill Adair

did say it was nerve-racking when I said, 'Here they come!'
At one point our wingman had his top turret shot off with
so much damage that we wondered what kept him up.
We could see the co-pilot wiping the blood away with one
hand while he flew the ship with the other. We lost him later.
As he slid off to oblivion, I said to Ralph we better get out of
here or we will all be dead. Ralph still had his sense of humor
and dryly said, 'Where would you suggest we go?' I scanned
the horizon and there were no other formations to be seen.

JOB DONE
Over the target, 382 tons of explosive were dropped on the factories
from heights between 16,000 feet and 21,500 feet. Sam Mastrogiacomo,
as a tail gunner, had the best view of target after the bombs had struck:
'There was snow on the ground and I could see below that they
had fighter planes out like they were ready to be delivered, and our
bombs hit right in the midst of that.'

Now the survivors, many already battle-damaged, had to negotiate
the defences on the journey home. Myron Keilman recalled:

No sooner had the wing left the target's flak than we were
accosted by German fighters again. Strung out in trail and
with some planes slowed down from flak damage, our three
squadrons became vulnerable to vicious attacks. For the next
hour and more, Messerschmitt, Focke-Wulf and Junker fighters
worked us over until our fighters could fend them off.

As deputy command pilot, I frequently changed off flying
formation with the airplane commander to keep occupied and
not have to watch the Jerries press their blazing gun attacks.
The interphone was alive with excited calls of enemy action.
Head-on passes and tail attacks, in singles and in 'gaggles';
rockets, 20-mm cannon, and even some cables, were thrown
at us. Seven of our B-24s were shot down. Many of us were
shot up, but it was not all one-sided. The gunners of the 22

airplanes that returned accounted for 16 German fighters.

Along with Myron, Sam Mastrogiacomo would make it back to base that day. So too would Hal Turell:

One of the many ironies of war was that the position we flew that day was high outside. The two most dangerous and exposed airplanes in a formation are high outside and low outside, commonly called 'coffin corner'. Both planes flying this most dreaded position survived! On the way back, two P-38s, each with an engine out, joined us for mutual protection. When we got to the Channel they waved us farewell. As we neared the English coast I turned on my radio-mapping box to home in on the base. I found it was not operating. I could not receive a signal. Trying to find the cause of the problem, I searched around. When I checked the aerial, I discovered it had been shot off. It was outside the ship, not more than a foot from my head.

Ours was the only crew of our squadron to return to our Tibenham base. The ship we were flying was incredibly shot up, yet we suffered no wounds. At the debriefing everyone was appalled and wanted to know what happened. There were a number of reporters there as well. We were still in shock and in disbelief that we had lived. Our squadron commander, Jimmy Stewart (yes, the actor), listened intently to us. We were the first crew into the debriefing room. He asked us details and then tears came to his eyes and he left the room for a little while.

At the debriefing our co-pilot, Lieutenant Milton Souza, was true to form and exaggerated. He said the guy in the chute that floated through our formation had to lift his legs up to avoid our props! The crew has a consensus to this day that only Milton could have exaggerated Gotha. There was a young American Red Cross girl there with candy for us. As the story of that day penetrated to her, she put her hand to her mouth and ran away. We cleaned out the candy. The bombing was the

*In the Battle of Britain, the aircrews of RAF Bomber Command were instrumental in the defensive victory won during the summer of 1940. Here the aircrew of 58 Squadron undergo a briefing by the station commander in the Operations Room at Linton-on-Ouse, Yorkshire, prior to an operation in June 1940.*

*A Bristol Blenheim Mark IV of 110 Squadron, at RAF Wattisham, Suffolk, June 1940. Armourers unload 250-pound general purpose (GP) bombs and small bomb containers (SBCs) of incendiaries from a trolley, while other groundcrew service the aircraft. The Bomber Command Blenheim crews were in the midst of the aerial battle during the Battle of Britain, and suffered accordingly, especially in daylight.*

An essential task for Bomber Command during the Battle of Britain was the bombardment of the German invasion barges gathering in ports on the other side of the English Channel. Concentrations such as that illustrated here at Boulogne Harbour, France, came within the sights of the bomber crews, who were successful in persuading the enemy Navy to rethink its invasion plans.

In the early years of the war, twin-engined Handley Page Hampdens were in the vanguard of Bomber Command campaigns. The two Hampden Mark I aircraft of 44 Squadron shown here were lost on raids over Germany later in the war.

*16 September 1940 – the shell-torn rear gunner's compartment of Handley Page Hampden Mark I, P1355 'OL-W', of RAF 83 Squadron, photographed at Scampton, Lincolnshire, the morning after returning from a night attack on invasion barges at Antwerp, Holland. It was during this sortie that the wireless operator/air gunner of the Hampden's crew, Flight Sergeant John Hannah, earned the Victoria Cross for his bravery when the aircraft was severely damaged and set on fire.*

*The special 'Thousand Bomber' raid to Cologne on the night of 30/31 May 1942 marked a turning point in the strategic air offensive against Germany. The city was hit hard, sending a shock wave through the Nazi hierarchy. This reconnaissance photograph taken over Cologne a few days after the raid shows widespread damage on either side of Luxemburger Strasse.*

*Prior to the historic Dambusters raid of 16/17 May 1943, the crews of 617 Squadron completed a rigorous training schedule. Here a practice 'Upkeep' weapon is attached to the bomb bay of raid leader Wing Commander Guy Gibson's Lancaster at Manston, Kent, while conducting dropping trials off Reculver, bombing range, Kent.*

*A still from a film recording, showing a 617 Squadron practice dropping the 'Upkeep' weapon at Reculver bombing range, Kent. As the bomb falls from the Lancaster, the aircraft begins to climb. The revolving 'bouncing bomb' then skims across the water to the target.*

The Dambusters raid – 16 May 1943. Leader of the raid, Wing Commander Guy
Gibson, climbs into his 617 Squadron Lancaster, followed by his crew.

Debriefing of Wing Commander Guy Gibson's crew following their return from the
Dambusters raid. Intelligence Officer Squadron Leader Townson questions, from
left to right: bomb aimer, Pilot Officer F. M. Spafford; navigator, Pilot Officer H.T.
Taerum; and rear gunner, Flight Lieutenant R. D. Trevor-Roper. Flight engineer
Sergeant J. Pulford and front gunner Flight Sergeant G. A. Deering are partly
hidden. Commander-in-Chief of Bomber Command, Air Chief Marshal Sir Arthur
Harris, and the commander of Bomber Command's 5 Group, the Hon. Ralph A.
Cochrane, observe. (Gibson is not in the picture.)

*An aerial reconnaissance photograph showing the breach in the Möhne Dam caused by 617 Squadron's raid on 16 May 1943. The Eder Dam was breached during the same operation by means of the 'bouncing' bombs designed by the brilliant scientist Barnes Wallis. The raid captured the nation's imagination and had tremendous propaganda value, although its practical results fell below expectations.*

*A typical ten-man crew of a US Eighth Air Force bomber. Pilot Bob Wolff, crouching third from the left, seems in good spirits with his crew as his bombardier Buzz White takes aim at the enemy. Bob, Buzz and thousands of their fellow Americans crossed the Atlantic to fight in partnership with their Royal Air Force colleagues.*

*Regensburg mission, 17 August 1943 – 100th Bomb Group Boeing B-17 Flying Fortresses over the Alps. Clearly visible is damage to the tail fin of the centre aircraft, Wolf Pack, flown by 2nd Lieutenant Bob Wolff. Despite the damage, causing drag that rapidly drained the aircraft's fuel, Bob managed to land the B-17 at an emergency airfield in North Africa.*

*Beirne Lay Jr, who wrote a compellingly graphic account of the 17 August 1943 mission to Regensburg, describing the intense fighting between American bombers and Luftwaffe fighters, and the sight of fellow airmen falling from the sky to their deaths. The losses suffered by the Eighth Air Force on missions such as that described by Beirne were unsustainable at the time, increasing the demand for long-range fighter escort.*

An aerial photograph taken on 23 June 1943 of Test Stand VII at the Army Research Centre, Peenemünde, prior to the famous RAF Bomber Command raid on the night of 17/18 August. Clearly visible at centre right inside the elliptical earthwork is a V2 rocket on its trailer. Two other trailers can be seen almost directly above.

Allied reconnaissance in the aftermath of the Bomber Command attack on the Peenemünde secret weapon research raid revealed widespread devastation. A heavily cratered Test Stand VII provides a case in point.

*Gaolbusters – the attempt to free Resistance members awaiting execution in Amiens prison, France, on 18 February 1944. Shown here is the 12-foot wide breach in the south side of the prison's outer wall, through which 258 prisoners escaped following the daylight raid by de Havilland Mosquito FB Mark VIs of 140 Wing, 2 Group, led by Group Captain 'Percy' Pickard.*

487 Squadron RNZAF de Havilland Mosquitoes FB Mark VI Series 2s, flying in
tight starboard echelon formation, with 500-pound medium capacity (MC) bombs
fitted on underwing carriers. 487 Squadron crews, along with 464 Squadron and 21
Squadron airmen, were charged with the precision attack on Amiens prison.

Mosquitoes of 487 Squadron RNZAF clear the target at low
level as the first 500-pound bombs to be dropped detonate near
the south wall of Amiens prison.

*A film still of Group Captain 'Percy' Pickard, Commander of 140 Wing, 2 Group, in October 1943, smoking his pipe by a de Havilland Mosquito FB Mark VI of 487 Squadron RNZAF, shortly before leading the squadron on a daylight bombing raid. Pickard would tragically lose his life on 18 February 1944, leading the Amiens prison raid. His final list of decorations – a DSO and Two Bars and a DFC – are a testament to his courage and skill.*

*The senior Allied air commanders. From left to right: Lt Gen. James H. Doolittle (who commanded the US Eighth Air Force during the* Overlord *campaign); Lt Gen. Lewis H. Brereton (US Ninth Air Force); Lt Gen. Carl 'Tooey' Spaatz (commanding the US Strategic Air Force in Europe); Lt Gen. Ira Eaker (who commanded the Eighth Air Force prior to 1944); and Air Chief Marshal Sir Arthur Harris (RAF Bomber Command's Commander-in-Chief).*

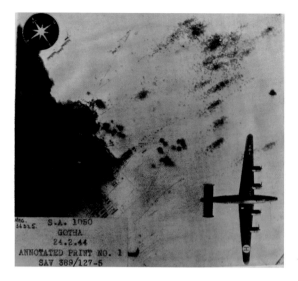

On 24 February 1944, the Eighth Air Force carried out a devastating raid on the Messerschmitt works at Gotha, one of the most accurate and effective attacks during 'Big Week' – the crucial all-out attack on the German aircraft industry. German aircraft can be seen silhouetted on the snow-covered ground to the right of the smoking factory.

Bombs falling away from a formation of Boeing B-17 Flying Fortresses of the US Eighth Air Force's 390th Bombardment Group on a daylight raid over Europe in 1943. The Americans believed in the defensive capabilities of unescorted bomber formations – a tactic that the Luftwaffe exposed as flawed. With long-range escorts, however, the resulting attrition rates eroded the German Air Force strength and the Allies gained all-important air superiority.

A typical seven-man Bomber Command crew stand in front of their four-engine
Halifax bomber. Arthur Darlow, third from the left, would take his British and
Canadian crew to Berlin four times during Sir Arthur Harris's 1943/44 Battle of
Berlin. On all Bomber Command raids to the German capital in this period, 625
bombers were lost and 2,690 airmen lost their lives. In total, 55,500 airmen were
killed serving with Bomber Command during the war.

Men from 77 Squadron, based at RAF Elvington, Yorkshire, look on as the
message 'we hope this hurts' is chalked onto a 500-pound MC bomb prior
to Bomber Command's attack on Berlin on 30 January 1944. Clearly set
up as a propaganda shot, most Bomber Command men were not interested
in revenge; their main motivation was to do their job to the best of their
ability, not let their crew down, and shorten the war.

*A graphic and shocking sight, as a B-24 Liberator bursts into flames. When flying into battle, bomber crews manned an aircraft filled with fuel, oxygen bottles and high-explosive bombs, and they often had little, if any, time to bale out when the aircraft was set alight. The crews in other nearby bombers could only watch, and fly on.*

*In the run-up to the D-Day assault on the Normandy beaches on 6 June 1944, Bomber Command carried out a successful campaign smashing the rail links to the battle area. Here an aerial photograph shows the devastation following an attack by 120 aircraft on the railway stores and repair depot at Chambly, France, on the night of 1/2 May 1944. The points and crossings shop and sleeper impregnation plant are almost totally destroyed, and the stores yards are saturated with craters.*

*A 12,000-pound MC deep-penetration 'Tallboy' bomb is hoisted from the bomb dump to its carrier at Woodhall Spa, Lincolnshire, to be loaded into an Avro Lancaster of 617 Squadron. An attack with 'Tallboys' by 9 and 617 Squadrons would result in the demise of the German battleship* Tirpitz *in November 1944.*

*617 Squadron's Willie Tait (on the left), who led the successful attack on the* Tirpitz *on 12 November 1944, stands with Air Vice-Marshal the Hon. Ralph A. Cochrane, Commander of 5 Group.*

*The German battleship* Tirpitz *lies capsized in Tromso fjord, attended by a salvage vessel. The ship had been finally sunk in a combined daylight attack by the Lancasters of 9 and 617 Squadrons on 12 November 1944.*

*June 1945. British people wave goodbye to the last B-24 Liberator of the 2nd Air Division of the US Eighth Army Air Force, as it takes off on the first leg of its trip home to the US. The Eighth Air Force's impact on the war in Europe was critical in securing victory, but the lives of 26,000 American airmen were lost.*

most accurate we ever did and destroyed the target. The 445th was awarded The Presidential Unit Citation for this action.

The 2nd Bomb Division lost 33 aircraft in total on the mission to Gotha – five men killed, 11 wounded and 324 who could only be listed as missing in the immediate aftermath of the raid (in addition five and 11 crews were lost on the Rostock and Schweinfurt missions respectively). But the attack was an extraordinary success. Reconnaissance and strike photos would certainly suggest such an outcome, which post-war analysis would confirm.

Over 400 high-explosive and incendiary bombs had fallen in the target area and 93 of these had struck buildings. In addition, a large volume of fragmentation bombs had been placed on the factory. Although damage to the buildings was extensive, a post-war investigation would find that the plant's machine tools had escaped lightly. Not that this detracts from the result of the attack, as the tangle of debris and girders prevented access, all of which had to be cleared. The United States Strategic Bombing Survey concluded that approximately 6 to 7 weeks worth of production was lost, equating to about 140 aircraft. The loss of production put a strain on the output at other Messerschmitt works and certainly inhibited the replacement of losses suffered by the Luftwaffe in the air.[4]

In combination with the other missions, on 24 February bomber gunners claimed 83 enemy aircraft destroyed, 22 probable and 42 damaged. Fighters claimed 38 destroyed, 1 probable and 14 damaged. These figures, as history has shown, were subject to over claiming: there could be no immediate decisive count in an aerial melee. Nevertheless, the Eighth had not only blasted the enemy aircraft in their nest, they had also maintained the unmanageable attrition rate in the air.

# 7
# GAOLBUSTERS: THE AMIENS PRISON RAID

*By 1944, the Royal Air Force could match up versatile bomber aircraft – the de Havilland Mosquito – with skilled aircrew and carry out extremely accurate bombing raids. One of the most famous special Mosquito operations, on 18 February 1944, was codenamed Jericho: the attempt to break down the walls of Amiens prison and release members of the French Resistance. These 'political prisoners' were needed to aid the Allies in the forthcoming invasion and time was of the essence, as many of those imprisoned were to face the death penalty within days.*

THE NEED FOR A MIRACLE
In the early hours of 18 February 1944, Mosquito pilot Maxwell Sparks was forced out of his slumber when, 'The loudspeaker broke rudely into my sleep.'

It barked through our hut with a list of aircrews who were wanted at the briefing room at once. My own name was on the list and I turned over with a groan. Like all things in the Royal Air Force, a speaker serves a purpose. It's what you might call a necessary evil. It's a system set up throughout a station in such a way that wherever you are you can't help hearing it. It brings you good news and bad news, orders and announcements. There are times when you feel like throwing your hat in the air on what it tells you. But there are other times when you feel like shooting it. It's as unwelcome as an Army bugler sounding reveille.
One of those times was that early English winter morning when it woke me up and told me I was wanted. Mutterings crossed the room from bed to bed. The lucky ones yawned and laughed and went back to sleep. But the rest of us, who were on the list, shivered and pulled on our clothes. We didn't feel any better

when somebody went to the window, pulled up the blind and announced that the weather was so good that even the birds were walking. Of all things, it was snowing. If we were being yanked out of bed to fly in that stuff it must be either some kind of practice or some kind of a practical joke. We were still wondering what it was all about as we swallowed a quick breakfast at the Mess and went down to the aerodrome. But when we found guards posted at the briefing room, and they asked us to prove our identities, we knew there was neither a joke nor a practice in the air. Those guards at the door could only mean that something very much out of the ordinary was going to happen.[1]

It certainly was something out of the ordinary. At this stage of the war, the RAF was committing its heavy bombers to the all-out attack on Berlin. But the RAF also had the flexibility to send small forces on special missions using the speed and versatility of the 'wooden wonder', the twin-engined Mosquito. One such 'special' raid was operation *Jericho*, the attack on the prison at Amiens by the Mosquitoes of 2 Group, then part of the 2nd Tactical Air Force, established to prepare for and support the forthcoming invasion. The French Resistance had been requesting a special attack on the Amiens gaol, in an attempt to release as many of their imprisoned colleagues as possible; and many were destined to face the death penalty, unless some kind of 'miracle' could be performed. More importantly, their imprisonment threatened the forthcoming D-Day landings; the contribution of the Resistance was a vital factor in the plans for the Normandy invasion. As author Jack Fishman surmised in his book *And the Walls Came Tumbling Down*, 'At risk was postponement for at least a year of the June 1944 Allied invasion.'[2]

Edward Sismore served with 2 Group headquarters and was involved in the logistical planning of low-level Mosquito operations. He was also actually planning to fly on this operation but, for security reasons, the commander of the 2nd Tactical Air Force curtailed any such thoughts:

The objective was to release some prisoners from prison who were in fact part of the French underground movement. Quite a lot of them had been moved into Amiens prison and we had this request to try to release them. Of course the first reaction was we'd probably kill them all in trying to do so. But there was considerable concern in France about their future if they were left in the prison. The AOC [of 2 Group], Basil Embry, decided that it would really be worth doing if we could try to knock the walls down without putting in too much explosive. I was involved in the planning, and of course the difficulty was to achieve this kind of success without killing a lot of people. We knew quite a lot about the prison. We had been provided with the details of the construction but we weren't quite so happy with the details of the effect of the bombs on that type of construction. It was a very difficult decision of what to drop and how much to drop. Obviously, we couldn't drop too little because we could not go back again, the defences would have been improved. If we dropped too much then we could negate the whole objective. So it was a very delicate operation.

The execution of the raid was allocated to 2 Group's 140 airfield, with the experienced Group Captain Charles Pickard, DSO and Two Bars, DFC, to lead 18 Mosquitoes: six each from 21, 464 and 487 Squadrons. Wing Commander Irving Smith was to lead 487 Squadron and in a post-war interview he intimated at an additional specific reason for the raid: that a certain notable member of the Resistance was under lock and key in the prison:

The Germans didn't know who he was or how important he was and he was due to be executed, along with some others for some other reason. It was vitally important that they be sprung before the Germans knew who he was. If they knew they could extract from him an awful lot of information.

Irving Smith is no doubt referring to a certain Monsieur Vivant, the Sous Préfet at Abbeville, who had been arrested by the Gestapo on 14 February 1944. An RAF investigation carried out later in the war surmised that it was 'probable that we were asked to carry out the attack mainly to effect his escape. Monsieur Vivant was a key member of the Resistance at Abbeville and probably had in his possession important secrets of the Resistance Organization.' Indeed, Vivant was a key member of the Resistance and had played an important role in the collection and dissemination of essential information concerning the planned invasion, such as the German coastal defence networks.

Irving Smith had only been commander of 487 Squadron a little over a fortnight before he took on the raid:

I flew with every one of these pilots at the squadron, first thing I did, see what they were like. The men I selected to fly to this particular target were not the two flight commanders (squadron leaders), but I had a flight lieutenant lead the second formation. My number two [in the first formation of three] was a pilot officer, a New Zealander; my number three was an English sergeant. The two in the second section with the flight lieutenant were both pilot officers. All very junior men, inexperienced, but all men I judged to have a necessary degree of skill and ability to do this job. This was what being a squadron commander is. It's no good just saying, 'you, you, you, you', pulling people out of hat. You selected people for the job. Ability is everything.

I was first told about the projected raid 2 days before it took place, along with the other two squadron commanders, Wing Commander Iredale, who commanded 464 Squadron, and Wing Commander Dale, who commanded 21 Squadron. The weather on the following day in the target area was impossible so it was put off for another day. The day of the actual raid was the last day it could occur if it was to have the success that was designed for it.

Each of the Mosquito squadrons was allocated a specific task, and the attacking crews were told that they would have Hawker Typhoon fighter-bombers as a fighter escort. In addition, a Mosquito of the Film Production Unit would fly with the attacking crews to record the results of the raid. Irving Smith recalled:

The feeling of the aircrews on this job was one of terrific determination to see that it was done properly. We knew that this prison was full of people arrested because they had helped our men escape or were suspected of being members of the underground movement. We also knew that they had all been condemned to death, though we did not know the day of execution. The thing had to be done whatever the weather . . . They had made a model of the prison and had rushed it up to us to study. Someone must have spent some time deciding what bombs would be required to blow open a prison wall 20 feet high and 4 feet thick and still do no damage to the prison itself.

It was a foul morning, with snowstorms and a low cloud base. We made to consider the plan, everybody wanted to go. There were a lot of niceties about the operation, for there were really two jobs to be done. Firstly, we had to blow the walls down to let the prisoners out of the yard, and secondly we had to blow the ends off the buildings to kill the guards who should be eating at that time. And thus open up the prison building itself so that prisoners could escape. It was a cruciform building, with guard houses at the end of the long arm, surrounded by the 20-foot wall. The timing of these jobs had to be in seconds. We had to release the prisoners from inside the building and wipe out the guards at the same time, or the guards might have been able to interfere; and it was absolutely essential that the outside wall should be pushed down first so that the prisoners wouldn't have anything to stop them once Bob and his crews had released them. Also, the operation was planned so that if the first squadron didn't break the outside walls, the second squadron would do so and a third squadron [21 Squadron] would come along to settle with the guard houses on the ends of the building.

So the plan was clear: blow the external walls down, then blow the ends of the prison buildings. This now had to be communicated to the participating crews.

THE DEATH OR GLORY SHOW
Maxwell Sparks, whose sleep had only recently been broken into, attended the briefing with some expectation:

So we stopped our nattering and sat in silence while the rest of the crews filed into the room. Six crews each from New Zealand, Australian and British squadrons. Then our group captain, Charles Pickard, arrived with the briefing officers and they brought with them a large wooden box. The lid was removed and we craned forward to see what the box contained. It was a model. The model of a building and it looked to me at once like a prison because of the high wall around it. As the briefing officers began to talk and the plan of our task unfolded, it sounded like a bit out of a dramatic novel. It was a prison all right; the gaol of Amiens in France and . . . Frenchmen were held there awaiting death; men of the French Resistance movement. Men who had fearlessly defied the German occupation of their country, who'd fought on in the secrecy of the underground movement and who'd helped our own airmen brought down in France to evade the Nazis and get safely back to England. Now those men had been arrested by the Germans and condemned to death. Whatever trial they had been allowed was over. They were going to die and soon. But before that could happen we were going to take our Mosquitoes over and try and break open that prison and get them out. This was something out of the ordinary. The idea of going to their rescue was simple enough but the very thought of it sent a thrill through all of us. But we could see the exact task of breaking

the prison open and doing it in such a way that the prisoners
would have a reasonable chance of getting away across the open
ground. It wasn't going to be so easy. It would call for the best we
could give to it in the best way of absolute accurate timing and
bombing . . . Briefly what we had to do was smash up the German
wing, killing as many of the guards as we could, blow open the
ends of the main building with as little force as possible, so that
the French prisoners wouldn't suffer too many casualties and so
they could climb out into the courtyard. Break down the wall in
at least two places to let them get away across the open ground
to the patriots who could be waiting in hiding to receive them.

It was to be the privilege of us New Zealanders to form the
first wave of the attack, with the specific task of blowing open
the walls. The Aussies would follow us in to do the job on
the prison itself. And the aircraft from the British squadron,
in which another New Zealander was flying as an observer,
were to be held in reserve and if necessary they would come
in and finish up anything that we and the Aussies had left
undone. Well, we studied the model from every angle. Fired
questions at the briefing officers and made sure that we
had everything as clear as possible in our minds. We were
determined to give everything we could to this job.

I remember Group Captain Pickard putting into words what
we were all beginning to feel when he said, 'Well boys, this is
a death or glory show. If it succeeds it will be one of the most
worthwhile ops of the war. If you never do anything else you
can still count this as the finest job you could ever have done.'

The plan was communicated to the crews. The aircraft were bombed
up and prepared, and the airmen dressed and gathered their kit.
Maxwell Sparks recalled:

So we went outside and looked at the weather again. It was
terrible. Snow was still falling, sweeping in gusts that every

now and then hid the end of the runway from sight. If this had been an ordinary operation we were doing it would pretty certainly have been scrubbed, put off to another day. But this wasn't an ordinary job. Every day, perhaps every hour, might be the last in the lives of those Frenchmen. We got into our aircraft, warmed up the engines and sat there thinking that it was no kind of weather to go flying in. But somehow knowing that we must. And when we saw the group captain drive up in his car, get out of it and into his own Mosquito, we knew for certain the show was on.

Irving Smith also had his concerns about the flying conditions:

The weather in the target area seemed impossible and our weather in England was appalling. Very heavy snow, enormous turbulence right across the south of England. There was no hope whatsoever of taking off in any sort of formation and maintaining any sort of formation in these cloud conditions. I had been nominated to lead the raid by Basil Embry. Why, I don't know. Perhaps because he knew me best of all the people. So I decreed that 487 Squadron would take off at 5-second intervals individually and fly absolutely strict to course, heights and speeds in this cloud until we popped out the other side of it near Littlehampton, which is what we should do if everyone had flown accurately and timed it accurately. We should all be in sight of each other and we should be able to join up into the right sort of attack formations.

Maxwell Sparks lifted his Mosquito from the runway at Hunsdon:

The 18 aircraft took off quickly, one after the other, at about eleven o'clock in the morning. We were going to hit the prison when the guards were at their lunch. By the time I got to 100 feet I couldn't see a thing except that grey soupy mist and the snow and rain beating against the Perspex window. There was no hope of either getting into formation or staying in it. So I headed straight for the Channel coast.

When the 487 Squadron Mosquitoes arrived over Littlehampton, Irving Smith brought his six aircraft in close formation, but they failed to rendezvous with the fighter escort:

We were supposed to have an escort of Typhoons and as far as I was concerned they never appeared. We crossed the Channel and flew sort of a reverse route, so that we could attack the right walls at the right angles. We flew round past Amiens down to Albert and then up the road from Albert to Amiens. There were no problems going to the target, except the leader of my second section had an engine fail. It was cruel luck; he couldn't keep up on one engine and although he started it again and tried, it caught fire. He put it out, stopped it again and he set off home on his own. So I arrived at the target with only five aircraft due to this mishap. We were all armed with 11-second delay 500-pound general purpose bombs. We flew from Albert down the long straight road to the prison, which we could see clearly sitting in the snow before us.

Two miles out from the English coast, Maxwell Sparks found himself out of the 'soupy mist':

The weather was beautifully clear, and it was only a matter of minutes before we were over France. We skimmed across the coast at deck level, swept round the north of Amiens and then split up for the attack. My own aircraft, a New Zealand wing commander's, and one other, stayed together to make the first run in. Our job was to blast a hole in the east wall. We picked up the straight road that runs from Albert to Amiens and that led us right to the prison. I'll never forget that road. Long and straight and covered with snow. It was lined with tall poplars and the three of us were flying so low that I had to keep my aircraft tilted at an angle to avoid hitting the tops of the trees with my wing. It was then, as I flew with one eye on the poplars and the other watching the road ahead that I was reminded that we had a fighter escort: a Typhoon came belting right across in front of us and I nearly jumped in my seat. The poplars suddenly petered out and there, a mile ahead, was the prison.

AIMING SURE

Thus the five aircraft of 487 Squadron prepared to attack. The appalling weather over England had resulted in an early return of two Mosquitoes from 21 and only four of the 464 Squadron Mosquitoes were later confirmed as having attacked. The filming Mosquito, flown by Flight Lieutenant Tony Wickham of 16 Squadron, had made it to the target:

I was flying the photographic aircraft which followed up the attack and took the recce pictures. We'd had a little bit of trouble getting off and had a few minutes to catch up to be there on time. We went flat out through the snow on this side of the Channel and caught up with the bombing aircraft over the continent. The weather had suddenly cleared, which cheered up my photographer, who'd almost given up hope of getting any photographs at all. We circled to the north of the target, watching the two squadrons making their attacks.

It was now time to prove the abilities of the crews. Irving Smith took his section straight in at right angles to the eastern wall:

My other section swerved off a few miles so that it would come in head-on to the northern wall. I never saw better flying and navigation in my life. It was like a Hendon display. We flew at the lowest possible height and at the slowest possible speed so that we could place our bombs exactly at the base of the walls.

The plan was that the first three aircraft, very tight echelon port formation, overlapping wing-tips, would attack the eastern wall, pull up over it and break to starboard and clear Amiens, leaving it to port. The second section of three aircraft, now two, were to swing out just short of the target, starboard and come in on a port turn and attack the northern wall. The leading section, my section, would go over the top of them by this time and they would be passing underneath. The whole thing had to be accomplished substantially inside the 11-second time delay on the bombs, otherwise the second section was blown up. They couldn't be more than 1 or 2 seconds behind the first section when they crossed. It required very precise and accurate flying on everyone's part.

The actual bombing was done by the leader of the section in each case. The other members of the section bombing on his bombs; the moment they saw a bomb release from the wing they then pressed their bomb release switches. They couldn't possibly look at the target, they had to be looking at the formation leader and depend on him entirely for the accuracy of the bombing, and secondly to pull up over the building and evade the second or first section as the case may be. I assessed the speed as the minimum I needed to have sufficient speed to pull up sharply over the wall and the building, since we bombed well below the top of the wall. It was impossible for us to see any results of the bombing because we had to clear the target area immediately, because 464 Squadron was to be 1 minute behind us to bomb the ends of the building.

To Maxwell Sparks the prison looked just like the model he had seen at briefing:

We hugged the ground as low as we could and at the lowest possible speed. We pitched our bombs towards the base of the wall, fairly scraped over it and our part of the job was over. There wasn't time to stay and watch the results. We had to get away straight out and let the others come in. And as we turned away we could see the second New Zealand section make their attack. As we headed back towards the coast we knew the Aussies would be going in with their bombs and suddenly on the radio I heard Group Captain Pickard's voice, 'Red, red, red, don't bomb.' And we knew from that almost for certain that our job had been successful, because that was an order to the reserve aircraft that they were not needed.

Wing Commander Robert Iredale and his 464 Squadron colleagues, following in the wake of 487 Squadron, had finished the job, ripping open the prison building walls:

After we crossed the enemy coast I didn't see Smithy again until I was on the deck and going down the long road toward Amiens. About 4 miles away I saw the prison and Smithy's three aircraft nipping over the top. I knew then it was OK for me to go in. It's always a worry on low-level attacks if you don't see the aircraft in front of you because you don't know when their bombs are going up and you might run into the blast. My squadron was divided into two sections, one to open each end of the prison. And it was now that one half broke off and swept round to attack the far end of the prison from the right. The rest of us carried on in tight formation straight at the prison. Four hundred yards before we got there Smithy's DA [delayed action] bombs went off and I saw they had breached the wall. Clouds of dust and smoke came up but over the top I could still see the triangular gable of the prison, my aiming point for the end we were going to open. I released my bombs at 10 feet and pulled up slap through the smoke over the prison roof. One of the things that worried me was the possibility of the two sections meeting at right angles over the prison. I

looked round to my right and felt mighty relieved to see the
other boys still 200 yards short of the target and coming in
dead on line. They bombed and we all got away from the target
OK, reformed as a section and made straight for base. We
could see the cloud of smoke and dust behind us and my only
worry was had we killed the prisoners as well as their guards?

So what were the RAF bombers leaving in their wake? Had the bombing
been too little, just sufficient, or tragically excessive? Monsieur Vivant,
probably the most important prisoner held by the Germans at the
gaol, was preparing to take lunch when the RAF arrived:

I had just taken off my jacket to go and wash my hands, when
there was suddenly the deafening roar of planes flying very
low overhead, followed by a tremendous explosion. At first I
thought a German plane must have crashed just outside, and
was rejoicing gleefully to myself, when the first explosion was
followed by several others. Instinctively I crouched for protection
in the corner of my cell, while the window shattered to pieces.
The left wall of the cell suddenly gaped open, and the air was
filled with dust. I didn't move, and by now I was thinking that
there must be an aerial battle going on overhead, and that planes
were crashing to the ground with their bomb loads. But as soon
as the dust cleared a little, I saw that my cell door had been
torn from its hinges. The corridor outside was a pile of stones
and smoking rubble! To the right, the prison buildings seemed
to be still intact, but to the left I could see my way open to the
country, the snow-covered fields stretching as far as the eye could
see! A wide gap had been torn in the high, surrounding wall.
   It didn't take me long to make up my mind. How many times
had I paced up and down in my cell, concocting wild plans of
escape – and now here was my chance, heaven sent! I couldn't
see my coat and hat anywhere, they had probably been whisked
away by the blast from the explosions. But there was no point in

hanging about looking for them now. Scrambling over the debris as best I could, I reached the breach in the wall at the same time as three or four other prisoners who were seizing their chance to escape. I set out in the opposite direction from Amiens . . . [3]

Some prisoners, however, were not as fortunate as Monsieur Vivant. A Monsieur M. Moisan, was also incarcerated in the gaol at the time of the raid, as a political prisoner. He was sharing a cell with two others at the time of the attack:

We saw the first plane and we heard the first bomb falling. Just a few seconds after that the cell dropped and I was buried in rubble. The bombing continued and I heard them falling and bursting. I could hear the voices of my fellows, from different directions, who were also buried in the rubble. After about 2 hours I was dug out, feeling very groggy and with numerous wounds over my body. But I was miraculously alive, no great injury. I was taken out, put on a stretcher and carried to a clinic in Amiens where I stayed for 3 months.

Indeed not all would be as fortunate even as Monsieur Moisan.

TRIUMPH AND TRAGEDY

Tony Wickham in the photographic Mosquito now had to record the scene for analysis back in the UK. He could see the clouds of dust and smoke rising and the other aircraft hurtling over the prison:

Then suddenly they were gone and it was our turn to go in. Frankly as we watched the bomb bursts, smoke and dust, it looked so concentrated that we expected the whole place to be flat. But it cleared a bit and when we came in on our first run we could see how accurate and successful the bombers had been. The ends were blown off, the building and the outer walls were breached. In the yard was a large group of prisoners making good their escape. Three of them had already got through the outer walls and were heading for the fields. Obviously, the operation had already succeeded and I called up the third squadron who were waiting to complete the attack if they were needed. I gave them the prearranged signal to take their bombs home, 'Hello Daddy, red, red, red.'

Meanwhile the fixed cameras in the aircraft were doing their job and the photographer, crouched in the nose of the aircraft, was using his hand-held camera. In fact it was his enthusiasm which made me stay longer than I considered healthy. After each run I tentatively suggested going home but his reply was, 'Oh no, come on, just once more.' However, finally even he was satisfied and we made back for base.

Everything appeared to have gone well. After attacking, Pickard circled the prison to see the results of the raid himself; a decision that cost him his life. William Dynes, an Irish civilian who lived close to the prison, witnessed the attack and Pickard's fate. When the bombs went off, 'I next saw nothing but smoke and dust in the air, everywhere.'

After the smoke and dust had died down a little I noticed an aeroplane still in the air, circling round the prison. He did so two or three times, after which he made off in the direction of England. He had stayed a good 4 or 5 minutes over the target. I then noticed two German fighters chasing him. Shortly afterwards he came down.

FW190s had appeared on the scene and Pickard's Mosquito was shot from the sky, killing Pickard and his navigator. Irving Smith recalled:

Pickard's job in this attack was to go round the target after 464 had bombed and assess whether the walls had been breached and the men were escaping. If not, 21 Squadron, which was to follow 10 minutes later, was to repeat the attacks. In the event, he sent 21 Squadron back and they did not bomb and he unfortunately was caught by fighters who took off from an adjacent fighter airfield. I think he stayed too long.

One other crew had also fallen to the guns of the enemy: a 464 Squadron Mosquito was forced down following a flak hit. The pilot survived but his navigator was killed. (In addition, two Typhoons would fail to return from the operation.)

With the walls breached, and liberated prisoners clambering over rubble to freedom, the remaining airmen set course for base. Maxwell Sparks recalled:

We still had to get home and one of our aircraft was already in difficulties. This was the leader of the New Zealand second section. He had been hit by flak near Albert and had to pull out of the attack. The pilot, an Englishman, received a wound in his neck that paralysed his right arm and leg. Our wing commander turned back to shepherd him home.

Right on the French coast, a little German pillbox opened up on us with some kind of cannon. We were still on the deck and I tried to get a shot at those fellows with my guns, but for my pains I got a direct hit in one wing and it grew into a hole big enough to crawl through. So I decided it was about time to go home. All the rain and snow of the morning was waiting for us half-way across the Channel. We were directed to another base, where we got emergency homings and made emergency landings.

Meanwhile, Irving Smith had found the leader of his second section who had aborted, Flight Lieutenant Hanafin:

On the way out of France, Hanafin called me up to ask for an escort because he had been shot at and wounded, and wasn't feeling at all well. I sent my crews back individually to land, went back, found Hanafin, and escorted him back to Ford. He had

had a splint of an explosive shell enter his neck, just above his shoulder, and he was paralysed all down the right side. He was on one engine, and of course the wrong engine for his left leg, so he had to put his left leg on the right rudder. He had to fly the aeroplane all sitting cross-eyed. He did very well to get the aeroplane back because conditions weren't ideal, with the very heavy snow showers. I was shot up going to collect him and was very lucky. I had an explosive shell in the main fuel tank on the port side. There was sufficient fuel and not enough air in the tank for it to quench the explosion. I had a great big hole and all the fuel ran out, and no fire and no explosion. I was very lucky indeed. But I only had 50 gallons left on that engine on that side.

Back at base the edge was taken off the excitement with news of the losses. Nevertheless, Maxwell Sparks, along with his colleagues, certainly felt a sense of achievement:

Back on the ground we compared notes among ourselves. We didn't talk about this show to anyone for months after. In fact, for a long time we didn't even put it in our logbooks. We just left a blank for that day. But we knew between ourselves that most of our bombs had done the job they were intended to do. My own squadron had breached the walls all right. Our second section had blown a beautiful hole through the north wall and the Aussies had made a mess of the guards' sleeping quarters and dropped a couple of big bombs into their dining room for pudding. Some of the chaps had even seen figures running out across the fields. Eventually we learnt that a high proportion of the prisoners had got away and a hell of a lot of Germans had been killed.

Our satisfaction was tempered only by the news of Group Captain Pickard's loss. We remembered what he had said about this op before we set out. About it being a death or glory show and well worthwhile even if it was the only thing a man had done in this war. All of us felt that way about it. The versatile Mosquito had given us scores of different jobs to do. We had bombed hundreds of targets by day and by night from 'zero' feet to 5,000 feet, from flying bomb sites to railway trains. But the Amiens prison attack was the one above all that I'll look back on with satisfaction as long as I live. Helping those prisoners to escape a cold-blooded death after all they had done for us was the kind of job that makes you feel you are doing something really definite in the war. It was an honour to be there.

Assessment of the raid was, of course, aided by the fact that the crews could watch a recording of their efforts. Tony Wickham appreciated the photographs obtained by the cameraman in his aircraft:

They showed clearly the flattened buildings and walls, black on the snow-covered ground, and the released prisoners running in all directions across the yard towards the open country. The photographs proved beyond all doubt the success of the attack made by the two squadrons.

Robert Iredale also came to appreciate what he and his colleagues achieved:

We saw the films taken by the recce boys who followed us in with cine cameras. We'd succeeded all right, the walls were breached and we had blown both ends off the main building. You could even see the first of the released boys running away from the prison, after they had got through the holes in the walls that Smithy made. The squadrons were rather proud too that of all the bombs dropped by Smithy's section and mine, only one went astray.

Time allowed a full assessment of the raid to develop. Jack Fishman's study in *And the Walls Came Tumbling Down* led him to conclude that, 'When D-Day was launched . . . Gestapo and Abwehr [German intelligence] mauled underground forces were sufficiently recovered, regrouped and revitalized to give effective support to General Dwight D. Eisenhower's invasion.'

The Resistance forces in northern France attacked German communications and provided information to the Allies during the momentous invasion campaigns. As Jack Fishman concluded, 'The job was done by men and women reinforced and heartened by the freeing of colleagues from Amiens prison and strengthened by the consequent deflection and disruption of enemy counter-actions.' An RAF investigation shortly after the Amiens area was liberated later in the war states that 258 prisoners escaped and 102 were killed by the bombing (of the latter only a few were political prisoners). The report also stated that 'the most important prisoner to escape was a Monsieur Vivant'. In addition, the Germans had to use considerable resources carrying out an extensive manhunt in the aftermath of the raid.

Another study of the raid, *The Gates Burst Open* by Colonel Livry-Level and Rémy,states:

Among the prisoners who escaped . . . many would certainly have been condemned to death. Twelve of them . . . had been due for execution on 20 February. Thanks to those escaped prisoners, who were immediately in touch once again with the Resistance movement, it was possible for them to identify at least 60 Gestapo agents. German counter-espionage in the whole region became comparatively useless, and thus many arrests were avoided that would otherwise doubtless have been made . . . and most important, the secret armies of the Resistance had been shown that the Allies were not forgetting them. [4]

The Amiens prison raid, despite the losses, is recorded in history as a military success. The Resistance movement did play a significant role during the battle for the beachheads in Normandy and the subsequent break-out. And what the raid also did was demonstrate the considerable flying skill and aircraft capability available to the RAF.

# 8
## BIG 'B': AMERICANS OVER BERLIN

*When the sun set on the Third Reich on 6 March 1944, the German people,
armed forces and political hierarchy were facing a stark reality. American
bombers, operating from England, had attacked Berlin in daylight.
It truly was a momentous and historic turning point in the war. Prior to the
attack, no one believed the Allies would dare run the gauntlet of a daylight
penetration to the 'Big City'. The RAF's night offensive had been ongoing,
but had failed to take out the Nazi capital; surely the Allies would not dare
send their bombers in daytime. Wrong. The Eighth Air Force would dare.*

In the early autumn of 1943, Albert Speer 'witnessed a dramatic scene
between Goering and General Galland, who commanded his fighter
planes.' Galland had informed Hitler that American fighter aircraft,
which had been escorting bombers, had been shot down over the
German town of Aachen. Galland passed on his concerns that there
was a real danger that American fighters in the near future may be able
to escort the bomber formations even further into German airspace.
Hitler passed the information on to Goering. The Reichsmarschall
was not pleased and confronted Galland, asking him why he had told
Hitler that American fighters had reached into Reich territory:

'Herr Reichsmarschall', Galland replied with imperturbable
calm, 'they will soon be flying even deeper.'
    Goering spoke even more vehemently: 'That's nonsense,
Galland, what gives you such fantasies? That's pure bluff!'
    Galland shook his head. 'Those are the facts, Herr
Reichsmarschall!' As he spoke he deliberately remained
in a casual posture, his cap somewhat askew, a long cigar
clamped between his teeth. 'American fighters have been
shot down over Aachen. There is no doubt about it!'
    Goering obstinately held his ground: 'That is simply not

true Galland. It's impossible.'
Galland reacted with a touch of mockery: 'You might go and
check it yourself sir; the downed planes are there at Aachen.'
Goering tried to smooth matters over: 'Come now, Galland, let
me tell you something. I'm an experienced fighter pilot myself.
I know what is possible. But I know what isn't too. Admit you
made a mistake.'

Galland maintained his stance and Goering suggested that the aircraft
had been shot down to the west, at considerable height, and glided
into German airspace before crashing:

> Not a muscle moved in Galland's face. 'Glided to
> the east sir? If my plane were shot up . . .'
> 'Now then, Herr Galland,' Goering fulminated, trying
> to put an end to the debate, 'I officially assert that the
> American fighter planes did not reach Aachen.'
> The General ventured a last statement. 'But, sir,
> they were there!'
> At this point Goering's self-control gave way. 'I herewith give you
> an official order that they weren't there! Do you understand?
> The American fighters were not there! Get that! I intend to report
> that to the Fuehrer.'
> Goering simply let General Galland stand there.
> But as he stalked off he turned once more and called
> out threateningly, 'You have my official order!'
> With an unforgettable smile the General replied, 'Orders are
> orders sir!'[1]

In the following months, Galland's fears were realized as the American
fighters did indeed accompany the bombers further and further
into Germany. 'Big Week' at the end of February 1944 was a historic
demonstration of the reach of the Eighth Air Force's escorted bombers.
In the first week of March, a further momentous demonstration was

to occur. The Eighth were going to Berlin. But before we join the Americans over the Big City, it is worth highlighting the reputation of this target, gained as a result of the RAF's previous battles over the German capital.

THE PRECEDING NIGHT ATTACKS – RAF BOMBER COMMAND
RAF Bomber Command's Sir Arthur Harris called Berlin the 'black heart' of Germany. In the previous months, RAF bomber crews had been there on numerous occasions, attempting to fulfil their commander's wish to bomb Berlin until **'the heart of Nazi Germany ceases to beat.'** As a result, RAF bomber wreckage was strewn along the approach routes to the city and RAF airmen had swelled the population of the various StalagLufts. Many RAF airmen now lay beneath German, Dutch, Belgian and French soil. Some lay at the bottom of the North Sea. A few could consider themselves fortunate and were in hiding, on the run in German-occupied territory.

John Martin of 620 Squadron went to Berlin on the night of 31 August/1 September 1943. John's account of the raid provides an insight into how a raid to Berlin in the early stages of Sir Arthur Harris's Battle of Berlin could affect one man:

> I've asked myself many times since the war ended, 'Was it all worth it, given the lives that were lost during the war?' I was at Waterbeach as a flight mechanic and I then went to train as a member of aircrew, and afterwards joined the squadron.
> I had flown about 25 bombing missions, I was an old sweat by that time. Everyone else had gone, and Taffy Whitfield [William Whitfield], the fellow who slept in the next bed to me, he arrived as a flight engineer. He was attached to an Australian crew.
> They went in to get briefed for their mission that night: it was an attack on Berlin. They came out from briefing and we went in for ours. I asked him whenever we came out, 'What do you think of the mission tonight?' He said to me, 'With this crew, I have got no hope, no hope in this wide world. Getting through with this!

They're hopeless.' We got to Berlin and I was in the astrodome. Berlin was like flying down Royal Avenue in Belfast, all the lights were on, everything was as clear as a bell. Once you start into Berlin, you never think you are going to get to the other end of the city. It's so long. While I was in the astrodome, I saw Taff going over ahead of me. The next thing I saw, a fighter came up and shot him down, and that was the end of Taff. It all happened right in front of me, he was shot down. I was able to read his aircraft registration on the side of his aircraft. That was Big Taff Whitfield. You realize just how close you were to being shot down yourself, and wonder how did you get through the war?[2]

William Whitfield had lost his life along with four others of the crew; two men survived and were captured. In total, 613 aircraft were sent on the raid: 47 failed to return, 225 men lost their lives, 108 became prisoners of war and one man evaded capture.

Further raids to Berlin would follow that winter and many other bomber airmen would come to share a common experience with John Martin. Canadian Alex Nethery was the bomb aimer on pilot Arthur Darlow's crew, and together they would fly operationally to Berlin four times over the autumn and winter of 1943/44. Alex reinforces Berlin's growing reputation:

If there was one dreaded target that we hated to hear as our objective, it was Berlin! Goering once said that no Allied bomber would ever reach Berlin, and he pulled a lot of fighter squadrons and guns from other parts of Germany to defend the German capital. In addition to the heavy defence, this was a long trip – 7 or 8 hours – and practically every fighter station in Germany got a whack at you going over as well as coming back.[3]

On the night of 2/3 December 1943, it would be the turn of an American, broadcaster Ed Murrow, to go to the Big City, and be able to tell his fellow countrymen of his experiences and what the RAF aircrews were enduring. Earlier that night Ed had attended a briefing at an RAF station, then joined a bomber crew as they prepared for the raid that night – to Berlin. Ed recalled the sight just after his aircraft took off: 'I looked right and left and counted 14 black Lancasters climbing for the place where men must burn oxygen to live.' And as they flew on and became part of the bomber stream, 'The blue-green jet of the exhausts licked back along the wing, and there were other aircraft all around us. The whole great aerial armada was hurtling toward Berlin.' Ed recorded his feelings as they reached the city, flying towards the blobs of yellow light:

Dead on time, Buzz the bomb aimer reported, 'Target indicators going down.' At the same moment, the sky ahead was lit up by bright yellow flares. Off to starboard another kite went down in flames. The flares were sprouting all over the sky, reds and greens and yellows, and we were flying straight for the center of the fireworks. D-Dog seemed to be standing still, the four propellers thrashing the air, but we didn't seem to be closing in. The clouds had cleared, and off to the starboard a Lanc was caught by at least 14 searchlight beams. We could see him twist and turn and finally break out. But still, the whole thing had a quality of unreality about it. No one seemed to be shooting at us, but it was getting lighter all the time. Suddenly, a tremendous big blob of yellow light appeared dead ahead; another to the right and another to the left. We were flying straight for them.

Jock [the pilot] pointed out to me the dummy fires and flares to right and left, but we kept going in. Dead ahead there was a whole chain of red flares looking like stoplights. Another Lanc was coned on our starboard beam. The lights seemed to be supporting it. Again we could see those little bubbles of colored lead driving at it from two sides. The German fighters were at him. And then, with no warning at all, D-Dog was filled with an unhealthy white light.

I was standing just behind Jock and could see all the seams on the wings. His quiet Scots voice beat in my ears, 'Steady lads, we've been coned.' His slender body lifted half out of the seat as he jammed the control column forward and to the left. We were going down. Jock was wearing woollen gloves with the fingers cut off. I could see his fingernails turn white as he gripped the wheel. And then I was on my knees, flat on the deck, for he had whipped the Dog back into a climbing turn. The knees should have been strong enough to support me, but they weren't, and the stomach seemed in some danger of letting me down too. I picked myself up and looked out again. It seemed that one big searchlight, instead of being 20,000 feet below, was mounted right on our wing-tip. D-Dog was corkscrewing. As we rolled down on the other side, I began to see what was happening to Berlin.

The clouds were gone, and the sticks of incendiaries from the preceding waves made the place look like a badly laid-out city with the streetlights on. The small incendiaries were going down like a fistful of white rice thrown on a piece of black velvet. As Jock hauled the Dog up again, I was thrown to the other side of the cockpit. And there below were more incendiaries, glowing white and then turning red. The cookies, the 4,000-pound high explosives, were bursting below like great sunflowers gone mad. And then, as we started down again, still held in the lights, I remembered that the Dog still had one of those cookies and a whole basket of incendiaries in his belly, and the lights still held us, and I was very frightened.

While Jock was flinging us about in the air, he suddenly yelled over the intercom, 'Two aircraft on the port beam.' I looked astern and saw Wally, the mid-upper, whip his turret around to port, and then looked up to see a single-engine fighter slide just above us. The other aircraft was one of ours. Finally, we were out of the cone, flying level. I looked down, and the white fires had turned red. They were beginning to merge and spread, just like butter does on a hot plate. Jock and Buzz, the bomb aimer, began to discuss the target. The smoke was getting thick down below. Buzz said he liked the two green flares on the ground almost dead ahead. He began calling his directions. Just then a new bunch of big flares went down on the far side of the sea of flame that seemed to be directly below us. He thought that would be a better aiming point. Jock agreed and we flew on. The bomb doors were opened. Buzz called his directions: 'Five left, five left.' And then there was a gentle, confident upward thrust under my feet and Buzz said, 'Cookie gone.' A few seconds later, the incendiaries went, and D-Dog seemed lighter and easier to handle.[4]

As the aircraft left the target, Ed recorded, '**I began to breathe, and to reflect again, that all men would be brave if only they could leave their stomachs at home.**' On the way back, the aircraft came close to a collision with another Lancaster, further aircraft were seen to fall in flames, and flak bursts came too close for comfort. After crossing the North Sea Ed recorded, '**We were over England's shores. The land was dark beneath us. Somewhere down there below, American boys were probably bombing up Fortresses and Liberators, getting ready for the day's work.**' Jock, described by Ed as, '**the finest pilot in Bomber Command**' brought the aircraft down safely and Ed was able to file his report. Other reporters had gone on the raid that night; two had lost their lives:

Berlin was a thing of orchestrated Hell, a terrible symphony of light and flames. It isn't a pleasant kind of warfare, the men doing it speak of it as a job. Yesterday afternoon, when the tapes were stretched out on the big map all the way to Berlin and back again, a young pilot with old eyes said to me, 'I see we're working again tonight.' That's the frame of mind in which the job is being done. The job isn't pleasant; it's terribly tiring. Men die in the sky while others are roasted alive in their cellars. Berlin last night wasn't a pretty sight.

Through this broadcast, Ed Murrow had informed America of the 'hell' of a raid to Berlin; something his country's servicemen had yet to experience at first hand.

## THE AMERICANS GO TO HELL

By March 1944, Sir Arthur Harris's Battle of Berlin had been raging for half a year. He had believed that with American help, a combined bomber attack could take out the German capital and possibly end the war. But at the beginning of March the Americans were yet to join their allies, mainly as a result of operational realities – the lack of suitable fighter escort and adverse weather. The Eighth Air Force bomber crews had yet to fly to 'Big B', as it became known. The RAF had not, to date, been able to take out the focal point of the Nazi Reich.

But now improving weather and improvement in fighter escort capability opened the window of opportunity. With the Eighth Air Force fighter pilots now able to accompany their 'big friends' into Germany, an all-out daylight assault on Berlin became a distinct possibility. And possibility became reality in early March, 1944.

The first attempt to reach the German capital on the third day of the month met with frustration: the weather. Although it is interesting to note that one fighter group did not receive the recall that was sent and pilots of the 55th Fighter Group were able to look down on Berlin from their cockpits. There was similar frustration owing to the weather the next day. The majority of the attacking force were recalled, turning back or bombing targets of opportunity. Only three squadrons reached Berlin, bombing through cloud. Two days later, the Eighth Air Force prepared to go back to 'Big B'. Mission 250 made a statement: the Eighth Air Force were not backing down from the challenge. Three primary targets were to be attacked, with 730 bombers despatched in 11 combat wings, accompanied by just over 800 fighters from 17 fighter groups and three RAF squadrons. The Flying Fortresses of the 1st Division would be in the vanguard of the bomber force, followed by the 3rd Division's B-17s and then the 2nd Division's Liberators. This day they would reach the 'black heart' in considerable force – but the cost was going to be high.

For William Mahn of the 96th Bomb Group, the mission to Berlin would be his twenty-fifth, 'my last one':

The Eighth had tried twice before within a few days. My crew was bragging that, 'Today we will make it – Captain Mahn never fails, etc.' We got there all right, in fact we circled the bloomin' town! Colonel Lemley was in the co-pilot's seat. He was the wing commander of the 45th Combat Wing. The day was like a wide-screen cinema. The 96th was neither leading the Eighth nor trailing; some place in the middle, en route to Berlin.[5]

Dana Morse served with the 91st Bomb Group, part of the 2nd Bomb Division, and recalled that on 5 March his crew were alerted that there would be a mission the next day:

On 6 March, up at 3 am with hardly no sleep, breakfast was at 4 am and then briefing. The crew was taken to our plane, 'My Darling Also', for boarding. The target again was for Berlin, a 9-hour flight. We had made attempts before in the early days of March, but had to abort.[6]

Hubert Cripe served with the 453rd Bomb Group, of the 2nd Bomb Division. He was woken, to go to work, at 02.30 hours on 6 March:

A GI orderly is sleepily making his way down the wet and muddy walk that leads past a row of Nissen huts where combat crews are sleeping. Already there are sounds of activity on the base. The orderly opens the door of one of the huts, turns on the light, and calls 'Lt Cripe?' 'Huh,' comes the sleepy answer. 'Breakfast at three o'clock, briefing at four.' He leaves at this and goes on to call other crews.

Lt Cripe, that's me, got up and shivered as the cold night air struck me. I called my co-pilot, Russ Anderson, and my navigator, Lt Dallacqua. Now I know how my father felt when he called my brother and me on a cold winter morning, only more so. Well, I got them up with lots of grumbling and cuss words. We put our helmets, oxygen masks, coveralls, and parachute harnesses in a C-3 bag, dressed and went to breakfast of powdered eggs and hot cakes.

Groups of men were grouped around the stove speculating on the target. However, trucks were waiting to take the crews to briefing so we cut it short and loaded up.[7]

Twenty-year-old Earl G. Williamson Jr of the 91st Bomb Group recorded his experiences of 6 March in a personal diary:

We climbed out of warm sacks in the pre-dawn darkness, went to briefing and found that our target was again Berlin. This would be our (my crew's) third attempt to bomb Berlin, since our group was called back due to weather on two occasions. Luring the Luftwaffe into combat was only one of the several valid reasons for daylight blows at the heart of Germany. The great ball-bearings works at Erkner (our target), in the suburbs of Berlin, was high on the list of priority targets.[8]

Hubert Cripe went to the briefing and gazed across the room to a large map of England and the continent:

The room soon filled and Major Hubbard directed the route he put on the map. A hush settled over the room as the S-2 men thumbtacked a thin sheet of Plexiglas in such a way that a red crayon line on the sheet disclosed our route. Groans went up over the room as the red line stopped at – Berlin!

Major Hubbard demanded order and called the role . . . Major Hubbard continued and assigned ships, told gas load, bomb load, and call signs. S-2 took over then and the first words they said were, 'Gentlemen, OUR target for today is Berlin.' Then the officer described our target, an electrical

plant on the south side of Berlin. Then he continued that if
we were unable to get back to England to head for Sweden.
'If you are forced to land in Holland or Belgium your chances
of contacting the underground are pretty good. However, no
such luck in Germany. Good luck, gentlemen.' Next came the
weather officer who described what kind of weather to expect.
The briefing officers had been up all night preparing this mission,
and with a few final remarks Major Hubbard dismissed us.

Back to the equipment room we went, drew parachutes
– mine was a new back pack – and the Mae Wests that were
to prove the factor to cheat death. The equipment I wore was
long underwear, blue bunny electric suit, coveralls, electric
gloves and shoes, fleece-lined boots, helmet with oxygen mask
attached, Mae West, and finally the parachute. I remember
I left a short coat, pink pants, green shirt, and my cap in my
C-3 bag in the dressing room. Past experience had taught me
to take along a winter jacket, as the electric suit might not
work. Thus equipped we went outside, loaded our equipment
and ourselves on a truck and went out to our hardstand.

The gas truck had just finished topping out tanks after pre-
flight. 'You'll have 2,700 gallons of gas,' Major Hubbard had
said and the crew chief was seeing that we had just that.
Dawn had not come yet and the lights were on inside the plane.
As I crawled into the bomb bay to put my equipment in the
cockpit I noticed the bombs. Eggs for Jerry, ten of them too. S-2
must have wanted the place bombed good. I rejoined the crew
who were checking the guns, ammo, and turrets. I was tense and
Russ and I walked away from the plane to have a last cigarette.

'She'll be a rough one today, huh,' said Russ. 'Yeah,'
I said, wondering if it would be like the mission 2 days
before when we got as far as Heligoland and were forced
back on account of weather. Well, I vowed, today would be
different. We'd blast that place wide open, I told myself.

Ten minutes before starting engines time, we (the crew) had

a final pep talk and boarded the plane. Russ read through the checklist and the engineer started the putt-putt. The clock on the instrument panel had come to engine starting time as Russ snapped on the switches and said, 'Starting number 3.' The starting motor gave a low whine and increased. 'Mesh number 3.' 'Meshing 3,' came the answer and the big prop started turning slowly. The 1,200-hp engine coughed, caught, blew out a cloud of blue smoke and burst into life. In such a manner the other three engines were started. After satisfying ourselves the engines were thoroughly warm, we waited for taxiing time. The lead bomber had already taxied past our hardstand and the others were following in order.

At the home of the 91st Bomb Group, Earl G. Williamson Jr's take-off appeared to be normal, and his Flying Fortress gained height. But little more than 5 minutes into the flight, fuel began to pour out of the wing close to the number 3 engine:

Someone must have left the gas cap off or at least didn't fix it very tight. Our pilot (Lt Wilkinson) and co-pilot (Lt Mughee) have always been extremely afraid of any gas, because one spark and 'you've had it' as the British say. Our pilot radioed for an emergency landing at our field but they told him he couldn't land for 15 minutes because other Forts were taking off. So – we flew over an adjacent fighter field only 3 miles away and radioed for an emergency landing. All communications between ground and air do not come over the interphone and the crew was ignorant of the fact that we were going to land so soon. The pilot should have let us know on interphone. The bombardier, ball-turret operator, radioman, and right waist gunner were all in the radio room. The navigator had just crawled out of the nose. The bombardier was in the radio room because in a short while (5,000 feet) he would have to pull the arming pins out of the bombs. The ball turret operator doesn't get in his cramped position until over the English Channel. The radioman was in his position, and the right waist gunner went up to check something in the radio room. The tail gunner was near the tail wheel adjusting and checking his equipment, and I was near him doing the same thing but still on interphone.

Suddenly Earl felt the flaps on the wings come down and the B-17 slow. He realized they were going to land:

The tail gunner looked back and noticed that our tail wheel was still up. This means that our main landing gear was still up also and that we were going to land. I ran to the interphone mike button to tell the pilot . . . Just as I pushed the button in, we hit, and all hell broke out. We were bouncing and hitting everywhere with ten 500-pound bombs, a full gas load and at 125 miles per hour with our wheels up. We were not even braced; at least most of us were not. There were a few seconds in which I don't remember what took place. I was going from side to side like a pingpong ball and I landed near the tail wheel when the plane stopped. I could picture the Fort blowing up, and I thought I could see myself floating around in the air; also there was the fear of getting struck by the ball turret since it protrudes lower than the fuselage and usually flies back toward the tail in a crash landing. All the pins were in the bombs but it was still a hell of a feeling. As the bomber came to a stop I heard gas sizzling, like those sizzling steaks in good old America. Sparks would fix things. I could hear ambulances, fire trucks, and crash crews with their sirens going full blast. I wondered about the others, and in my daze I knew that I had to get out of the plane in a hurry but for some reason I was frozen. The next thing I remember was the fellow coming from the radio room telling me to hurry. I stepped out and the other fellows were close behind, and we almost ran over the ambulances and fire trucks getting away from that bomber. I looked back to see the co-pilot coming out of the cockpit window and the pilot and navigator close behind. Crash crews and crew personnel began to swarm out near the plane with fire extinguishers and fire-fighting equipment. We got a safe distance from the smoking and badly battered plane and everyone seemed all right except for the fact that it was very hard to light a cigarette. It was hard to keep moving about and everyone was shaking like a dog that had just been doused in water, only we couldn't help it. The doctor looked us over and we were told we were all right.

The pilot had forgotten in all the excitement to put the landing gear down. The engineer (Wilson) had gone back to check the landing gear with a crank but before he could do so the pilot was hollering for him to call out ground speed and so he rushed back. The pilot said, 'Sorry boys, I just forgot to put the wheels down. I've made worse landings with my wheels down.' He had controlled the plane considering everything. How a crew can walk from a wreck is beyond me. We were plenty lucky and everyone realized it. In a few minutes the colonel and a captain from our field were over there. Trucks came, and after we had gathered our equipment, took us back to our base. This was the third time we had started out for Berlin and still had not gotten over the capital.

Hubert Cripe's crew would have no such misfortune. They would be going to Berlin that day. At the 453rd Bomb Group's Old Buckenham base, Hubert prepared to take off with his colleagues:

We were flying off Lieutenant Witzel's wing and when I saw him begin to move I released the brakes, increased the RPM and slowly made our way to the taxi strip. By the time we had taxied half-way to the end of the runway, the lead plane was taking off. He was airborne before the end of the runway and the other planes followed in order. They all showed evidence of their heavy load: bombs, 2,700 gallons of gas, plus ten men and

ammunition for ten machine guns, a total of nearly 35 tons.
We stopped at the run-up area and went through the take-off
checklist: 20 degree flaps, high RPM (2,700), manifold pressure
47 inches of mercury. We taxied to the opposite side of the
runway Lt Witzel used, in order to escape his prop wash, and held
our brakes awaiting the green light from control. Hatches closed,
cowl flaps closed, auto rich, brakes set, and 25 inches of mercury.
  There's the green light and here comes the white knuckles.
Brakes released and we're rolling. Throttles wide open and
the 4,800 Pratt and Whitney horses bellow their song.
Full military power, we get 49 inches mercury, maximum
from the ram effect. Sgt Garrett, replacement engineer, stood
between Russ and me and like Cool Hand Luke he calmly
called out the airspeed: 60 – 65 – 70 – 80. Come on baby, come
on, we're already past half the runway length: 90 – 95. She's
getting lighter, keep that nose wheel down, don't let her fly
off yet: 100 – 105. Back pressure on the wheel: 110 – 120 and
we're in the air just over the end of the runway. 'Gear up! Gear
up!' I screamed. Why does it seem I'm the only white-knuckled
guy aboard? Russ calmly answered, 'Gear coming up.' And
the massive gear swung out and upward. Use brakes to stop
the spin of the wheels or they will be just like a gyro. Yeah, we
sure got a load of baggage. We can scarcely climb but we are
gaining. Five minutes of maximum military power are the limit
and Russ lowered manifold pressure and RPM and milked up
the flaps. Our speed increased and we started our climb.

Almost as soon as the wheels were retracted, Hubert took his aircraft
into a climbing turn:

If you don't, you will be miles away from the formation.
We started turning almost as soon as our wheels were off
the runway. By turning inside of Witzel we soon caught up
with him and assumed our position off his right wing. He

had already assumed his position and the plane that took off behind us got into position off his left wing. Our section got into a semblance of a formation and closed up. Our position was number two in the high right element – the Purple Heart element. After our group had formed we started looking for the other two groups in our wing – the 389th and 445th. All the B-24s are in the second division and after much manoeuvring in banks, rolling in prop wash, and racing engines, the entire division was formed. Planes seemed to be everywhere.

At 12,000 feet, Russ and I put on our oxygen masks and at 15,000 feet, I ordered the crew to put theirs on. It was going to be a long raid and a long time on oxygen, so save all you can. The choppy, cold North Sea was beneath us now. We seemed to be standing still but the airspeed indicator read 165. After what seemed to be hours the coast of Holland came into sight. Enemy territory!

The engineer had finished transferring gas out of the Tokyo tanks and was back at his top turret searching the sky for enemy fighters. High above us were many single contrails. Fighters! Maybe they are our own. Sure enough, as they got closer the wing and tail positively identified them as P-47s. If any enemy fighters were present they kept away from us while we had fighter protection.

We were well inland now and Spike, the navigator, called up and said we would be over the German border in 7 minutes. Well, so far, so good. No flak yet. The gunners were keeping a line of talk going over the interphone. For myself, I was comfortable. Electric suit OK. Oxygen mask OK. Plane OK, except number 3 was getting pretty warm.

Suddenly, out of nowhere, dark smudges of black smoke appeared in the group ahead of us. Flak! Hope they leave us alone. I didn't see any apparent damage but by then we were in it. It wasn't too accurate though and we flew on unhindered.

Our route took us out of most of the flak areas and we flew

on, seeing light flak occasionally and many of our own fighters, which had changed to P-38s. We'll change again before the target to P-51s. We were well over Germany by now and Spike called again to tell me we would change course for the IP in 15 minutes. Well, so far this had to be a milk run. I would have been plumb happy, only we were 250 miles inside Germany.

We changed course for the IP all right, but 10 minutes later Witzel suddenly pulled out of formation. Well, being out of formation 100 miles from Berlin is like slitting your own throat, but I followed him. He was definitely in trouble. And sure enough, he feathered number 3. What to do? Why didn't the dumb fool try to stay with the formation? But no, he was going home. ?!*%?!**!! Well, I've got to catch the formation or my goose will be cooked. I gave her full throttle and caught my group just after they had passed the IP but I got the wrong section! I was in the first one and my own was behind me.

Hubert decided to stay where he was.

LET BATTLE COMMENCE

Up to that point, enemy fighters had not caused Hubert and his crew any problems. As he said, 'It seemed a milk run.' But the Luftwaffe was climbing and was indeed taking up a position to oppose the Eighth's bombers. At midday the bombers of the 3rd Bomb Division were the first to confront the enemy fighters: an estimated 100-plus Me109s and FW190s. William Mahn recalled:

The Luftwaffe hit us like a ton of bricks. I could easily see them, like a bunch of angry hornets buzzing all around us, in and out, hitting the wing just in front of us. We could see the damage by the planes falling out of formation, chutes billowing, etc. But though just a mile in front of us, maybe a bit more, they didn't bother us. Occasionally one bandit would float past within our gun range. They acted as though we didn't exist.

At approximately 12.50 hours, bombers of the 1st Bomb Division grew in the sights of the Luftwaffe fighter aircraft. For Dana Morse, everything appeared to be 'fairly smooth' until they reached the IP. But his participation in the mission was nearing its end:

The fighters came in on our group and tail-end Charlie was knocked out. First Lieutenant Bob Tibbets Jr thought it best with our experience over the crew or wingman that we should fill in the tail-end position, which we did. As I recall, enemy fighters were being called in from every position on our plane. To the best of my knowledge, we had made the turn at the IP when we were hit and knocked out of the formation. The intercom was out, so I moved my chute and put it back near the escape hatch. Later, a hole was blown in the spot where my chute had been. I went back to firing my gun at, I believe, a Messerschmitt 110 and could see my machine gun holes going down at least a third of its fuselage; he could not have been more than 50 yards away and came in from nine o'clock low. Others were firing their guns and it reminded me of the first mission when we had to ditch into the North Sea and had to fire the guns to get rid of our ammunition.

One German fighter pilot then went to the extreme in taking out one of his adversaries: a FW190 rammed Dana's aircraft:

Walter J. Davis, the tail gunner, survived the collision. The fighter had aimed at the area between the tail assembly and the tail gunner. The plane was jarred and I was knocked from my gun, and then my gun was shot out and I felt a burning sensation on my left thigh. Sydney A. Barratt Jr, the right waist gunner, was holding his stomach and had been hit bad. I looked out the right-waist window and saw that we were on fire and sliding off to our right and going down. I could see no one at all up through the plane due to the smoke and knew we were in deep trouble. I tried to arouse

Harold J. Rhode, the ball turret gunner, with no results.

Then I tried to help Barratt, but he was out cold, so I tried to open the escape door but it was jammed. I was finally able to kick it out. I could see no movement from the ball turret and the right waist gunner was still laying there. I could not move him. I took one look out of the escape door before jumping and saw the right horizontal elevator torn off near the fuselage. I could not see Davis in the tail section. I jumped and waited some, but probably not long enough and I was jerked hard. The chute opened and I floated toward the west. I heard a loud explosion and when I tried to locate our plane, I could not find it. At the same time a fighter came in on me, an Me109. I was not sure at the time if it fired at me, but later when I looked up at my chest-type chute, it had at least 25 to 50 holes in it. I drifted over one big town and several small towns. It seemed that the wind was strong and blowing me. I tried to steer the chute as I was heading into the woods and I don't know if I did any good, but I landed hard into some type of thorn bushes. People were coming in from all sides as I drifted down, so I just lay there. I had lost a lot of blood and had no more strength.

There were many civilians with guns pointed at me and they stripped me of my chute and anything else that they wanted. The German Army came up and knocked the guns out of the hands of the civilians. I guess they were thinking of shooting me, because of all of the loud talking. The Army then placed me in an oxcart and it was not long before Sgt Davis came up and tried to give me some morphine, but they would not let him. By this time, I did not know if Sgt Davis had gone. All I know was that it took a long time and was a long ride. When I came to, I was in a building and on a stretcher and taken to a room where they held me down on a table. I thought that this was it, so I fought like hell. I came to some time later in an old theater. It was in the town of Magdeburg, Germany. I was later transported to be interrogated and sent to a POW camp.

Back in the sky, the 1st Bomb Division had opened the bombing, hampered by cloud, attacking secondary targets in the east of Berlin. They were followed by the 3rd Bomb Division, including the 96th Bomb Group, detailed to attack the Robert Bosch electrical works, but cloud cover also forced a switch to secondary targets. William Mahn described the problem caused by the cloud, which became apparent on the run up to the target:

We approach the IP just south of Berlin. Colonel Lemley taps me on my right shoulder. I look at him. He places an 8 x 11 sketch of a map in front of me to see, showing three lakes in a string, way south of Berlin. Lemley points to the lakes on the map and points out the window to the south. Sure enough, three lakes are glistening in the sun. He then points on the map where it indicates I should make a 90 degree left turn. I point down toward the nose wherein we have two navigators and two bombardiers, indicating to the colonel to call them on the interphone. The navigator usually calls me and tells me each major turn and number of degrees turn and change of altitude if any. So the colonel calls the navigator/bombardier. I don't recall the actual conversation. I must have been on the interplane because I anticipated the other groups would wonder why I had not turned. I don't ever recall getting a call from the nose. I don't recall whether or not my interphone was functioning because the colonel and I usually conversed by sign language. Anyway I did get a bit startled when several B-17s from one of the other groups made a 90-degree left turn and brushed rather close to us. The colonel attempted at least twice to raise the nose. I was not aware the intercom was out – I don't think it was. Anyway, up ahead was the 5,000 foot thick overcast that for days had covered Berlin and was now about 100 miles east of it. So I belatedly made a left turn.Incidentally, looking toward Berlin, you could not see anything – not so much clouds as heavy haze.
By circumstance, an element of three planes in the low

squadron to my left and low did not drop their bombs when we dropped on a target of opportunity. So fortunately as it turned out, a town appeared. We were now headed west (probably north-east of Berlin) and the pilot of this element called for permission to pull out and drop on the town.

I Looked at the colonel, nodded my head to indicate it was OK with me, so the colonel nodded OK. So either I, or the colonel, called to the pilot and said to pull out and drop.

Shortly after he dropped his bombs, white smoke rose up about 1,500 feet, so he hit something worth hitting. The group had previously dropped on what looked like a small industrial set-up. No smoke was seen rising from it, although we believe we hit it. We kept looking for enemy activity but never saw any, no flak, no fighters, just heavy haze. We must have skirted to the north of Berlin. All this time we not only didn't see any enemy action, but no friendly activity either.

As we approached Belgium or Holland, at ten o'clock low about 5,000 feet below us and 3 miles away was a B-24 box. About eight enemy fighters were harassing them. This was my twenty-fifth mission and I didn't want it to be my last in but one meaning. I pondered a bit whether to veer toward them to go to their aid or to continue straight ahead. I made a slow casual left turn, a descending turn, both to pick up airspeed and lose altitude. As we got near to the activity, the bandits broke off and away from us. It was amazing! Going to Berlin, I knew it was coincidental that they didn't jump us specifically, but here I asked for it and they beat it!

As Hubert Cripe's Liberator had neared the target, flak, as opposed to fighters, which he had so far managed to elude, was to be his main worry:

Berlin, here we come. Jerry had the welcome mat turned upside down and inside the door. Over the target was the

most concentrated flak barrage I have ever seen. It was almost
a solid black cloud with red bursts of exploding shells. We
could see it 50 miles off and it filled me with dread. Right then
I preferred fighters to flak. We kept approaching our target,
the lead plane using the bombsight and making corrections.
Our bomb bay doors were open and we were going to drop our
eggs when the lead plane did. Suddenly we were in the flak.
It was everywhere. When you can hear it, it's too close – and I
heard plenty. Spent pieces of flak bounced off our ship like BBs.
A burst directly to one side rocked the ship. Boy, a hit in our
bomb bay and we've had it. There go the bombs! Instantly the
bombardier hit his bomb release. They're off. After what seemed
like ages we are out of the flak and the bomb bays closed.

From the bombers that attacked Berlin, which was later acknowledged
as 'generally scattered', just short of 10,000 bombs fell – 520 tons. In
addition, 2.5 million leaflets were also released to give the Berliners
an Allied perspective on the course of the war. So the Americans had
now turned the threat of a large-scale bomber attack on Berlin into
a reality. But the mission was far from over. Not all the remaining
bombers would make it back to their English bases. Hubert Cripe
would be in one of these:

We were now going home. The only apparent damage I could
see was a tiny flak hole the size of a dime just in front of the
windscreen. Immediately after releasing our load I noticed the
manifold temperatures started lowering, a good sign as we
could close the cowl flaps. The formation was pretty ragged
but it got better as we started letting down to 14,000 feet, the
altitude on the return leg. I tried to get into a position but was
chased out by other planes, so rather than brush wings I let
them have it until I finally got on the left wing of Lt Tobin,
who had one engine feathered. We didn't know then that that
was a mistake, as he started lagging behind. Flak was negligible

and neither Russ nor I saw any enemy fighters. Things were going too well. Sporadic conversations were coming over the interphone so I let Russ fly and I tuned in the radio to the fighter-bomber frequency. Enemy fighters were around. As the airwaves were full of frantic calls to our fighters to come to our aid, I glanced around. Our formation was quite a ways ahead of us and we were letting ourselves wide open for attack!

We were in the Dummer Lake area where lots of enemy fighters were concentrated. Should I leave Tobin, chance getting to the formation, or try to give the stricken Tobin what protection we could? The Jerries settled that question. One minute all was tranquil, the next I heard an explosion in our ship. We were under attack and we had been hit! Almost immediately I saw a large gaping hole appear in the trailing edge of Tobin's left wing, as a 20-millimeter shell exploded. The attack was from the rear. I jerked my head to the left and looked out the side window. There was one of our attackers. He was making a graceful left bank and the black crosses on the wing were plainly visible. Why don't the waist gunners get him? He's a sitting duck! I got on the radio and called for fighters. A cool Texas drawl came back, 'Don't get excited, sonny, poppa's coming.'

Almost immediately two P-47s appeared and chased the Me109s. I didn't look to see if they got them, as more pressing business was at hand. Tobin evidently had had it. A figure appeared in his waist window and baled out. Then my engineer called from the top turret and said we were on fire, left wing. I looked out. Sure enough, flame was coming out of a 20-millimeter hole that had punctured the tanks. If the engineer hadn't left about 20 gallons of gas in there when he transferred, the fumes would have exploded, undoubtedly blowing our wing off. However, now just the gas was burning. Should we or shouldn't we bale out now? Maybe we can slip out the flames. We tried but to no avail.

Meanwhile, we were nearing the Holland border. My decision was to try to ditch in the North Sea. That was a bad one. Trying to ditch a 24 is bad enough without it being on fire. The radio operator, as soon as he heard my decision, started sending SOS on his radio. The cockpit was filled with gas fumes, so he cracked open the bomb bay doors. Russ took off his oxygen mask and suggested smoking a cigarette, as we probably wouldn't get any for a while. I ordered him not to and to get ready to bale out. Over the interphone I ordered the crew to stand by to bale out, as we might not reach the North Sea.

Then I started losing altitude. At 10,000 feet we entered a cloud and the flames mounted higher. We weren't going to make it. I unfastened my belt, took off my mask and clamped down on the alarm bell, the signal to bale out. Spike's face appeared in the astrodome. He grinned, waved and vanished. Dineen had baled out before him through the nose-wheel door. Russ climbed out of his seat and went back to the bomb bay. I tried putting the ship on automatic pilot but it wouldn't work. To hell with it, I'm leaving. I crawled out, walked through the radio room and saw Russ on the catwalk fastening his Mae West. I thought everyone had left her. Russ and I shook hands and he jumped. I saw his hand on the ripcord and with just a little bit of fear I stepped off into 2 miles of space.

My first sensation was a 170 mph slipstream hitting me and – quiet. I felt no sensation of falling. My last glimpse of the plane was flame all over the left wing and fast getting to the fuselage. I must have been on my back when I saw her. I grabbed for the ring and yanked. Instantly there came a loud report as the nylon caught the wind, followed by a hard jerk that I hardly noticed, then – silence. I didn't even seem to be falling; instead I seemed to be going up! I was in a cloud bank and didn't get to see the ship crash. However, I heard it. When I floated out of the cloud I looked below. Water. It was the Zuider Zee and a piece of wreckage was still burning on the surface. I looked up and counted the chutes. All I could see were seven, including my own. I'll never know what happened to the other three.

On the water below were objects I took to be fishing boats. Suddenly the water seemed close and I tried to unfasten my chute and slip out but I was too late. I hit the water with a splash. Boy was it cold! I went under and came up blubbering. Treading water I tried to unfasten my chute but I couldn't get hold of the snaps. Then I tried to jerk the cord to inflate my Mae West. I missed. I tried again and missed.

God must have heard my silent prayer because on the next try I got it and yanked. Instantly the tiny cylinder filled with carbon dioxide and inflated one side of the Mae West and kept my head above water. I rested, and then I unfastened my chute, which was tangled around one leg.

Russ had landed about 100 yards from me and he was about all in, too. One of the fishing boats had pulled alongside him and taken him on board by the time I had swum to the side of the boat. The Dutchmen on the boat hauled me aboard, a dripping cold, half-drowned man who was very thankful to be alive. Once aboard, Russ and I shook hands and almost bawled to each other. The fishermen were very kind and while we were stripping off our wet clothes they asked us, 'Drink?' Nothing bashful about us, we said yes, expecting maybe some schnapps, but no, it was water! We only had about half the Zuider Zee inside us and they wanted to know if we wanted water. However, they finished taking our clothes off and put us to bed. They would have been very helpful in getting us back to England, I think, but a German harbor patrol launch pulled alongside and took us on board. In the cabin was Spike. We three were the only survivors of Crew 44. Much later, I received information that the bodies of the other seven men were washed ashore in the Amsterdam area and were buried.

Hubert's crew were far from being the only ones who would fall on the journey home. Further fighter attacks claimed American bombers and lives. In total 69 bombers would be lost.

Berlin had cost the lives of hundreds of RAF aircrew, and now Hubert Cripe's crewmates and numerous other American names could be added to the lists. Fourteen lifeless crew members had returned in bombers, 38 were wounded and 708 next-of-kin had to be notified that their sons, brothers and husbands had not returned. Claims were totalled of 178 enemy aircraft destroyed, but this was a clear demonstration of over claiming. The actual figure of Luftwaffe aircraft removed from the battle was 66.

Despite the losses, on 8 March the Eighth Air Force sent 623 bombers back to Big 'B' at a cost of 37; and on a mission the next day, despite poor weather, 526 bombers went to Germany, two-thirds of them to Berlin. The weather had kept the Luftwaffe, which was also trying to regroup, on the ground and only eight bombers were lost. Had the Americans' first few missions been worth the cost? In the middle of March, General Galland filed a report that clearly showed they had:

The strained manpower situation in units operating
in defence of the *Reich* demands urgently the further
bringing up of experienced flying personnel from other
arms of the service; in particular for the maintenance of
fighting power to the air arm, tried pilots of the ground
attack and bomber units, especially officers suitable as
formation leaders, will now also have to be drawn on.

Berlin was again targeted on 22 March, and further missions in the run-up to D-Day would keep the pressure on. But the cost must never be forgotten. In March 1944, the Eighth lost 570 aircraft and 3,290 airmen had exited the daylight air battle. Further evidence of what they had achieved came from an enemy signals decrypt, intercepted at the end of the month:

The extraordinary difficult situation in the air defence
of the homeland requires with all emphasis:
1. The speedy salvage of all fighter and heavy fighter
aircraft and their immediate return for repairs.
2. The unrestricted employment of salvage personnel
for salvage tasks. Subordinate units are expressly
forbidden to employ them for any other purpose.
3. That spare parts be acquired by repair and salvage units by
removal from aircraft worth salvaging only in case of
absolute necessity.
4. That repair of aircraft in your area be energetically speeded
up in order to increase serviceability and to relieve supply.

The Eighth was clearly winning the daylight attrition battle. General
Doolittle summed up his appreciation of the work done by his crews
with a broadcast at the end of March 1944:

Our immediate goal is the destruction or neutralization of
the German Air Force . . . In our most recent operations the
German fighters have shown little inclination to come up
and fight, an indication that their losses are now exceeding
their replacements and that they are conserving their forces.

It had yet to be actually proved, but the Eighth Air Force and the RAF
had put the Luftwaffe firmly on the defensive in Western Europe.
The bomber crews had created the space over Normandy in which the
Allies could utilize daylight air superiority supporting the advances of
the ground troops.

# 9
# NIGHT BATTLES OVER FRANCE, D-DAY

*The Allied heavy bomber forces made a significant contribution to the success of the D-Day landings on 6 June 1944. In the 3 months leading up to that eventful day, the bomber aircrews played their part in a special campaign softening up Hitler's Atlantic Wall and isolating the prospective battle zone from rapid German reinforcement. It proved to be another turning point in the war: the bomber boys 'set the scene' for the success of the airborne and seaborne assault.*

A successful re-entry into mainland Western Europe centred on gaining a foothold on the beaches of Normandy, breaking the German defensive crust, securing the beachhead and then breaking out inland and beyond. The initial success of operation *Overlord,* the Normandy campaign, would depend largely upon which side could locally muster the required force to overpower their adversary. The Allies had to get enough men, equipment and supplies into the battle area before German reinforcement arrived, attempting to throw them back into the sea. Air power was going to be a critical factor in winning the battle of the build-up. The hard-fought daylight air superiority, in the main won by the American bomber incursions over Germany, would be utilized in harassing any daylight movement of German troops and weapons with Allied fighters and fighter bombers.

Much of the German reinforcement would have to travel to the battle area by rail. The Allies planned to counter this by bombarding the transport focal points – the marshalling yards in French and Belgian towns and cities – utilizing both the RAF and American heavies. This campaign against the railyards would escalate in the 3 months prior to D-Day and would indeed make a significant contribution to the winning of the Normandy campaign. But there was going to be a cost in carrying out this plan, deemed a military necessity, which would have considerable political impact. This cost had to be kept to a minimum. At the end of March 1944, British Chief of the Air Staff, Sir Charles Portal, wrote to Winston Churchill:

> In the execution of this Plan very heavy casualties among civilians living near the main railway centres in occupied territory will be unavoidable, however careful we may be over the actual bombing. Eisenhower [supreme commander for the forthcoming invasion] realises this and I understand that he is going to propose that warnings should be issued to all civilians living near railway centres advising them to move. I hope you will agree that since the requirements of *Overlord* are paramount, the Plan must go ahead after due warning has been given.[1]

Despite such representation, Churchill and the War Cabinet still had their reservations. Did the military justification outweigh the potential political implications? Eisenhower's stance on the matter remained firm:

> We must never forget that one of the fundamental factors leading to the decision for undertaking *Overlord* was the conviction that our overpowering Air Force would make feasible an operation which might otherwise be considered extremely hazardous, if not foolhardy . . . I and my military advisers have become convinced that the bombing of these centres will increase our chances for success in the critical battle, and unless this could be proved to be an erroneous conclusion, I do not see how we can fail to proceed with the programme. I admit that warnings will probably do very little in evacuating people from the points we intend to hit. On the other hand I personally believe that estimates of probable casualties have been grossly exaggerated.
>
> The French people are now slaves. Only a successful *Overlord* can free them. No one has a greater stake in the success of

that operation than have the French . . . I think it would be sheer folly to abstain from doing anything that can increase in any measure our chances for success in *Overlord*.[2]

In using the term 'grossly exaggerated', Eisenhower was demonstrating his faith in the skill and application of the Allied bomber crews.

At the start of this chapter a few examples of the special bombing operations carried out by RAF aircrews against targets in occupied France will be explored through the words of some of the participants. Yes, the flights to the targets were shorter, with less time spent in enemy airspace. And yes, in general there was less risk than on deeper penetrations into Germany. However, this was still a dangerous business, as the following will show.

MASTER BOMBER

Accuracy, for the reasons mentioned above, was of paramount importance, a point highlighted to all operational crews at briefings prior to the attacks on the rail systems in the occupied territories. There was also a considerable burden of responsibility on the men who would be controlling the raids directly over the target – the master bombers. These crews, along with the 'deputy master bombers', would be orbiting above the target, using radio (VHF – very high frequency) to maintain contact with the raid target markers and the crews of the main force. The master bombers could assess initial marking, correct any errors by instructing subsequent markers and then direct the main force to bomb or ignore the pyrotechnics as they saw fit. The task of the master bombers was crucial in this kind of raid – a target in the centre of a 'friendly' built-up area. But they would be at great risk. Once the raid started, the defences would be alerted, thus exposing them to the guns below and the guns of the nightfighters.

The RAF bomber campaign against the rail targets began on the night of 6/7 March 1944, when 261 Halifaxes and six Mosquitoes carried out a successful attack on the Trappes railyards. Over the course of the next 6 weeks further railyards were attacked, and there was, in the main, considerable success and losses were actually light in comparison to the attrition of the winter of 1943/44. Occasionally however, the bombing did go astray, such as on the night of 9/10 April 1944, when the bombers inflicted considerable damage to the Lille railyards, but an estimated 456 French people also tragically lost their lives. Military necessity, nevertheless, still required a continuance of the rail plan, a continuance of the demand of accuracy on the RAF bomber force and a continuance of the demand on the master bombers to do their best to control the raids.

Details of some RAF Bomber Command crew experiences on the night of 22/23 April 1944 now follow, when Bomber Command sent 181 aircraft to the railyards at Laon. They provide a graphic example that these raids were still dangerous, particularly for the master bombers, who had to spend more time over the target than the main force, controlling the raids. At this point, it is also worth mentioning one other feature of the raids to rail targets in France and Belgium: Bomber Command decided not to count the operations as 'whole' operations with respect to a Bomber Command tour. A tour for a main force crew was normally 30 operations; however, crews who flew on numerous rail target operations often went way beyond the 30 mark. Bomber Command had decided that there was a lessening risk when attacking the rail targets, and that crews would also reach their tour limits far too quickly, not having contributed in the way that the crews of the earlier campaigns had. There seems to be some inconsistency between how the Bomber Command Groups allocated these operations against tours; some as a third of an operation, some as two-fifths. But the raids were still risky and as one Bomber Command veteran recalled, 'If you were killed, you weren't a third killed, you were killed.'

Inexperience would often weigh in against bomber crews. One 419 Squadron Halifax crew, who flew on the Laon raid, is a case in point. Five of the crew were on their first operation. The pilot, an American, was flying his second sortie and the air bomber, the most experienced man on the crew, only had eight operations to his name. Flying Officer

Thomas lifted his Halifax from the Middleton St George runway that evening at 20.36 hours, gained height and crossed the French coast at 10,000 feet. On course for the target, Thomas lost height. A few minutes before reaching the marshalling yards, target flares lit up the sky ahead, dropped by the Pathfinders. It had been easy so far, and then flak bursts a few hundred yards to starboard of the Halifax demonstrated that the bombers' presence was not welcome. Thomas and his crew settled into the bomb run, at which point the mid-upper gunner Sergeant Greene, peering through the tail blister, reported a Junkers 88 outlined against the flares, at 100 yards range and 50 feet below. Sergeant Knox, the rear gunner, was not prepared to wait and see what developed, barking down the intercom, '**There's a kite on our tail, corkscrew port.**' The official report of the incident takes up the story:

> The fighter closed in to 50 yards, firing all the time, but the
> rear gunner got in first and the mid-upper gunner saw strikes
> on the enemy's port motor and 'tracer clustering round
> the nose'. A fire started below the enemy's port motor and
> informant claims to have seen it go down and crash in flames.

The Halifax had not come out of the encounter unscathed, however. The Luftwaffe pilot had managed to get a burst in at the bomber. Flight engineer Sergeant Thompson glared out of a window, his face illuminated by the fire developing in the port inner engine:

> The bomb doors were open and bombs on board at the time.
> The captain, who had not heard the gunners' warning, executed
> a moderate corkscrew, and turned northward. He then cut the
> port inner engine, but was unable to feather the propeller; he
> operated the extinguisher but it had no effect on the fire. About
> a minute after turning off track, bombs were jettisoned, but the
> captain does not recall whether the bomb doors were closed.

The sound of machine gun fire from the rear turret then made it clear to the rest of the crew that Knox was trying to ward off further unwanted company:

> The mid-upper gunner heard bullets strike the fuselage above his head and all the forward part, and saw a fire start in the under part of the starboard wing. The engineer did not report the damage caused in the second attack, which severed the intercom system, but the pilot states that it was more serious than the first. The tail plane was hit and the aircraft tended to dive to port, so the captain increased boost to +6, revs 2,850. A fire started amidships, but the mid-upper gunner managed to kick it out with his flying boot. The captain had two skin wounds in his left side, and the back of the mid-upper gunner's head was grazed by shell splinters.

Height was now down to 5,000 feet and Thomas, deciding the situation was hopeless, ordered the crew to bale out:

> Those in the front were instructed verbally; the gunners were called by light signal, but did not reply. All except the rear gunner left by the front exit. The navigator, air bomber, wireless operator, flight engineer and mid-upper gunner had all jumped about a minute after the order was given. The pilot remained in the aircraft a couple of minutes, diving and climbing in the hope of putting out the fires, but the starboard wing and port inner engine were blazing fiercely. He baled out from about 4,500 feet. It is no known whether the rear gunner baled out. The captain saw the Halifax crash and explode, 4 miles north-east of Laon, and he landed about a mile west of the aircraft. The mid-upper gunner landed in the target area, and the raid continued for half an hour after he landed. [3]

The flight engineer and wireless operator were captured. The other four men managed to evade capture, and two of them reported the events of the night to RAF intelligence officers in August 1944. At that time the fate of the Sergeant Knox, the rear gunner, was not known. In fact he had lost his life.

Above are the details of the loss of one relatively novice crew. But experience was absolutely no guarantee of safety. The rear gunner on a certain Squadron Leader Ken Bond's 77 Squadron Halifax, Flying Officer Bill Jacks, was able to report on the loss of another aircraft that night when he returned to England a few months later. Jacks was on his 52nd operation (having flown 41 operations in the Middle East):

At 23.50 hours, informant sighted accurate light flak bursts astern. He reported this to the pilot, who acknowledged the report but took no action. It was a moonless night with average visibility and there was no cloud, and no searchlights. The Halifax was flying straight and level and in accordance with instructions, Monica [tail warning radar] was not used. Directly after reporting the flak astern, informant heard and felt a succession of thuds on the bottom of the aircraft, which he is positive were caused by cannon shells from a fighter. No one gave warning of the attack and there was no return fire, and no one saw the fighter. Informant saw no tracer and considers that the fighter must have been right below the Halifax as the rear half of the aircraft aft of the mid-upper gunner's position was undamaged. Immediately after the attack, sparks were starting to fly past the rear turret.

When informant received the 'bale out' signal on the emergency intercom system, he tried to call up the pilot on the intercom. But, finding it out of action, he opened the turret doors, seized his parachute, and ran forwards towards the escape hatch. Then he was thrown onto the floor as the Halifax lurched downward (possibly caused by the pilot putting in 'George' [autopilot]). At the hatch he found the mid-upper gunner wounded in the foot and hardly able to see (informant states that the mid-upper gunner had bad sight, for which he wore goggles) and after giving him his parachute, informant rushed up to the cockpit to make sure that the pilot could not fly the aircraft home. Informant found no one in the cockpit so he returned aft, put on his chute, and opened the hatch. The Halifax had been losing height rapidly and was possibly below 2,000 feet when informant jumped. He pulled his ripcord at once. In the light of the burning aircraft he saw the mid-upper gunner's parachute open and then informant hit the ground heavily. The Halifax crashed about a minute later.

Informant considers that less than a minute had elapsed between his receipt of the 'bale out' signal and abandoning the aircraft. He had little time to find out what damage had occurred, but saw flames coming from the bomb bay. The inspection panels were not in position, and the sides of the aircraft were burning amidships. When he opened the escape hatch, sparks were blowing past it.[4]

Bill Jacks, of course had managed to evade capture, as did the flight engineer. Charles Hobgen, the navigator on Ken Bond's crew, had also initially managed to evade capture for the night but was caught the next day, when he went to the aid of the wireless operator, who was badly injured. The bomb aimer and the mid-upper gunner were also captured. The wireless operator and mid-upper gunner both had serious leg wounds and had to have below-the-knee amputations. Pilot Ken Bond, suffering serious injury, was taken to a hospital, but died on arrival.

Above are the details of two of the losses from the main force that night. Master bomber on the raid was 635 Squadron's Wing Commander A. G. S. Cousens, in an aircraft flown by Pilot Officer Courtenay. While the destructive payloads were falling from the bomb bays of the main force onto the railyards at Laon, Courtenay orbited and Wing Commander Cousens directed the attack. For a total of 20 minutes Courtenay held the Lancaster just 4,000 feet above the target area, exposing his crew to a greater risk of ground fire. Finally, when Cousens was satisfied, and with the master bomber role completed,

Pilot Officer Courtenay set course for home, hauling the bomber back up to 10,000 feet. Then, without any warning, an enemy nightfighter unleashed a hail of fire at the Lancaster. The first Courtenay knew of it was the sound of machine gun bullets hitting the aircraft. He immediately threw the bomber into a corkscrew, diving to port, and he managed to catch a glimpse of a fire developing in the starboard wing. Courtenay focused hard on his instrument panel, but within a few seconds an explosion blasted him from the aircraft. An RAF report recorded Courtenay's experience:

To quote the pilot's own words, 'Everything suddenly went black. I was conscious, but it was like being in a completely dark room and I was being thrown all over the place. I did not know if I was on my head or my heels.' The next thing the pilot remembers is being in the air. At first he seemed to be standing still in mid-air without any sensation of falling. Then he saw the aircraft below him, a mass of flames, and realized that he was no longer in it. He surmises that a wing fuel tank or tanks had exploded and that the blast had blown the whole canopy off the cockpit and thrown him clear.

After a few seconds, Courtenay pulled his parachute ripcord, but then lost consciousness. He eventually came round, on the ground at the foot of a tree. Courtenay would manage to evade capture and return to England, where he was able to report on the events that night, including news of the fate of other members of the crew.

Informant [Courtenay] learned from the French that the wreckage of the aircraft, which was completely burned out, contained five bodies. Two more bodies were found a considerable distance away without parachutes. The nose turret was also found a long way from the main wreckage. It looked as if it had been cut clean off with a knife.

In addition to the accounts of the crews above, Bomber Command lost further aircraft. Nightfighter attacks led to the deaths of the entire crews of a 7 Squadron Lancaster, a 90 Squadron Stirling, a 149 Squadron Stirling, a 405 Squadron Lancaster and a 582 Squadron Lancaster. And a nightfighter sent a 218 Squadron Stirling burning to the ground, resulting in the death of the pilot and one other member of the crew. In total, nine aircraft were lost and 46 airmen were killed. Despite the losses, the raid was deemed a military success and there was severe damage at the railyards.

Into May 1944 and the rail attacks continued, with further success, and further losses, although not on the scale of Bomber Command's campaigns of the year to date when over Germany. However, Ronald Ivelaw-Chapman provides us with another example of the fact that night operations over France were still very dangerous. Ronald had served as a pilot in the first global conflict of the twentieth century, and had held numerous high ranking administrative roles in Bomber Command and the Air Ministry. As 1943 closed out, Ronald took up duties as a base commander at Elsham Wolds:

> During the next 3 or 4 months I did what I could to appear at briefings, debriefings, intelligence rooms, dispersal, hangars and workshops at each of my three stations as frequently as possible, apart from coping with the inevitable admin. work at my base HQ. Nevertheless, I felt I was not really being much use as a base commander and was not likely to be until I had at least one operational sortie (in the current war) to my credit. I had had some dual on the Lancaster but I was far too aware of my shortcomings as a pilot to offer myself as a 'second dickey'.

As base commander, Ronald was aware of the policy of not counting the attacks in Northern France as a full op with respect to a tour of 30:

> The crews, and I shared their views, thought this a little unfair and it crossed my mind that it might help things if

I signed on for one of these sorties as an extra aircrew.

Accordingly, at 00.15 hours on the night of 6/7 May 1944, with my group commander's permission, I took off from Elsham Wolds as 'extra aircrew' in a Lancaster of 576 Squadron with Flight Lieutenant Shearer of the Royal New Zealand Air Force as captain of our aircraft. Our target was a German ammunition depot at Aubigne, 25 miles south of Le Mans and not more than some 120 miles inland from the Normandy coast. There were about 50 of us 'Lancs' in the stream for that target that night. Shearer took us out there with no untoward event at some 18,000 to 20,000 feet in a three-quarter moon and with no cloud cover. As we neared the target I crouched alongside Sergeant Ford, of the Royal Australian Air Force, in the bomb aimer's cubbyhole as a ringside spectator. On the appointed dot second the marker flares went down. I was amazed at the accuracy and the skill with which these marker chaps had found this depot, which later I discovered to be a nondescript wood with no prominent or lead-in features nearby and stuck well out into the countryside. How they did it astounded me.

Half a dozen of the stream may have bombed before us and by the time we were running in to the target it was well alight and the conflagration, with its periodic vast explosions, was a sight I shall never forget. Even Sergeant Ford, with his long tally of ops behind him, said he had never seen anything like it before. By the time we left the target it was not so much a 'Brocks' benefit, as a burning fiery furnace.

We had settled down on the first leg of our homeward run for about 5 minutes when our rear gunner suddenly opened up, shouting down the intercom to his skipper, 'Corkscrew!' which Shearer promptly did. Within seconds there was a flash from a nightfighter flare and cannon shot riddled our Lanc all down its fuselage, followed by the acrid smell of burning . . . Then came the first sign of flames in the middle of the fuselage and almost immediately our captain's order to 'bale'.

Sergeant Ford snatched his 'brolly' and was away. Mine was strapped to the side of the fuselage just below the second pilot's seat. I remember grabbing it and making for the bomb aimer's exit but at that moment an explosion occurred in one of the petrol tanks and I found myself in the air suspended by a parachute to which, in my panic, I had only managed to get myself attached by one buckle instead of the more orthodox two. By moonlight from 15,000 feet or so I could see the flat countryside of Normandy below me . . . Our poor ill-fated Lanc, with all its crew save Sergeant Ford and myself, had become a ball of flame and I saw the wreckage hit the earth at least a minute before the trees on the edge of the forest loomed up alarmingly close below me. I landed with a bump, badly shaken but otherwise all in one piece.

For the next 10 minutes, mindful of the briefing I had been given at Elsham some 6 hours earlier, I dug like a beaver and buried my parachute as best I could and was making for such cover as the locality offered.[5]

Ronald, with the aid of the Resistance, managed to evade capture for a month. His helpers in fact received instructions from no less than Churchill himself that they were to try and arrange a return to England. If, however, there was a possibility of capture, then owing to his knowledge of D-Day plans, they were to kill him! Indeed Ronald did fall into the hands of the Gestapo, but they failed to realize his seniority and potential, and he was passed down the line to a regular POW camp. Ronald was the most senior RAF officer to fall into German custody during the war.

BLASTING THE PANZERS

This chapter has, so far, recounted examples of the experiences of airmen shot down on operations to targets in France, in the run-up to D-day. Yes, the operations were still dangerous, but generally, as anticipated by the commanders, the loss rates were low. However, there could be the occasional exceptional night of heavy losses, as the following shows.

Support to operation *Overlord* was not limited to the attack on the rail system feeding the proposed battle area. Other targeting systems came within the directives issued to the Allied bomber commands. Coastal gun batteries, bridges, airfields and radar stations were also on the target lists, as was targeting the German Army direct. Lawrence McGowen flew with 467 Squadron on one of the latter operations. On the night of 3/4 May 1944 Bomber Command would suffer one of its highest loss rates to a target in France, of the entire war. Lawrence wrote:

3 May – war again. This time the target was Mailly le Camp, not far from Paris. At briefing we were told that a Panzer division had camped there and consisted of 20,000 German troops and tanks. The object was to destroy as many Germans and their equipment as possible. Most of us had second thoughts about bombing French targets because of the damage to the French population. This was different. Now we could really hurt the enemy and so it was with anticipation and some excitement that we took off. [6]

Sidney Lipman served as a flight engineer with 166 Squadron and also flew that night:

There were 21 Lancasters on our squadron. On the first operation that I was involved in, to Essen, Germany, we lost two Lancasters and were down to 19. On the second raid, over Nuremburg, Germany, we lost another four . . . The loss of six Lancasters out of 21 in my first two flights brought home to me the full extent of the terrible odds that were stacked against the bombing crews.

The first two raids that I flew in were with strange crews which were short of a flight engineer while waiting for my own crew to be ready. Subsequent to those first two flights I flew a further 29 operations with my own crew, piloted by

Alan Gibson (Gibby), the New Zealander. Many of those flights were very eventful and hazardous . . . the flight which will be forever etched in my mind is the trip to Mailly le Camp.[7]

Wireless operator Ron Storey, from 166 Squadron, would also have this night etched into his memory. Early in his operational flying career, Ron came across an example of the acceptance of 'fate' present amongst some bomber airmen:

Karlsruhe was our second operation, on 24 April 1944 – this one I remember very well. When the call came for briefing I was standing in the doorway of our Nissen hut when a fellow from another crew stood up at the end of his bed and calmly announced that a crew from this hut was 'going for a Burton tonight'. I gazed at him in astonishment when he confidently said, 'It's OK mate, it won't be you.' We duly took off, the whole trip being fairly uneventful for us. We returned to our beds only to be awoken at 05.30 in the morning, the door opened and in came the service police to pick up the other crew's personal belongings.

Ron enjoyed a few days' leave, then on his return ops were back on:

We were detailed for an operation against Mailly le Camp, the night of which I clearly remember. I was detailed to do an air test for a wireless operator who was late back off leave. I hated flying with a crew other than my own. However I did it and briefing time came. There was a model of the Mailly le Camp area for us to study, and our squadron's task was to bomb the ablution block. All high explosives were to be used. The commanding officer said, 'It will be a piece of cake chaps, just like falling off a log, tonight there will be no nightfighters, very little ack-ack, just go in and wipe it off the map and come home.' We were to bomb from 8,000 feet. On reaching the assembly point, we were to circle the avenue of flames, and await the instructions from the master bomber, [also often referred to as the controller, or master of ceremonies] who would then give the go-ahead to head for the target and bomb precisely on the markers. It all sounded so simple, and we were in such good spirits. This was to be a real military target, manned mainly by the Panzer regiments. I met the wireless operator for whom I had air tested, and let him know that I was not very pleased with him. He replied by saying that he'd had a rotten leave, he had fallen out with his girlfriend, didn't like tonight's operation as it was out of Gee [radio navigation system] range, and without it his navigator was useless. His final words were, 'This operation, we've had it.' We had a good laugh and parted. He was lost with the rest of the crew that night.

Bomber Command's 1 and 5 Groups put 346 Lancasters and 14 Mosquitoes into the air that night, accompanied by two Pathfinder Mosquitoes. Sidney Lipman would fly in one of the 1 Group Lancasters:

The briefing was optimistic; a 'piece of cake', we told each other afterwards. We collected our parachutes from the stores, took our log books and made sure we each had our lucky mascots. The uncertainty and danger bred an atmosphere of superstition and I never flew without a little toy monkey to bring me luck. We were looking forward to getting going as we fastened our flying helmets, donned silk gloves and pulled on leather fur-lined boots to protect us from the severe cold of the altitude. The code name for our Lancaster was 'K' for King and we waved regally to the loyal WAAFs who stood outside the runway to wave us off.

In moonlight the bomber force crossed the Channel. The route to the target from the coast was the shortest possible. The bomber force met little opposition at the coast; the German fighter controller expected a penetration into Germany and had positioned the majority of his fighters accordingly. A Mosquito diversion to Ludwigshafen aided the deception. However, some nightfighter aircraft did manage to pursue the bomber force as it neared the target. Nevertheless, there should have been time to bomb and set course before they had a chance to interfere. Wing Commander Leonard Cheshire was the 'marker leader' on the raid and after the initial marking he ordered the main force crews in. But the main force controller was unable to do so owing to interference from an American force's broadcast, and his transmitter being incorrectly tuned.

Squadron Leader Sparks, on his twenty-first operation, was flying an 83 Squadron Lancaster. His responsibility was as 5 Group Deputy Controller on the raid, his 'bomb' load consisting of ten red spot fires, four green target indicators and three flares. Five minutes before zero hour Sparks reached Mailly and, in bright moonlight, began to circle the target. Between 5 and 10 minutes after zero hour the controller ordered Sparks to release all his red spot fires. A post-raid official report then takes up Sparks's recollection of the development of the bombing:

About zero + 15 informant's wireless operator reported he was not receiving W/T messages from the controller, so he called him up on VHF and asked him what was wrong. Controller acknowledged this message but still no W/T messages were received from him and after a few minutes informant again reported this to the controller, and stated he would himself send out by W/T the message to bomb. As bombing had in fact been in progress for some time, and informant considered this was falling towards the S.E. end of the target he gave the message to bomb 300 yards ten o'clock from the concentration of spot fires – that is the opposite end of the camp. This message was received by Group and immediately re-broadcast.

At about zero + 40, i.e. after circling the target for three-quarters of an hour, informant called up controller on VHF and suggested it was time to set course for base. Controller answered, 'OK. Let's go.'

The report would also state that Sparks had seen that many aircraft going down over the target that he could only give an estimate of the number: 'two dozen aircraft', containing of course 24 crews and 168 airmen. The delay over the target was going to prove fatal to many of the aircrew that night. Ron Storey recalled:

We arrived over Mailly le Camp on time, and flares almost like daylight lighted the whole scene. A bright moon shone, the assembly point marked and the flares to the target were very prominent. The radio somehow was being jammed, and it was very difficult to pick up instructions from the master bomber.

The attack should have taken place between 23.56 and 00.25 hours but the delay extended the attack a further 19 minutes:

My job over the target was to stand in the astrodome to report sightings of aircraft being hit, and if possible record the position according to a clock dial. Suddenly I saw a burst of green tracer fire flash across the sky, then another and so it went on and there were aircraft going down in all directions. I was busy giving Nick our navigator the sightings, and after a few minutes he called to me to say, 'Don't give me any more, I am too busy.' In that time I had counted 17 aircraft shot down. It was very hectic, and the master bomber was being constantly called by a number of anxious crews who were told in no uncertain terms by a booming Canadian voice to 'pipe down'. After this a dead silence pervaded the airwaves, then we were given the orders by the master bomber to go in and bomb. This we did, and thankfully we were lucky to come out without a scratch.

Lawrence McGowen also recalls the intensity of the battle:

Fighter opposition was fierce, although we were not attacked. Cannon fire from the fighters was distinctive, like a row of pretty blue lights. I saw many poor wretches being shot at and on fire. One of my friends, Stan Jolly, was shot down but survived.

Despite the deadly fight in the air, the bomber crews still managed to attack the target. Sidney Lipman remembered:

As usual we flew in formation like a flock of birds each protecting the other. We were birds of prey tonight, carrying in our bellies the weapons of destruction . . . Approaching the target, the bomb aimer gave instructions to our pilot to enable him to line up directly above the target in readiness for dropping the bombs. Gibby managed this time to avoid being caught in the searchlight, although others that night were not so fortunate and we watched them helplessly as they weaved and turned like moths around a flame. Bombs were dropped and 'K' for King lurched up sharply, relieved of all that extra weight. Our mission had been accomplished; now for the return flight home.

On the bombing run, Lawrence McGowen could see lines of burning huts and numerous explosions:

At this stage we were carrying a 4,000-pound blockbuster and a mixture of 1,000-pound bombs and incendiaries. We were now flying at 5,000 feet and as the safety height of the blockbuster was 4,000 feet, any lower and we could have blown ourselves out of the sky. As it was, turbulence made the aircraft difficult for the pilot to control and extremely difficult for the bomb aimer to bomb with accuracy.

After the bombs had fallen on the target from Sidney Lipman's aircraft, his crew began to consider relaxing a little. Such an idea was short-lived:

We congratulated ourselves on a job well done and were

looking forward to a well-earned tipple when we arrived back
at base. However, as we came away from the target we saw
really heavy flak: tiny sparks of light shooting up into the
sky like beautiful fireworks. We had no time to admire the
display. They were German anti-aircraft guns, aiming at us with
German thoroughness and German precision. We watched in
horror as two of our companion planes burst into flames.
We managed to pick out a tiny figure escaping from his inferno,
looking like a little toy parachutist suspended in mid-air.
We weaved in and out to escape the same fate, when a German
fighter flew across from starboard to port and then came
into port quarter down. He hit us and we opened fire at him.
The enemy aircraft continued to strafe us. We experienced
damage to the control surfaces, petrol supply system, edging
starboard mainplane, coolant, flank, magneto system and
engine structure and the pipelines to mid-upper turret were
severed. Apart from these minor irritations we were unharmed!

The German fighter followed us for about 8 minutes, taking
pot shots from approximately 600 yards, and our pilot weaved
and lost height. He attacked us again from port quarter down,
determined to finish us off this time. At 500 yards our rear
gunner, Alf, opened fire with a 3-second burst and tracer
was seen to enter the fighter's front cabin. A huge explosion
followed when the enemy aircraft burst into flames.
'I've got the basket,' shouted Alf and we cheered with relief as
we watched the enemy aircraft plunge to the ground. We were
out of immediate danger but were conscious of the terrible
damage that had been inflicted on 'K' for King and aware that
the bomb aimer's parachute had opened during the fighting
and was strewn about the cockpit. This meant that he would
be unable to parachute out in an emergency as we didn't carry
spare parachutes. The conflict had lasted about 12 minutes over
a distance of 35 miles, but we still had a long way to go home.
We were down to 2,000 feet and climbed up to 14,000 feet on

track. Taking stock of the damage, I feathered the starboard outer engine as it was giving trouble and noticed that the fuel gauge was very low, obviously due to the leaking pipeline. I tried to balance the fuel to no effect. We crossed the French coast.

The damaged Lancaster lost height crossing the sea:

Fuel was now very low and we sent out a distress call. We were desperate to cross the Channel before the fuel gave out, but all we could do was hope. For a long time we received no signal but at last, to our relief, we received confirmation that our distress call had been accepted. Finally, our hearts in our mouths, we crossed the coast . . . Gibby knew that our engines were about to cut; he lowered the wheels, as all the red lights had come on. He gave the order for the crew to assume the crash position. Although it would have been perhaps safer for us to have baled out, no order was given to parachute because the bomb aimer would not have been able to parachute with us as his 'chute was damaged. So we stayed in the Lancaster and took our chances with him.

Shortly after crash positions were taken, all engines cut as fuel ran out and Gibby decided to make a glide landing. As we came in to land, an aerodrome with three ambulances was seen, prepared for the inevitable casualties. Incredibly, the landing, with 30 degrees flap and no engine assistance, was faultless (one of the best we ever made) and none of us needed medical assistance.

'Miraculous' was the word the newspapers used to describe the landing, which was carried out in darkness and without any engine assistance. I felt very keenly that nothing short of a miracle could have brought us through our ordeal unscathed. Although I am not an emotional person, instinctively I kissed the ground with relief after jumping down at last from the aircraft. I shall never forget the moment of truth when each of us knew that our innermost prayers had been answered.

We now return to Squadron Leader Sparks's 83 Squadron Lancaster, which had just turned for the home flight. Sparks was making sure his crew kept a 'sharp look-out for fighters'. As they left the target area, at 4,000 feet, he noticed a fighter midway between his Lancaster and the ground, and threw his Lancaster into 'irregular combat manoeuvres'. Sparks's official report takes up the encounter with the enemy:

Considering that his aircraft was at the extreme end of the bomber stream, he now decided to set a direct course back to England instead of the long route south of Paris. The rear gunner and air bomber followed visually the movements of the fighter, and each time informant banked he sighted it himself, clearly discernible in the bright moonlight. About 2 to 3 minutes after first sighting the fighter, both rear gunner and air bomber reported they had lost sight of him. The Lancaster was in a turn at that moment. Within a few seconds a burst of cannon fire struck the starboard wing.

Fire broke out in the starboard wing and, thinking this was located in the starboard outer engine, informant stopped it and feathered the propeller. Informant then realized the fire was definitely seated in the petrol tank between the engines. He had considerable difficulty in controlling the aircraft, which was vibrating strongly. No report was received from the gunners after the attack although the intercom was working satisfactorily. Informant heard a groan on the intercom just after feathering the engine but had no chance to ascertain whence it came as at the same time the whole wing from fuselage to starboard outer engine went up in flames, which soon burnt right through the wing. The order to bale out was given immediately, and the visual air bomber jettisoned the front hatch and jumped directly after this. He was followed by flight engineer, H2S [ground radar] operator, navigator and wireless operator. Informant called up the gunners on intercom and call lights, but there was no response, so he baled out himself. The Lancaster was then in an uncontrollable turn to starboard, with three engines running, height unknown.

Sparks came down in a tree approximately 25 miles from the target area; his parachute had only been fastened on the left side. Fortunately, all of Sparks's crew survived. Two men were captured, and the others, including Sparks, evaded capture. Sparks would later report that whilst evading, he heard that bodies were still being dug out of the wreckage at the target area 14 days following the attack.

It truly had been aerial carnage that night over Mailly le Camp. Further examples concerning lost aircraft graphically describe what some aircrews had to endure. Sergeant Viollet was a wireless operator on Flight Sergeant Sanderson's 166 Squadron Lancaster. His fourteenth operation was to Mailly le Camp. Sanderson flew his crew to the target area without incident but then had to keep his bomber in an orbit for three-quarters of an hour awaiting the order to bomb. Whilst in the 'holding ring' Viollet heard Sanderson call that the Lancaster had been hit by flak and that the port inner engine was on fire. The engine was feathered; in the meantime Viollet went to the astrodome and peered out, his face illuminated by the flames spewing out of the engine, back under the wing. Within seconds, however, the fire went out.

Sanderson took his crew into and through the bombing run and 30 minutes after midnight set course for home. Ten minutes later Viollet was listening in to an incoming message and was off the intercom. The first he knew of the nightfighter attack was cannon shell exploding and the lurching of the Lancaster as Sanderson threw the bomber into a corkscrew. Viollet looked down the inside of the Lancaster, where a fire had broken out just aft of the mid-upper turret. He reported the fire to Sanderson and along with the navigator, their helmets removed, he went to see if anything could be done with the fire. Viollet's official report takes up his story:

They [Viollet and the navigator] found that the mid-upper gunner had left his turret and was apparently on the other side of the fire which stretched right across the fuselage immediately behind the turret. There was a great deal of smoke and fumes and the informant formed the impression that the hydraulic system must have been hit and the mixture ignited. He considered that the fire was much too serious to be dealt with by any of the extinguishers. He opened the escape hatch above the rest bed to admit a current of air to disperse the fumes. The flames seemed to die down momentarily and then flared up again as fiercely as ever.

Viollet turned and went forward to report the situation to his pilot, coming across another fire, centred on the port side well below Sanderson's feet, but smoke billowed and flames flicked over his boots and into the cockpit. The navigator had also returned and began the detonation of his equipment. Viollet did not see him again; his official report continues:

Finding himself in between fires, the wireless operator proceeded to make his escape by way of the hatch immediately above the rest bed. Parachutes had been donned on the orders of the captain, after the Lancaster had been hit by flak. Sergeant Viollet climbed on to the rest bed and put his head through the hatch, got his arms over the edge and began to lever himself out facing aft. When he had got his shoulders through, his pack caught underneath the lip of the hatch. While he was struggling to get through it got very hot around him and flames seemed to be coming up round him out of the hatch and he burned his hands considerably. After a few seconds the strings attaching the pack to the harness broke, the pack slipped down and he was able to haul himself up. He seemed to lie on top of the fuselage for a second or two and then fell away into space, he does not know exactly how. The Lancaster seemed to be still under control but in a slight dive when he left. He pulled the ripcord at once and the parachute functioned satisfactorily. As he came down he saw two aircraft hit the ground and three or four more going down in flames. He landed in a small ploughed field surrounded by woods somewhere due north of Troyes. As he made his escape through the woods he saw the wrecks of three heavy bombers believed to be Lancasters. He could not distinguish any identity marks on them, but in one he saw the dead body of the rear gunner.

Viollet was able to evade capture and return to England and make his report. Four of his crew saw out the war behind barbed wire and the other two crew members, the two gunners, lost their lives.

Sergeant King was a wireless operator on Flight Sergeant Leslie Lissette's 207 Squadron Lancaster. Lissette was on his fourth operation, having flown one previous as a second pilot. His crew were on their third operation. Lissette and his crew had met with little difficulty on the way to Mailly le Camp, which they bombed at 00.30 hours. At 00.55 hours, flying straight and level at 6,000 feet, Sergeant King was asked to watch the Monica set by Flight Sergeant Pittwood, the navigator. King immediately became aware of an aircraft on the port beam, at 1,000 yards. As King made his crew aware, the unidentified aircraft closed then made its intention known, opening up on the Lancaster at 600 yards. The bomber's gunners fired back and Lissette threw his aircraft into a steep dive to port, the fighter passing overhead. Lissette continued the churning corkscrew and then levelled up, at which point a second attack was made, from the same position, with the same inconclusive outcome. A third similar attack was made, then a fourth, and each time Lissette twisted his Lancaster out of trouble.

By this stage the Lancaster was down to 3,000 feet, and moments after the fourth fighter attack, Sergeant Wesley, the bomb aimer, told Lissette they were under fire from flak and, '**For God's sake do something about it!**' Lissette plunged the bomber into a dive, but flak smashed into the port outer engine, which burst into flame. The cover also came off the dinghy compartment on the starboard wing. Lissette now had to make a decision. The aircraft was damaged and they had lost considerable height. An official RAF report, based on Sergeant King's recollection, takes up the incident:

The pilot at once gave the order to bale out but the crew protested that they still had three good engines and could reach base on them. The pilot therefore stopped and feathered the damaged engine. He probably also used the graviner as the fire soon went out. Monica, however, was rendered useless and the wireless operator started to connect it to the generator on the starboard outer engine. While he was doing so the fighter attacked again from the same direction as before. Informant does not think the gunners sighted it as they did not fire. There was one burst of cannon fire of about 3 seconds and shells entered the fuselage and started a fire close to the rest bed, and it seemed to spread down into the bomb bay.

The air bomber had removed the hatch cover when the first order to bale out was given. The captain now repeated the order to bale out. The wireless operator detonated the IFF and tried to make his way aft to the rear exit. He was unable to do so because the fire was spreading rapidly and the flames were too fierce. It seemed to be alight underneath both the wireless operator's and the navigator's compartment. The wireless operator therefore came back on to the intercom and asked and received permission from the pilot to leave by the forward escape hatch. While he was on the intercom he heard the rear gunner say, 'I've had it.'

Sergeant King then followed the navigator forward. He noticed as he passed that the navigator's altimeter registered 1,000 feet. He therefore pulled his ripcord while still in the aircraft. The pilot parachute came out normally and part of the main parachute. He gathered it in his arms, rolled himself in a ball and went out head first, receiving a kick from behind from the pilot. The air bomber, flight engineer and navigator had already left.

As he made his descent, informant passed quite close to another parachute. He called out to ask who it was and got the reply that it was the mid-upper gunner. The fighter was still in the vicinity and it attacked another aircraft just before his own Lancaster dived almost vertically into the ground, burning from stem to stern and exploded. Informant landed comfortably at 01.10 hours on soft ground, in a wheat field . . .

Two men lost their lives from the crew: the rear gunner, 25-year-old Ronald Ellis, and the pilot, 26-year-old New Zealander Leslie Lissette,; the two airmen now sharing a joint grave in Chaintreaux Communal Cemetery, France. Lissette had stayed in his aircraft as long as possible, despite having ordered his crew to bale out once already. A decision that duty may have expected, but that cost his life.

The extremes of night combat detailed above really only provide a snapshot of what many Bomber Command airmen endured that night. Of the 346 Lancasters and 16 Mosquitoes on the raid, 42 of the heavy bombers were lost; 1 Group, in the second wave of the attack, lost 28 out of the 173 aircraft sent. This raid yielded one of the highest Bomber Command loss rates of the war. Had it been worth it? Lawrence McGowen was one of those who had returned safely from the raid:

The next morning I anxiously went down to the bombing section to see the photographic results of my bombing. To my chagrin, I had missed out on an aiming point, bombs were plotted just outside the target area. I put this down to air turbulence, but some consolation was that they had landed in a vehicle park.

There had indeed been widespread destruction: 114 barrack buildings, 47 transport sheds and ammunition stores were hit. One hundred and two vehicles were written off, 37 of which were tanks. Two hundred and eighteen German soldiers' lives were ended, with 156 injured.[8] A success in terms of material support to the forthcoming invasion, but at an extraordinary cost. For the airmen who took part it was a night that remained etched in their minds for years to come. Ron Storey recalled:

It was a night that I shall never forget, and I think that a lot of boys were turned into men on that raid. I remember at the debriefing, the commanding officer came over to a group of crewmembers demanding to know what had gone wrong. A flight sergeant who was on his third tour, in the region of 90 operations including trips to Berlin, turned round on the commanding officer and told him to (expletive deleted) off, 'And don't you talk to me about falling off a log, give me Berlin any time.' The commanding officer quickly disappeared. The flight sergeant was a pilot that had refused a commission, as he wanted to be with his own crew at all times and was very keen on operations. I have always wondered if he survived the war. I have returned to Mailly le Camp on two occasions, to attend the remembrance ceremony held by the French. Each time the memories return to me of that eventful night. They are vividly impressed on my mind, and I often wonder if the sacrifices made at that time were really justified.

If the sacrifices had been made in an attempt to ease the fight for the beachhead in Normandy and the subsequent breakout, then history can now show that the bombing campaign in the run-up to D-Day made a significant contribution to the success of the Normandy campaign. Below are just a couple of examples evidencing the effect of the bombing. On 15 May the German Transport Ministry reported:

Large-scale strategic movement of German troops by rail is practically impossible at the present time, and must remain so while attacks are maintained at the present intensity ... In assessing the situation as a whole it must further be borne in mind that, owing to the widespread destruction and damage of important construction and repair shops, the maintenance and overhaul of locomotives has been considerably disorganized; this causes further critical dislocation of traffic.[9]

A report on Radio Paris of 23 May gave further indication of the success of the RAF's attacks:

The French railway system is in complete chaos. The Allies have successfully pulverized into rubble whole marshalling yards. They have destroyed countless locomotives and have made scores of railway stations unusable.

The rest of the destructive work, which could not be done by the Allied pilots, has been accomplished by experienced squads of saboteurs, who have blown up railway tracks and directed attacks against goods trains and other rolling stock.[10]

THE DAY OF DAYS
As May 1944 closed out, RAF Bomber Command had been bombing in preparation for the Normandy beach assault for nigh on 3 months. The Eighth Air Force too had played its part, although to a lesser extent, as it maintained the attacks on German targets. At this point, we will look at the day itself, D-Day. Re-entry into Europe had been the primary Allied objective as the European war ground towards its fourth anniversary. This had been achieved in the first instance through Sicily and Italy. Into 1944, and the assembly of men and material in the UK gathered pace. On D-Day, 6 June 1944, the Allies would throw their might at the beaches of Normandy. It was a joint logistical enterprise, unprecedented in scale: land, sea and air forces combining to put Allied soldiers back onto French soil.

Here we will look at the experiences of RAF and USAAF bomber crews on this historic day, through the words of a selected few. RAF Bomber Command would open the proceedings, with a variety of tasks. One of the most unique was that carried out by the 617 Squadron crews, who would try to confuse the enemy, simulating an invasion fleet on course for the coastline of the Pas de Calais. Leonard Cheshire recalled:

Basically what we were asked to do was to create a high radar reflector by dropping this *window* [foil strips]. That meant having

eight aircraft in perfect formation spaced by 2 miles advancing
from a starting point for 8 miles, then doing a very slow right-
hand turn. That was to take 1 minute, then coming back to the
return leg, then repeating it each time 20 seconds short and
throughout the period of the forward and backward leg.
I think our great worry was whether we would make a mistake
because we had been told that if one mistake was made the
German radar would notice it; they would then realize that we
were doing a spoof; they would then recognize the urgency of
getting all their armour across to the Normandy beachhead, and
we were really not trained for this kind of flying.
At briefing we were unexpectedly given a bird's eye view of the
whole of the D-Day operation. It startled us because it made you
realise we were just one tiny cog in a vast operation, but at the
same time you were one of those cogs that could not afford to
go wrong; if you made a mistake then perhaps everything would
suffer. You had that feeling that so many people [who] were
taking the brunt of the invasion landing on the beachheads were
depending upon us for something we weren't quite sure we could
really do.[11]

Other Bomber Command crews would be also be carrying out special
tasks: 218 Squadron was also involved in the dropping of the 'window'
to simulate an invasion fleet; Halifaxes and Stirlings would drop
dummy parachutists inland of the invasion beaches, and Lancasters
jammed German nightfighter controller instructions. The role of the
main force crews was to bombard and blast the gun emplacements
that defended the sea approaches to the beaches prior to the seaborne
assault from the landing craft – a clear requirement for night precision
bombing. This would be achieved with partial success, with only three
aircraft lost in these attacks. Seven thousand RAF Bomber Command
airmen were operational that night in the attacks on the coastal
batteries. Many, not knowing that this was the start of the actual
invasion, returned with tales of what they had seen: 'I looked out of the

cabin window and I suddenly saw all these ships, dozens of them,' 'We reported the fact that there was a hell of a lot of activity in the Channel,' 'When we broke over the French coast the Channel was full of ships,' 'Marvellous sight coming back as the sun came up. We on the way back and the Americans on the way out.' As the RAF bomber crews flew back to their airfields, in their wake were 10,000 men of the Eighth Air Force, and beneath them the invasion fleet edged onwards. Eugene 'Gene' V. Lipp served with the 453rd Bomb Group:

It was two o'clock in the afternoon in northern England on a mid-week day, 5 June 1944. I was at my desk doing my duties and meeting my responsibilities as the 453rd Bomb Group and Air Base Sergeant Major when my phone rang (certainly nothing uncommon), and I was quickly informed, 'Sergeant, this is General Griswold, 2nd Air Division.'

'Yes, General – Yes sir,' I replied. The general was the Deputy Commanding General, 2nd Air Division, Eighth Air Force. General Griswold asked first for Colonel Ramsey Potts, Base Commanding Officer, and when I replied that he was not anywhere in headquarters, the General said, 'Let me speak to Lt Col. Harris' (second in command).

'Sorry General, neither he nor Lt Col. Stephenson are here at this time and neither is Major Pringle,' I replied. Pringle was the group and base adjutant and my immediate superior. Our desks were only 10 feet apart.

'General,' I said, 'I'm sorry sir that I cannot explain their absences.'

He said, 'Very well, Sergeant, you will have to act in their absence. I will hold you fully responsible, do you understand?' I cannot possibly forget his words after going over them for the last 49 years.

'Yes sir, yes General,' I said in response.

'Sergeant,' he said, 'I am ordering you to close the base as soon as I finish here. I want the base closed in the next 10 minutes, and nobody, absolutely nobody, may leave the base. You may allow officers and enlisted men to come back on the base where they belong, that only. Do you understand Sergeant?'

'Yes, General, I do indeed sir, and I am ready now to implement your orders, sir,' I replied.

'Very well, Sergeant. I am holding you fully responsible.'

'Yes sir, I understand General. Goodbye, sir.'

With that I immediately called our base provost marshal, a captain and the equivalent to a chief of police in civilian life. He quickly understood the orders from General Griswold. Within 10 minutes the base was closed. I made the announcement on the PA system that operated from my office in the headquarters compound. Unlike the Navy, we did not address our base personnel with, 'Now hear this.' My announcement always began with, 'Your attention please,' a slight pause and again, 'Your attention please,' and then the announcement. This day the announcement centered upon the instructions from General Griswold, and I made it very clear that the base was closed upon the orders of the Deputy Commanding General, 2nd Air Division.

Well, you've certainly guessed it by now. It was the first official action, the prelude to the commencement of D-Day the next morning, 6 June. The base closure announcement did indeed cause a really gripping tenseness that dominated, permeated the minds and hearts of the entire base population because 'invasionitis' and D-Day talk had been prominently in the forefront of general daily conversation for many weeks. Our base personnel sensed we were very, very close to D-Day, and the announcement fully convinced them. 'This is it guys, at any moment.' [12]

Paul Roderick was a pilot with the 398th Bomb Group and flew a mission the day before the big event:

On 5 June we flew a combat formation and bombed German gun emplacements on the coast of France. We had very little opposition and landed after only 4 hours and 45 minutes of flight. It was what we termed a 'milk run'.

We knew the invasion was coming soon, because suddenly we were flying these short missions to the coast of France instead of deeper into France and Germany itself.

After landing on 5 June, which was our ninth mission, we ate dinner and then checked the bulletin board for the next day's combat crews. Our crew was listed, so immediately the anxiety began, with each man on our crew handling it in a different way. There was usually a poker game going on in our hut. That seemed to occupy minds and prevent thoughts of what may come tomorrow. I liked to visit my B-17, 'Madame X', and the Crew Chief, Master Sgt Leroy Smith. We would sit in the cockpit and talk about her problems and what he and the other two ground crew were doing to keep her in good condition.

We went to bed about 10 pm that night. We needed as much rest as possible because we worked very hard flying formation nearly every day, but going to bed early, knowing what was facing us the next day, was useless. We slept very poorly at night. Our good rest was in the afternoon before dinner. At 11 pm the corporal who usually shook me awake before a mission wakened me. He always stayed and talked to me until he was certain that I was awake. I then woke Scribner, Harvey, and the bombardier, Harry Houchins.[13]

Some were in the know, but most airmen were oblivious to the fact that this was the 'Day' until briefing, or even until they were sitting in their aircraft. But there was considerable optimism. The 381st medical diary recorded:

6 June – Today is D-DAY!!!!! This is the day we have all been waiting for. We were gotten out of the sack at 00.30 hrs this

Tuesday, and alerted for enemy action. Everyone on the base was under arms, tense and excited. The station defence was out in force and most of us were [more] afraid of trigger-happy defence boys than we were of enemy action.

Speculation was of course rife. The airmen knew that the invasion was going to take place any day; they had seen the build-up of troops and equipment. But when exactly? Further clues were provided, as Paul Roderick recalled about the early hours of 6 June:

We dressed and went to the Mess Hall for breakfast. We had an hour to eat and took full advantage of it. Before going on a mission, we had fresh eggs, some kind of meat, and all the toast and orange marmalade that we could hold. We had no idea of when we'd sit down to eat again . . . if ever. We ate and talked for the whole hour. That night, because of the hour, we speculated that today would be the BIG day. On the way to the Mess Hall, we saw two P-51 fighters cross our field at a low enough altitude. We could make out the black and white stripes that were painted on the wings to indicate they were Allied planes and would be flying at very low altitudes. Those stripes were painted on only the day before.

After a welcome breakfast, Paul Roderick attended briefing at 01.30 hours:

It was there that we learned that this was 'IT' for sure. Our target was Courseulles, France, and we were bombing Juno Beach in support of Canadian troops who were scheduled to make their landing at 06.20. We dressed in our battle gear, and arrived at the plane at 03.30. Started engines at 04.05, taxied out to the runway at 04.15, and the first ship took off at 04.30. It was still very dark, and as each radio operator took off in the tail gunner's position, he constantly flashed a code signal to the plane behind him, to enable that pilot to follow the Group to the assigned altitude to assemble into formation. I believe that altitude was about 13,000 to 14,000 feet. I flew on Capt. Dwight Ross's left wing as the Deputy Leader. If something happened to prevent Ross from leading the formation at any time, I was to take the lead.

Eighth Air Force stations put up a staggering 1,805 bombers that morning. It was a historic moment, but the crews could not let the occasion get to them. Yet once in the air, the crews could do little but see that they were part of an immense operation, as Eugene Lipp recalled:

At 06.28 the next morning, the combined air, water and land strike commenced. Everything that could fly or float was either in the air or on the water in the greatest military undertaking, the greatest military spectacle of all time. True, the base was closed, but it was anything but down. Come dusk, then darkness, the base was certainly alive, really humming, just plain peaking with activity. Mission briefings began well before midnight for all four bomb squadrons comprising our 453rd Bomb Group.

Take-off for the B-24 bombers, and then the rendezvous of the four squadrons in the Group, began about 03.30. The same was true for the other thirteen bomb groups of the 2nd Air Division. After much time spent, the fourteen groups successfully joined together as the Division. After considerably more time had gone by, the 2nd Air Division met up in a giant rendezvous with the B-17s of the 1st and 3rd Divisions. What a strike force – the full Eighth Air Force now in position to strike just beyond the coast of France. And strike they did.

Once in the air, the Eighth's airmen could see for themselves the weather conditions. They were not ideal. The Allied commanders were fully aware that this would be the case prior to launching the invasion, but time had been running out, and it was deemed acceptable.

Paul Roderick, high above the English Channel, summed up the conditions:

The weather was not too good, with heavy cloud cover below us. However, my crew was able to see part of the naval armada in the Channel just as we left the English coast where the sky was clear for a short time. Neither Roger Harvey nor I were ever able to see directly below the plane from our positions, so we always missed 'the good stuff'. Shortly after entering above the Channel, the weather closed in below us. Our lead ship in the 36-ship formation was a 'Mickey Ship'. It was equipped with the best radar available at the time, and with a specially trained crew. During briefing, we were warned not to drop any bombs in the Channel, as was our custom if we got into trouble. There were too many boats in the water. Another caution was not to count on being picked up by boats other than the English Air/Sea Rescue in the event we were forced down in the Channel. All invasion ships were on a strict timetable and could take no time to stop for us.

We dropped our bombs over the target 10 minutes or so ahead of the first wave of Canadians. We dropped our bombs with the Mickey Ship as our guide. As we approached the drop spot, Harry Houchins watched their bomb bay. When the first bomb dropped from the leader, he released our bombs. We received no visual indication regarding where they fell, but could only hope they were on the mark. We had no flak or fighter opposition. I could only think how lucky I was to be in the air and not down there in the water, about to try to storm a hostile beach. For us, it was a 'milk run'. After the bombs were released and Harry Houchins made his usual announcement of, 'Let's haul ass outa here,' we made a wide right turn, staying in line behind the formation ahead. There were so many planes in the air that we had to maintain a rigid traffic pattern to avoid interfering with planes behind.

Wesley R. Williams served with the 492nd Bomb Group, and recorded his memories of the day, commenting on the problems with the cloud cover:

We invade Europe. We also take off and assemble in the dark to be over the landing beaches by dawn. En route I note what seems to be every ship built since the dawn of time. I would not have been surprised to see a Viking galley pulling for the beach. We also know that if we bale out, they would not stop to pick us up. Couldn't bomb. Low clouds. Hauled our bombs inland a ways and dropped through the murk. Someone got a nasty surprise. Hairy part was milling around like sheep in the dark with a zillion other aircraft. Probably were mid-airs. Didn't see any flashes.[14]

Duane Heath also flew with the 492nd Bomb Group. He mentions a common experience for the Eighth crews: the lack of opposition:

Target was a beachhead or town. Coastal guns. Bombed from 15,000 feet, bomb load was 250 anti-personnel bombs. This was the big day for all of us. Yep, D-Day. I was one of the first ones over in the first wave of bombers that opened the second front. Never seen so many damn planes before. Was cloudy but I could see one hell of a lot of boats down in the Channel. Damn glad I'm up in the air and not down there. No flak or fighters today. Too damn many of our planes around.

The cloud cover did have an adverse impact on the effectiveness of the bombing that morning. Of the 1,805 aircraft sent, 1,114 are recorded as 'effective'. But much of this bombing was actually inland of the targets. Unsurprisingly, without being able to see the target, crews had feared bombing their own troops and held on that split second longer.

One statistic was certainly well-received with respect to the first mission that day: only three bombers were lost. But D-Day was far from over for the crews of the Eighth Air Force. Later in the day a further 782 aircraft took part in bombing operations. For some this would be their first mission of the day. For others it was a return to the skies above the beach assault. Major Marvin Bowman was the 100th Bomb Group's intelligence officer:

The invasion began this morning. Briefing at 23.00 hours last night, 12.15 hours, and 14.15 hours today . . . Crews' morale bounced up 100 per cent. First take-off at 02.30 hours. First two waves bombed coast using PFF, third wave had Falaise for a target but returned with bombs when no PFF could be found. Last wave of the day left at 17.00 hours, returned at 23.15 hours. Had a good view of the invasion, the undercast having broken away. Told of hundreds of ships unmolested off the coast, indicating that shore batteries have been silenced. Hundreds of gliders going in; no air opposition at all. German radio is something to hear, are reporting the invasion a complete flop – a few parachutists who were quickly eliminated. Whom do they think they are kidding? . . . Standing down tonight – we have temporarily ran out of bombs.[15]

Duane Heath's diary entry recorded his second flight to enemy skies that day:

Target was a rail and road center. Bomb load was twelve 500- pound . . . Bombed from 15,700 feet. This was the second mission of the day for us and the third for the group. More damn planes and boats. Really some sight to see too. We bombed PFF (Pathfinder) and did a good job on that target. No fighters or flak this time either. Met one continuous stream of C-47 and gliders on the way back. Jerry is going to catch plenty of hell tonight. Wished I could fly two a day like this till I got all mine in. Only 20 more to go. Long time off yet.

Paul Roderick returned to Nuthampstead from his first mission of the day, 5 hours after take-off:

Mission number 10 was completed. The gunners removed the thirteen 50-caliber machine guns and cleaned them. A truck arrived to take us to the armor shop to store the guns and then on to the briefing room where intelligence officers would interrogate us as to what we observed on the mission. This was the normal procedure that was followed after each trip.

But this was not to be a normal day. As the truck arrived, a jeep driven by Major Pete Rooney, my 602 Squadron CO, pulled up with Colonel Frank Hunter, the 398th CO. As I walked to the jeep, Pete told me to send the truck along without me, and to also have Roger Harvey come with me in the jeep. Then after a word by Colonel Hunter he said to also send Harvey with the crew in the truck. I did, and climbed into the back of the jeep, not knowing what was up. Pete handed me a sandwich and a cup of coffee. I recall the coffee was loaded with sugar and milk, but it still tasted good.

Pete drove us into a hangar where a strange (to me) aircrew was waiting. Then they told me they wanted me to take that crew and bomb a bridge that was about 20 miles inland in France, near Carentan. We were to fly at a very low level to be sure to knock out the bridge. The crew had already been briefed. The navigator knew the route in and the bombardier had his target well in mind. This crew had just arrived at our station and this was their first mission. Their co-pilot was remaining on the ground and the pilot was to ride as my co-pilot. I recall how excited they all were. Then Col. Hunter told me the mission was a 'secret'. We were not to discuss the flight with anyone, including my crew. He also told me he was sorry, but there was to be *no credit* for this mission – a *freebie* !!?? In those days one did not question authority. One listened and did what he was told. A plane (not the Madame X) was loaded with heavy demolition bombs and fuelled up for us. I felt little fear, for after all, the first trip was a breeze and reports indicated the German Air Force was operating at low level that day. They had their hands full trying to repel the ground forces.

Paul's take-off and flight across the sea went without incident:

Just before we reached the French coast we began to descend through the overcast. We broke into the clear just as we came over land. I don't know the altitude because a rapid series of events began that left no time for sightseeing in or out of the cockpit. A sudden burst of flak disabled the number 2 engine. The ball-turret gunner reported a massive gushing of oil from the engine. The co-pilot, at my order, shut down the engine and feathered the prop . . . Before we could take a breath of relief another burst of flak took several feet off our right wing-tip. I think perhaps 6 or 8 feet. I had knocked off the autopilot and was flying manually and it felt like half the wing was gone. The same burst set fire to the number 4 engine. The co-pilot pulled both built-in fire extinguishers in that engine to no avail . . . I pushed the throttles for the remaining number 1 and number 3 engines to their stops to attempt to maintain altitude. Then we found one of those engines was failing due to stress and only able to develop about half the power. We had turned around and were out over water. We could not salvo the bombs into the water, nor could we bale out. The Channel was very cold and if we were not picked up at once we would die of exposure. We also could not let the aircraft go down at random with all of the boats in the water. The fire worried us, but appeared not to increase in intensity. As long as it did not burn back into the 400-gallon fuel tank that fed from behind the engine, I thought (prayed) that we would be all right.

The co-pilot called the Air Sea Rescue, providing heading, speed, rate of descent and location. 'A very calm Englishman,' told them that all his rescue boats were already in use, locating fighter pilots and who had first call owing to a small life raft and being more difficult to find:

The crew knew their jobs and we prepared to ditch the plane. The engineer, using the fire ax, broke out both the co-pilot's and my side windows. Roger and I had discussed that many times. We had heard of all the crew getting out of ditched planes except the two pilots, who were trapped when those windows jammed shut. That was the pilot's only exit during ditching. Then the crew all sat on the floor on the radio room, which is in the center of the plane; a large ceiling escape hatch in that roof was unlatched, and blown off. The two five-man life-rafts were located in compartments topside of the radio room. The crew sat with their backs to the forward bulkhead, for their protection upon impact. The bombardier and one of the gunners replaced the cotter pins in the bomb fuses, making them safe upon impact. I had read that in a manual, but always wondered about it being true.

The Channel was very rough and we had lost track of the wind direction, so we had to do the best we could. There were no boats around when we landed. We hit with a terrible jolt, landing on top of one swell and then submarining through the next swell. I thought we were going straight to the bottom. We wound up hitting the third swell and stopped. Still alive! We had taken off our heavy flight clothing and just had on our flight coveralls, our chute harness with our Mae Wests (life jackets) over those. I skinned out of that little window as if it were 6 foot square. The top turret gunner had turned his guns so they were pointed forward. The co-pilot and I could grab them to help pull us from the plane.

I jumped down on the wing of the plane and noticed the life

raft on my side was already deployed and inflated. It was one of the duties of the engineer to pull two handles in the radio room when the ditching was complete. That jettisoned both raft compartment doors and automatically began inflation of the rafts. They were attached to the plane with a cord that would withstand a 10-pound pull. I hit a wet spot on the wing and slid down towards the raft. As I slid, I inflated my Mae West, also with carbon dioxide. A couple of gunners grabbed me and pulled me into the raft. It was crowded and very wet, but at the moment was worth a million dollars!! One of the gunners yanked the cord loose and it seemed that was all that kept the plane afloat. It sank at once! We think it floated less than a minute. The crew said its back was broken at the rear of the radio room. I was too busy trying to get the salt water out of my eyes to see it.

The two rafts were tied together and SOS signals were sent out. Paul was the first to become seasick, followed soon after by other members of the crew:

In a short time a boat arrived and a seaman with a bullhorn invited us aboard. I told one of the crew, who could still talk . . . to find out where they were going. When we were told 'France', I told him to decline the invitation. I was not that sick!! A short while later an LST [landing ship tank] pulled up alongside us. It seemed like a very large ship. They were going to England, so we were happy to be taken aboard. An officer told us to climb up the rope nets that were slung over the side of the boat. A couple of the crew were able to make it, but most of us were so weak, we had no chance. A sailor climbed down and hooked a cable on our parachute harness after removing our Mae Wests. They hoisted us aboard with a small crane. Once on deck, my stomach settled down very quickly.

We found an odd crew on the boat. The crew was all US Coastguard with a Navy Lt as their commander. They gave us blankets for protection from the wind, which felt good. They were loaded with US paratroopers who had been wounded during the drop the night before. Some were in very bad shape. I believe a few died before we got back to land. They also had a few high-ranking German officer prisoners on board. They were all standing in a sunken section of the deck where they were visible only from the waist up. Some very hard-looking paratroopers were guarding them. One German was very talkative and was constantly being told to 'shut up'. He spoke English most of the time, but also lapsed into German too. He said something to our crew in German and laughed. One of the guards, who understood, told him to be quiet, and told us he was making fun of our poor condition. The German said something else towards us and the guard 'smashed' his hand that was on the deck with the butt of his rifle. The German screamed in pain and then began to cry. We couldn't laugh at him.

They soon arrived back on friendly shores. Following a few shots of whisky whilst clothes were dried, and some questions about the ditching, Paul and his colleagues were flown back to Nuthampstead:

As soon as we landed, Colonel Hunter and Pete Rooney met us. They had received a teletype informing them of our whereabouts, but did not know if we had completed our mission. They were disappointed that we had failed, but did not disapprove of how we handled the situation in any degree. They both congratulated me for my pilot skills, and stated they were sorry to put us in danger. Again, we were instructed to say absolutely nothing about the mission. I never did say a word to anyone in the 398th until after the war over. By the time the 398th reunions began, Col. Hunter and Pete Rooney were both dead. There is nobody to tell me the reason for the mission, and why it was a secret.

As for the anti-aircraft fire that was so deadly that day, I'll always be convinced it was a mistake and just 'friendly fire'. There was some dead-eye Navy gunners out there that day. We were lucky to live through the day. I believe there was a special hand on my shoulder helping me out.

As night drew in on 6 June, the Allied commanders could satisfy themselves with the knowledge that the hard-fought battle for the beaches had been won. But this, of course, was only the beginning. What is so special about the missions flown by the Eighth Air Force on D-Day? Not so much the tangible results of the raids, but the fact that there were so many sorties with so few losses. To those in the ships below and the men assaulting the beaches the sight that day and in the following days of armadas of Allied aircraft was a considerable boost to morale. This is what the men of the RAF and the Eighth Air Force had won: the opportunity for the vast armada to assemble in the United Kingdom and then cross by sea to Normandy, without serious hindrance from the Luftwaffe. The Allies had clearly gained air superiority over the battle area. The attrition of missions already featured in this book – Schweinfurt-Regensburg, Second Schweinfurt, Big Week, Big B – had not been in vain. The Luftwaffe had been forced to retreat to the defence of the homeland, away from Normandy, and had suffered crippling loses. The Eighth Air Force had won that 'hidden' daylight victory against the Luftwaffe.

# 10
## _TIRPITZ_: SINKING THE BEAST

_In November 1944, RAF Bomber Command demonstrated its
precision bombing capabilities with a historic and extraordinary attack
on the German battleship_ Tirpitz. _This special operation captivated
the public imagination at the time and its success released some of the
pressure on the Royal Navy, allowing the 'Senior Service' to redeploy
much needed shipping and resources to fight the war in the East._

The last chapter of this book provides a clear demonstration of the
advances in RAF bombing capability since the days of the Battle of the
Barges back in 1940. RAF bombing had been through the optimism
of daylight precision bombing, then night-time precision bombing,
then night-time area bombing, back to relatively successful precision
bombing in darkness in support of _Overlord_, and now back to daylight
precision attacks. Scientific investment in bombsights, navigational
aids, bomb ballistics and aircraft technology, along with the hard
lessons learned in 5 years of air battle passed on to crews and raid
planners, resulted in precision targeting being an option. Nothing
demonstrates this more than the attack on the German battleship
_Tirpitz_ in November 1944.

The _Tirpitz_ had been the proverbial thorn in the side of the Royal
Navy since the early days of the war, threatening forays into the
North Sea and Atlantic and tying down British naval forces that
were certainly needed in the other theatres of war. The British Prime
Minister, for one, was keen to nullify the threat of the 'beast', as he
nicknamed _Tirpitz_. Various attempts had been made on the beast
throughout the war to eliminate its potential, using conventional
bombing, midget submarines and even 'chariot' torpedoes. There had
been partial success: the _Tirpitz_ had received some damage, but some
was not enough. While still in existence, the 'beast' was still a threat.

In the autumn of 1944 the _Tirpitz_ was holed up in the Norwegian fjords, and it was now deemed time to call in the specialist bombing techniques of the Royal Air Force's 9 and 617 Squadrons. Their task was simply to sink the battleship; and for this they had for their use 'Tallboys', 12,000-pound penetrating bombs designed by aeronautical engineer Barnes Wallis. Following his success with the dams raid, Barnes Wallis had been asked to develop one of his earlier ideas – a 10-ton bomb. He set to work on his vision, and in the first instance produced a 12,000-pound 'earthquake' bomb, which came to be known as a Tallboy (and he would go on to see production of the 22,000-pound 'Grand Slam' bomb). Described as 'ballistically perfect', the Tallboy would break the sound barrier on descent, slice into its target at high speed, penetrate deep and explode. It was first used operationally on the Saumur rail tunnel on the night of 8/9 June 1944, in an attempt to black the passage of Panzer reinforcements to the Normandy battlefield. The raid was a success and one Tallboy penetrated 18 metres through the hill to explode in the tunnel. Tallboy's destructive power was unprecedented, and perhaps it provided the answer to the *Tirpitz* problem. It just needed to be flown to the target, aimed and dropped. No easy task, requiring the expertise of Bomber Command's 9 and 617 Squadrons.

FRUSTRATION

The first attempt on the *Tirpitz* by Lancasters of 9 and 617 Squadrons was made in the middle of September 1944. The planes had flown to Russian bases prior to the attack, in order to bring them within range. Thirty-eight Lancasters departed British soil on 11 September to fly to Russia. In one was air gunner Ralph Briars of 617 Squadron:

The big one against the German pocket battleship *Tirpitz*, which had so far led a charmed life despite a variety of attacks by everybody except the Army, and survived the lot. As the vessel was out of range from Britain the plan was to fly to Yagodnik, an island airfield upstream from Archangel; refuel, carry out the raid, refuel again in Russia and return to Lincolnshire. As additional petrol had to be carried, the top turret was removed, together with much of the ammunition from the rear turret, some of the radar and the exhaust cowls from each engine, which seemed rather extreme and may have been done under the old dictum that every little helps. A 250-gallon fuel tank was installed in the fuselage, and the length of the tank necessitated the departure of the top turret. We carried twelve 450-pound bombs, which I have a feeling were a sort of sea mine [Johnny Walker mines], and others had the 12,000-pound Tallboy.

[Ralph's diary entry:] Took off at 19.00 hours, headed for Norway at 2,000 feet, climbed to 6,000 feet at coast to clear mountains, bit cloudy, saw glimpses of peaks at times. Sweden well-lighted, even saw neon signs occasionally, some flak on one area, one kite damaged. As it became lighter we dropped to avoid cloud at 500 – 1,000 feet, crossed White Sea very low, looked somewhat inhospitable and cold. Eventually found Archangel in mouth of river, and after some searching came across the airfield on an island down stream. Heavy landing on grass with bombs aboard. Quarters in an old river steamer, clean but lousy washing and sanitary conditions. Meals good generally, plenty of eggs, butter and sugar. Tea without milk – in glasses – slightly sour bread and Spam will be remembered! Swapped cigarettes for cap badges, coins, paper money and buttons. Entertained every night with concerts, films and dances. Band could even play 'Lambeth Walk'. Sand and grass field, weather slightly colder than at home.

Re-reading the diary reminds me of the proficiency of our navigator, James Barron, who so skilfully guided our way to Russia and back, basically with only his expertise, map and six pairs of anxious eyes to assist. No navigational aids in that part of the world. Several aircraft force-landed in the area when fuel ran out in their vain search for the field . . . the Russians brought them along in various ancient light planes at intervals.

There is a nice photo of a downed Lancaster, its 12,000-pound Tallboy hurled free on the landing impact and laying forlornly in the mud a considerable distance in front of the aircraft. The aircrews involved eventually came home in other aircraft.

The Russian films were terrible, long affairs of continual war scenes, and I seem to recall that the Royal Navy contingent at Archangel sent along some cartoons which cheered us up and left our hosts baffled. Living around the airfield in various primitive huts were some of the Russian staff, including, no doubt, the ladies who fell about on being asked for hot water to shave with – such Western decadence. The men spent much time playing cards on the river bank. Their wives only appeared when called to have large tree trunks, that had floated down from the Urals, hoisted on to their sturdy shoulders by their caring partners; it was a peaceful scene, only disturbed by the sound of chopping and sawing whilst the interrupted card game continued. Lenin would surely have approved. I jest a little. Within the limitations of the times, the Russians we met were generally kind, generous hosts. They beat us handsomely at football too. The wait for suitable weather accounted mainly for the few days that passed before attacking the *Tirpitz*, and the time was probably useful to enable some aircraft servicing to be done . . .

[Ralph's diary entry:] Took off 09.30 hours on 15 September, loose gaggle, 1,000 feet, route over Finland, Sweden and Norway, a god-forsaken countryside of hills, rivers, timber and marshes. We led JW [Johnny Walker's] force and came in from different direction. Saw smoke generators start up a few minutes before bombing, nuisance. Saw JWs swinging down on 'chutes, weird. Flak scattered and inaccurate, surprising as we bombed at 11,000 feet, no fighters. One kite only damaged.

Took off 19.45 on the 16th to return home. Weather dull, poor visibility, 1,500 feet over Finland, climbed to 7,000 feet over sea and Sweden. Dark night, saw some 'dromes lighted, occasional light flak. Bad weather just after leaving Sweden, had to drop to 4,000 feet to clear cloud and heavy and rain. Off track, ran over north Denmark, searchlights evaded by using cloud cover, flak ships a darn nuisance off coast. Carried three of Ross's crew, bet they were cold in fuselage. Glad to see English searchlights and 'dromes again – and real egg, bacon and chips![1]

Only 27 Lancasters were able to take part in the raid on 15 September, along with a photographic Lancaster. The element of surprise did work to some effect, and the defensive smokescreens were late in starting; a few Tallboys did cause some damage, although not fatal.

As far as the RAF was concerned, the attack had had little effect and another raid was arranged for late in October, involving 18 Lancasters from each of 9 and 617 Squadrons and a Lancaster from 463 Squadron detailed to film the raid. Since the previous raid, the *Tirpitz* had moved south to Tromsø Fjord, bring it within range, just, of the UK. Ralph Briars scribed the following entry into his diary:

29 October 1944: Took off from Lossiemouth at 2 am and landed back at 2.55 pm – did I feel done. Crossed Norwegian coast at dawn and flew north over Sweden, looked very bleak and cold. Had to orbit at rendezvous, both squadrons went on to target, became very hazy even at 15,000 feet with 7 – 8/10ths cloud below. Ship hard to find, Al finally bombed on fourth run. Bags of flak, but very inaccurate, one kite hit badly, landed in Sweden. Terrible stooge home, saw no land for 4 hours – had 16 hours sleep at Lossie' tho'!

Rear gunner Fred Whitfield flew on a 9 Squadron Lancaster:

For this trip the mid-upper turret has been removed, making it possible to carry more fuel for the raid; approximately

2,400 gallons for the 2,250 miles covered . . . In order to give the Lancaster more power it was necessary to replace the engines with larger Merlins. I was well kitted-out for this long journey to Tromsø in Norway. I would have been a good advert for Michelin Tyres with all the gear I was wearing.

We flew very low, only a few feet above the sea, until we reached Norway, and had avoided the German radar, then the skipper was able to make height.

When we were 5 miles away from the target, the flak came up thick and heavy. As we were on our bombing run I felt a stabbing pain in my foot and I called the skipper to tell him that I'd been hit. He told me to wait until we had got out and he would send Larry down to get me out. I put the turret dead astern, opened the door and pulled myself into the rear of the aircraft. I proceeded to take off my flying shoe and was met by a puff of smoke. My electric slippers had shorted out with the sweat from my foot. I was burned, not shot. I climbed back into the turret and reported what had happened; I won't put into print the skipper's reply.

The fuel tanks were hit by flak and we lost a lot of fuel before the self-sealing tanks sealed up the holes. Larry, our flight engineer, and Jim, our navigator, got together to calculate how far it would be possible to travel and it was decided to try and make Sumburgh on the Shetland Isles.

When we were over the North Sea our wireless operator, Jack Facheux, was instructed to send out an SOS. We were all surprised at how quickly a Catalina flying boat from Coastal Command was flying alongside. He gave us an escort to Sumburgh, and on arrival Flying Control gave us permission to fly straight in. It was just as well, because immediately we touched down the engines cut out: we were out of fuel. We had no brakes and when we finally managed to stop we were only a few feet from a Nissen hut.[2]

But what of the results of the bombing? Bobby Knights was the pilot of a 617 Squadron Lancaster and flew on the 29 October raid. As the RAF's bombers neared the target it appeared that conditions were just right. But there was going to be further frustration:

> In October, when we arrived at Tromsø, the whole thing was perfectly clear and it was lying just off one of the islands. We started our bomb run and just as we did cloud began to appear over the target and by the time our bombsight was ready to go the bomb aimer told me the target by then had gone under cloud. I remember saying to him, 'Is it a good run?' He said, 'Absolutely perfect.' So I said, 'Well, let the bomb go.' We thought we had sunk the *Tirpitz* in fact. I didn't see it because I was flying straight, to get a photo, but he saw it and he said he thought he sunk it, because it went right down the side of the ship and rocked it over onto its side. But then it righted itself and came up. We were rather disappointed.[3]

On return, it was not just Bobby's crew that were disappointed. The *Tirpitz* was still afloat, the raid had failed, and the beast remained.

WITH TIME RUNNING OUT

It was imperative to mount a follow-up raid, with haste; the days were shortening. The daylight window of opportunity, particularly as far north as Norway, was rapidly diminishing. On 12 November another long flight north was scheduled for the aircrews of 9 and 617 Squadrons, once more carrying their Tallboys, with a 463 Squadron Lancaster armed with a camera. Ralph Briars would not be taking part in the next *Tirpitz* raid: 'Broke my finger whilst trying to fix an escape hatch during night practice bombing – clot! Went u/s until after Christmas.' Willie Tait, the Commanding Officer of 617 Squadron, led the raid:

We took off from the north of Scotland about 02.30 on the morning of 12 November 1944. When we were approaching Tromsø the sun was resting on the horizon so the snow-covered mountains were turned pink in its light. The sky was cloudless, the air calm and the aircraft rode easily without a bump to disturb the bomb aimer's sights. We sighted the *Tirpitz* from a range of at least 20 miles, lying squat and black amongst her torpedo nets, like a spider in a web; silhouetted against the glittering blue and green waters of the fjord and surrounded by the beautiful hills. Down below everything was quite still. The whole scene – water, mountains, sky – blazed in the cold brilliance of the arctic dawn.[4]

Fred Watts was a pilot with 617 Squadron:

We flew over at about 1,000 feet across the sea until we got up into the Scandinavian area and then we climbed all the time heading round for the *Tirpitz*. We climbed up to bombing height and we spotted it 20 to 30 miles away. It was so gin clear and I remember saying to my bomb aimer, 'By God Mac, she's had it today.'[5]

Bruce Buckham was flying the 463 Squadron film Lancaster:

It was a magnificent sight to see the large snow-covered island of Tromsø as we climbed to height and *Tirpitz* anchored facing towards us. We still had about 15 minutes to fly and vast explosions were occurring in the middle and around our loose gaggle of aircraft. She was firing her 14-inch main guns at us with short delay fuses. Closer in to our target there was some sporadic ack-ack from guns lining the fjord and by now the *Tirpitz* ack-ack and gunfire from two flak ships on the fjord 'hotted' things up.[6]

Willie Tait led his crews on into the flak:

Suddenly, when we were still about 5 miles away, the ship fired
her main armament and was almost hidden in rolling smoke.
These shells burst about 20 seconds later, ahead of us and below,
and the air was filled with smoke puffs as all the guns of the
ship, and all those along the shore, combined the fusillade.
But no aircraft deviated from the formation. The first bomb
down hit the ship and all her guns stopped firing. I turned and
dived hard to port to see what was happening. The ship was
almost hidden in smoke, a jet of white steam was gushing out
and amidships she blazed fiercely. She stayed afloat for about
15 minutes, listing heavily, but the crew remained at their
stations trying to correct the list and the order to abandon ship
came too late.

Fred Watts completed his bombing run:

. . . and I then hung around for a little while to see if I could spot
anything. I couldn't and thought, 'Well you're pushing your luck
a bit now.' So we went home.

Meanwhile Bruce Buckham had taken up a position from which to
film the bombing:

We went in at 6,000 feet as Willie Tait and the others lined
up to do their individual bombing runs, but this was too
unhealthy, so we descended to about 2,000 feet and isolated the
guns lining the fjord. One of the flak ships became somewhat
pestiferous so we shot her up a bit and she disappeared up to
the end of the fjord; the other kept a respectable distance.
    The bombers were right overhead now, doing a perfect
bombing run, bomb doors gaped open, the glistening Tallboy
suspended. Now they were released. To us they appeared to

travel in ever so graceful a curve like a high diver, heading with deadly accuracy towards one point, right amidships of *Tirpitz*. Suddenly there was a tremendous explosion on board. The *Tirpitz* appeared to try to heave herself out of the water. Carried away by this turn of events, and the suddenness of it all, we had descended to 200 feet, cameras had been whirring at their task of collecting photographic evidence of the action.

Willie Tait had been the first to release his Tallboy, and was credited with the first strike on the ship. Not all those in his wake were as successful, but further hits or near misses were made. As Tait recalled:

> She capsized quickly, and all those below, about 800, were trapped. They had not surrendered. They knew it was coming to them after they had seen the damage one of our bombs had done at Alten. But the ship fought to the last. Finally we should remember the Norwegian Resistance, who always watched the *Tirpitz* as she crept from one Norwegian cranny to another under cover of the frequent fogs on that coast. If they had not constantly watched and wirelessed her movements to London it would have been very difficult to keep track of her.

The camera in Bruce Buckham's Lancaster continued to record the final death throes of the beast:

> We flew over it, around it, all about it and still it sat there with dignity under a huge mushroom of smoke which plumed up a few thousand feet in the air. There were fires and more explosions on board; a huge gaping hole existed on the port side where a section had been blown out.
> We had now been flying close around *Tirpitz* for 30 minutes or so and decided to call it a day, so we headed out towards the mouth of the fjord. Just then the rear gunner, Eric Gierch,

called out, 'I think she is turning over.' I turned back to port to have a look, and sure enough she was, so back we went again. This time we flew in at 50 feet and watched with baited breath as *Tirpitz* heeled over to port, ever so slowly, and gracefully.

We could see German sailors swimming, diving, jumping, and by the time she was over to 85 degrees and subsiding slowly into the water of Tromsø Fjord, there must have been the best part of 60 men on her side as we skimmed over for the last pass. That was the final glimpse we had as we flew out of the fjord and over the North Sea.

After a 14-hour flight, we landed back at our base Waddington, where the interrogation was conducted by Air Marshall, now the late, Sir Ralph Cochrane.

When asked how it went, my one remark was, 'Well we won't have to go back after this one; *Tirpitz* is finished.'

For the returning crews, there was speculation on the flight home. Had the attack been successful; indeed would they have to try again? When Fred Watts learnt of the outcome of the raid, he celebrated in a time-honoured fashion:

It wasn't until we got back that a photographic reconnaissance came back with the news that it had capsized. And we all got very drunk.

Bruce Buckham and his rear gunner Eric Gierch, flying in the 463 (RAAF) Squadron film Lancaster were interviewed after the raid. The nature of the interview, jovial and spoken without pauses, does suggest that it was somewhat staged. The propaganda opportunity of such a story had not been overlooked. The beast was no more and Bruce and Eric would tell the world of its dying moments. The interviewer opens by asking Bruce Buckham about the previous two raids on the *Tirpitz*:

*Bruce Buckham:* We were filming on both those occasions and she was a lucky ship in so far as weather conditions hampered our operations. However the boot was on the other foot this time. For instance, on the first attack there was too much cloud for us to see what was going on. Combined with the weather, the Germans had a very effective smokescreen in operation. Weather conditions were slightly worse on the second attack so again we couldn't see the results.

*Interviewer:* So we come to this final and successful sortie.

*Bruce Buckham:* We thought that something big was coming up. We heard that it was the *Tirpitz* again and I remember thinking of the *Bismarck* and how hard she was to sink. But the war has progressed in our favour and now we have five and a half ton bombs and these we thought out to be able to shift the *Tirpitz*.

*Eric Gierch:* They certainly did shift it from what we can see. We arrived at Tromsø Fjord shortly before 10.30 Sunday morning. The weather was bang on. We could see everything. I got a sneaking suspicion Jerry didn't know what he was in for. We arrived with the first mob because on a job like this we like to be in at the beginning and film everything possible.

*Interviewer:* Did you see the first bomb go down?

*Bruce Buckham:* Yes I saw it go down and it overshot very slightly. A second one was even closer and the next bomb hit it roughly amidships. The guns had been firing and there was the usual smoke from them but there was something different about this hit. A few seconds later there was an explosion, then flames came up, followed by a column of black smoke. But we didn't feel a thing where we were.

*Interviewer:* Was it then that the *Tirpitz* keeled over and sunk?

*Bruce Buckham:* No. Further hits were scored but she still remained afloat. I thought then after all these hits that the myth of the unsinkable *Tirpitz* was true and we were thinking about going home. We'd actually turned off when Eric came up on the intercom, 'Hey Skip. I think she's keeling over, have a look.'

*Interviewer:* Was she?

*Bruce Buckham:* Well, I tried to get around and see this but it was all too quick, as she was on her side. All I could see was the red lead hull gleaming in the morning sunshine.

*Interviewer:* Well Buck, I hope you got some good movies of the action. Some of the still pictures in the London papers are pretty wonderful.

*Bruce Buckham:* I think so too. During the attack the cameramen were working hard and I think they shot some pretty good films.

*Interviewer:* I hope we'll have an opportunity of seeing them because there must have been some very fine bombing. From the tail turret Eric, you could get the best view of that, I suppose.

*Eric Gierch:* It looked all right to me. From what I could see of it the boys had done a really fine bit of work and I bet they spoiled the captain's breakfast.[7]

The airmen of 9 and 617 Squadrons, utilizing their flying skill and technological advances, had further demonstrated that high-level precision daylight bombing was achievable. The sinking of the *Tirpitz* takes its place in the history of aerial bombardment as one of the most outstanding high-level bombing attacks ever carried out.

The European war had another 6 months to run, not that this could be predicted with any certainty in November 1944. Hitler and his Nazi followers were not prepared to agree to 'unconditional surrender' as stipulated by the Allies. Russian and Allied forces would have to fight their way through Germany before the Third Reich finally fell. The bombers would play their part, inflicting total defeat upon the German nation, and post-war debate has often focused on the bomber 'overkill' in the last months of the war. This has tended to suppress acknowledgment of the vital contribution that the bombers actually made in progressing the war from the defensive days of 1940 through to victory in 1945.

At the end of May 1944, the Luftwaffe had 565 fighters in *Luftlotte*

*Reich* and *Luftlotte 3*. These, along with 82 twin-engined aircraft employed as bombers/destroyers, defended German airspace. In darkness, the Luftwaffe had 474 aircraft of the nightfighter force to oppose RAF Bomber Command. Anyone who seeks to examine the Allied bombing policy must take these figures into consideration. If there had been no Allied bomber offensive these aircraft would have been operating over the UK, the Russian front and the Mediterranean. As it was, at one stage, on the Eastern Front, the Luftwaffe could muster only 372 single-engine fighters that could fly into battle. And *Luftlotte 2*, at one point, only had 75 day fighters and 48 bombers to oppose the Allies' Italian campaign.[8]

The bomber airmen of the USAAF and the RAF focused the Luftwaffe over the Reich. The defence of Germany became the primary role of the Luftwaffe, drawing resources in from the campaigns on the periphery: Normandy, the Mediterranean and Russia. The Allied bomber offensive put the Luftwaffe on the defensive, unable to support in any material way the land campaigns. The day and night battles over Germany were, without doubt, instrumental in the achievement of final victory. As one distinguished RAF Bomber Command veteran stated, '**We moved the air battle from the skies over London to the sky above Germany.**' But the cost was high: 55,500 Bomber Command and more than 26,000 Eighth Air Force airmen respectively lost their lives. And approximately 28,000 Eighth Air Force aircrew populated German prison camps by the end of the war, along with just short of 10,000 of their Allied colleagues from RAF Bomber Command.

# EPILOGUE

The closing remarks to this book are provided by WAAF Jean Barclay, whose recollections opened the book:

So it goes on, several nights of the week. Off to bed, the night's doings revolving on one's mind, and to sleep like the dead, one's last waking thoughts being of one gunner in the sickbay to whom, perhaps, alone out of the silence of the vast airfield, sleep will not come. Or perhaps sleep does come, eternally. In the back of my diary I seem to have written, in one of my 'browned-off' moments, grieving over some old and bitter losses, lines by Philip James Bailey:

THE BRAVE
Die never. Being deathless, they but change
Their country's arms for more, their country's heart.
Give then the dead their due: 'tis they who saved us,
Saved us from woe and want and servitude.

They came straight home to me, a relief and a rebuke. One is so cowardly when things go wrong. If only the danger was to oneself one would perhaps cope more successfully. Because it isn't: there is no glory to keep courage alive, only the promise one made to the dead one knew and loved and admired that one would cope, whatever happened, and see that, come what might, their deaths should forever have been worthwhile.

# ENDNOTES

**Prologue**
1. IWM (Imperial War Museum) documents archive, 8497

**Chapter 1**
1. Quoted in Shinkfield, H. *Esse Potius Quam Videri, To be rather than seem. A brief history of 77 Squadron RAF, 1939–1945* (privately published, 2000)
2. Wilf Burnett, www.rafbombercommand.com
3. Account by Jim Moore in Bingham, V. *Attack – Blenheim Operations, June–October 1940* (J. & K. H. Publishing, 2002)
4. Ernest Chuter, IWM sound archive, 14592
5. Account by Mike Henry in Bingham, V. *Attack – Blenheim Operations, June–October 1940* (J. & K. H. Publishing, 2002)
6. Ken Dobbs's letter, the accounts by Jan de Wolff and Mrs van Kempen and the Air Ministry report are all from the IWM documents archive, 11742
7. Bomber Command loss rate figures are from Middlebrook, M. and Everitt, C. *The Bomber Command War Diaries* (Midland Publishing Limited, 1995)
8. Letters to Douglas Mourton, and his account, are from the IWM documents archive, 2706
9. Quoted in Ramsey, Winston G. (ed) *The Blitz Then and Now* (Battle of Britain Prints International Limited, 1988)
10. Quoted in *The Blitz Then and Now*
11. George Parr, IWM sound archive, 12991
12. German Naval Staff report in Shirer, W. *The Rise and Fall of the Third Reich* (Secker and Warburg Limited, 1991)
13. Rod Rodley, www.rafbombercommand.com

**Chapter 2**
1. Harris, Sir Arthur. *Bomber Offensive* (Greenhill Books, 1998)
2. Hamish Mahaddie, IWM sound archive, 2897

3. Alex Shaw, IWM sound archive, 25279

4. Ian Robertson, *WW2 People's War,* www.bbc.co.uk/ww2peopleswar

5. Peter Ward-Hunt, *WW2 People's War,* www.bbc.co.uk/ww2peopleswar

6. Tom Tate, IWM sound archive, 3593

7. Victor Martin, *WW2 People's War,* www.bbc.co.uk/ww2peopleswar

8. At this point in the sound recording, the memory of the events leads Gordon to get somewhat emotional

9. George Mellor, IWM sound archive, 28650

10. Tom Dailey, *WW2 People's War,* www.bbc.co.uk/ww2peopleswar

11. Quoted in Barker, R. *The Thousand Plan* (Pan Books, 1967)

12. Flying Officer Friend, IWM sound archive, 2150

13. Geoffrey Hall, *WW2 People's War,* www.bbc.co.uk/ww2peopleswar

14. From the *London Gazette,* 23 October 1942

15. Leornard Pearman, IWM sound archive, 11191

16. Speer, A. *Inside the Third Reich* (Phoenix, 1995), pp. 382–383

17. Dr Chave, IWM documents archive, 6625


**Chapter 3**

1. The following quotations are from the IWM sound archive: Dave Shannon, 8177; Edward Johnson, 8204; Harold Hobday, 7298; and George Johnson, 17970

2. Quoted in *Enemy Coast Ahead* (Goodall Publications Ltd, 1995)

3. 617 Squadron Operation Record Book, National Archives, AIR 27/2128

4. All Guy Gibson quotations are from his book *Enemy Coast Ahead* (Goodall Publications Ltd, 1995)


**Chapter 4**

1. *Target Germany, The US Army Air Force's Official Story of the VIII Bomber Command's First Year Over Europe* (HMSO, 1944)

2. *Target Germany* (HMSO, 1944)

3. *Target Germany* (HMSO, 1944)

4. Quoted in Murray, W. *The Luftwaffe 1933–45: Strategy for Defeat* (Brasseys, 1996)

5. Courtesy of 100th Bomb Group Foundation, www.100thbg.com
6. Author's correspondence with Bob Woolf
7. Courtesy of the 381st Bomb Group website, www.381st.org
8. Accounts by Robert Hughes courtesy of the 100th Bomb Group Foundation, www.100thbg.com
9. David Hutchens, 381st Bomb Group website, www.381st.org
10. Author's correspondence with Bob Slane
11. Arthur Glenn Foster's account courtesy of Bob Slane
12. Published by Brasseys, 1996

**Chapter 5**
1. Middlebrook, M. and Everitt, C. *The Bomber Command War Diaries* (Midland Publishing Limited, 1995)
2. Translation by Randall Bytwerk, available at www.calvin.edu/academic/cas/gpa/goebmain.htm
3. Quoted in Middlebrook, M. *The Peenemünde Raid* (Bobbs-Merrill Company Inc., 1983)
4. All John Searby quotations are from the IWM sound archives, 14193, and personal printed recollections, 78/2269
5. Wilkie Wanless, www.rafbombercommand.com
6. IWM sound archive, 15112
7. Dennis Slack, *WW2 People's War,* www.bbc.co.uk/ww2peopleswar
8. Quoted in Shinkfield, H. *Esse Potius Quam Videri, To be rather than seem*
9. Accounts by David Balme courtesy of 207 Squadron Association
10. John Martin, *WW2 People's War,* www.bbc.co.uk/ww2peopleswar
11. Sam Hall, www.rafbombercommand.com

**Chapter 6**
1. Accounts by Myron Kielman and John Cihon are from the 392nd Bomb Group website, www.b24.net/392nd/index.html
2. Lieutenant Ackerson, IWM documents archive, 5865
3. Accounts by Hal Turell and Sam Mastrogiacomo are from the 445th Bomb Group website, www.445th-bomb-group.

com/index.html
4. United States Strategic Bombing Survey; and Frank, W.
and Cate, J. L. *Argument to V-E Day, January 1944 to May
1945,* www.ibiblio.org/hyperwar/AAF/III/AAF-III-2.html

**Chapter 7**
1. Accounts by Maxwell Sparks, 2240; Irving Smith, 2236 and 11754;
Tony Wickham, 2236; Robert Iredale, 2236; Edward Sismore 10988;
Monsieur Moisan, 2237; and William Dynes, 2239, are from the
IWM sound archive
2. Fishman, J. *And the Walls Came Tumbling Down* (Souvenir Press,
1982)
3. Monsieur Vivant quoted in Livry-Level, Colonel and Rémy
(translated by Pamela Search). *The Gates Burst Open*
(Arco Publishers Limited, 1955)
4. Livry-Level, Colonel and Rémy (translated by Pamela Search)
*The Gates Burst Open* (Arco Publishers Limited, 1955)

**Chapter 8**
1. Speer, A. *Inside the Third Reich* (Phoenix, 1995), pp. 397–398
2. John Martin, *WW2 People's War,* www.bbc.co.uk/ww2peopleswar
3. Account by Alex Nethery in Darlow, S. *Lancaster Down!*
(Grub Street, 2000)
4. Ed Murrow, IWM sound archive, 2181
5. Account by William Mahn courtesy of 96th Bomb Group historian
Geoff Ward
6. Dana Morse, 91st Bomb Group website, www.91stbombgroup.com
7. Hubert Cripe, www.453rd.com
8. Quotes from Earl G. Williamson's diary courtesy of his son, Steve
Williamson

**Chapter 9**
1. Sir Charles Portal quoted in Lord Tedder, GCB. *With Prejudice*
(Cassell 1966)

2. Eisenhower quoted in Lord Tedder, GCB. *With Prejudice* (Cassell 1966)

3. The official reports mentioned in this chapter are the 'K' reports, held in AIR 14 at the National Archives, Kew

4. Accounts by Bill Jacks are from the 'K' reports

5. Ronald Ivelaw-Chapman, IWM documents archive, 10867

6. Lawrence McGowen, 463 and 467 Squadron website, www.467463raafsquadrons.com

7. Sidney Lipman and Ron Storey, *WW2 People's War*, www.bbc.co.uk/ww2peopleswar

8. Middlebrook, M. and Everitt, C. *The Bomber Command War Diaries* (Midland Publishing Limited, 1995)

9. Quoted in Tedder GCB, Lord *With Prejudice* (Cassell, 1966)

10. Quoted in Tedder GCB, Lord *With Prejudice* (Cassell, 1966)

11. Account by Leonard Cheshire in Darlow, S. *D-Day Bombers: The Veteran's Story* (Grub Street, 2004)

12. Eugene Lipp, www.453rd.com

13. Author's correspondence with Paul Roderick

14. Wesley Williams and Duane Heath, 492nd Bomb Group website, www.492ndbombgroup.com

15. Accounts by Marvin Bowman courtesy of the 100th Bomb Group Foundation, www.100thbg.com


Chapter 10

1. Ralph Briars, IWM documents archive, 5843

2. Author's correspondence with Fred Whitfield

3. Bobby Knights, IWM sound archive, 9208

4. Account by Willie Tait in Darlow, S. *Five of the Many* (Grub Street, 2007)

5. Fred Watts, IWM sound archive

6. Bruce Buckham, 467 and 463 Squadron website, www.467463raafsquadrons.com)

7. Bruce Buckham and Eric Gierch interview, IWM sound archive

8. Price, A. *The Luftwaffe Data Book* (Greenhill Books, 1993)

# BIBLIOGRAPHY

Barker, R. *The Thousand Plan* (Pan Books, 1967)

Bennett, D.C.T. *Pathfinder* (Frederick Muller Ltd, 1983)

Bingham, V. *Attack – Blenheim Operations, June–October 1940* (J. & K. H. Publishing, 2002)

Chorley, W.R. *RAF Bomber Command Losses of the Second World War – 1939–1940* (Midland Publishing, 2005)

Chorley, W.R. *RAF Bomber Command Losses of the Second World War – 1941* (Midland Publishing, 2006)

Chorley, W.R. *RAF Bomber Command Losses of the Second World War – 1943* (Midland Publishing, 1996)

Chorley, W.R. *RAF Bomber Command Losses of the Second World War – 1944* (Midland Publishing, 1997)

Chorley, W.R. *RAF Bomber Command Losses of the Second World War – 1945* (Midland Publishing, 2004)

Churchill, W. *The Speeches of Winston Churchill* (Penguin, 1990)

Clutton-Brock, O. *Footprints in the Sands of Time* (Grub Street, 2003)

Cooper, A. *Beyond the Dams to the* Tirpitz (Goodall Publications, 1991)

Darlow, S. *Five of the Many* (Grub Street, 2007)

Darlow, S. *D-Day Bombers – The Veterans' Story* (Grub Street, 2004)

Darlow, S. *Sledgehammers for Tintacks* (Grub Street, 2002)

Darlow, S. *Lancaster Down* (Grub Street, 2000)

Falconer, J. *Bomber Command Handbook* (Sutton Publishing, 2003)

Fishman, J. *And the Walls Came Tumbling Down* (Souvenir Press, 1982)

Freeman, R. *Mighty Eighth War Diary* (Jane's Publishing Company Limited, 1981)

Gibson, G. *Enemy Coast Ahead* (Goodall Publications Ltd, 1995)

Harris, Sir Arthur, *Bomber Offensive* (Greenhill Books, 1998)

Livry-Level, Colonel and Rémy (translated by Pamela Search). *The Gates Burst Open* (Arco Publishers Limited, 1955)

Middlebrook, M. *The Peenemünde Raid* (Bobbs Merrill Company Inc., 1983)

Middlebrook, M. and Everitt, C. *The Bomber Command War Diaries*

(Midland Publishing Limited, 1995)

Murray, W. *The Luftwaffe 1933–45: Strategy for Defeat* (Brasseys, 1996)

Price, A. *The Luftwaffe Data Book* (Greenhill Books, 1997)

Ramsey, Winston G. (ed) *The Blitz Then and Now* (Battle of Britain Prints International Limited, 1988)

Shinkfield, H. *Esse Potius Quam Videri, To be rather than seem. A brief history of 77 Squadron RAF 1939–1945* (privately published, 2000)

Tedder GCB, Lord *With Prejudice* (Cassell, 1966)

# PICTURE CREDITS

1 Bomber command © IWM/CH 218; 2 Bristol Blenheim Mark IV © IWM/CH 364; 3 German invasion barges © IWM/MH 6657; 4 No. 44 squadron in flight © IWM/CH 3478; 5 Shell torn plane © IWM/ CH 1347; 6 Aerial over Cologne © IWM/C 2550; 7 Practice 'Upkeep' weapon © IWM/HU 69915; 8 Upkeep' bomb test © IWM/FLM 2365; 9 Dambusters' crew © IWM/CH 18005; 10 Dambusters' debriefing © IWM/CH 9683; 11 Breach in the Möhne Dam © IWM/CH 9687; 12 Bob Wolff and crew © 100th Bomb Group Foundation; 13 Regensberg mission © Bob Wolff; 14 Lt. Colonel Beirne Lay © 487th Bomb Group; 15 Peenemunde (before)© IWM/C 4782; 16 Peenemunde (after) © IWM/C 4783; 17 (and back cover) Raid, Amiens jail © IWM/C 4740; 18 No. 487 Squadron in formation © IWM / CH 12412; 19 Operation Jericho © IWM/C 4732; 20 Group Captain P C Pickard © IWM/CH 14106; 21 Bomber commanders © Mighty Eighth Air Force Heritage Museum; 22 Eighth air force raid © The National Archives; 23 B-17 Flying Fortresses © IWM/HU 4052; 24 Bomber command crew © Steve Darlow; 25 Men from No 77 Squadron © IWM/CH 12232; 26 B-24J Liberator on fire © IWM/EA 36158; 27 Depot at Chambly © IWM/C 4329; 28 2,000-pound MC deep-penetration bomb © IWM/CH15363; 29 Tait and Cochrane © ww2images.com; 30 Tirpitz, capsized © IWM/CL 2830; 31 B-24 Liberator departs © IWM EA 52996

Cover image: Martin Smith
Inspired by the painting *Impossible Mission* by Robert Taylor. Thumbnail courtesy of the Military Gallery. The copyrights to all Military Gallery images are jointly owned by the artists and the Military Gallery.

# ACKNOWLEDGMENTS

I extend a big thank you to those who agreed to contribute their experiences to this book. I have a particular respect for the American airmen who crossed an ocean to fight in the defence of my country. My grandfather Arthur Darlow, who served as a Royal Air Force Bomber Command pilot, was shot down on his thirty-second operation and taken prisoner. Arthur was defending his family, his home, his freedom. The Luftwaffe bombing of London during the Blitz, and the V1 flying bomb and V2 rocket attacks were examples to him of acts of aggression directly against everything he held dear. His motivation for fighting with the RAF is obvious. But the men of the American air forces were fighting for another country's freedom; a distant country at that. Their lives were on the line for a more indirect cause. The trial they experienced took them to the extremes of life and death. They will always have my respect, and by helping publish their recollections, I hope that their memory will survive for generations to come.

A book such as this requires the generous help of many people. Thanks to Lloyd Morris for allowing me access to the stories on the 453rd Bomb Group website (www.453rd.com). My appreciation to Ron Scott of the Blenheim society and Victor Bingham for allowing me to quote from *Attack – Blenheim Operations, June–October 1940.* Thanks to David Higham Associates for permission to quote from *Enemy Coast Ahead.* Thanks also to the Trustees of the Imperial War Museum for allowing access to their collections, and to Peter Collins at the IWM Duxford, for access to their resident B-17. The BBC have been kind enough to allow me the use of extracts from their WW2 People's War website – an online archive of wartime memories contributed by members of the public and gathered by the BBC. The archive can be found at www.bbc. co.uk/ww2peopleswar.

The following people deserve acknowledgement for their support to the project – thanks to you all: Pamela Reid, Jim Sheffield, Geoff Ward, Richard Balme, Steve Perri, Lloyd Morris, John Howland, Bob Wolff,

Bob Bowen, Paul Roderick, Michael Faley, Jay Boehm, Robert Slane, Chuck Harris, Ken Decker, Geoff Easterling, Harry Shinkfield, Mike Simpson (Unit Historian of the 445th Bomb Group), Randall Bytwerk, Peter Elliott, Peter Johnson, Earl and Steve Williamson, Norma and Bill Beasley and Paul Fishman. Thanks also to Alex Beetham, Doug Radcliffe and the Bomber Command Association.

And finally, thanks to Neil Baber and Demelza Hookway, at David & Charles, for their work supporting the project.

*Index*

*285*

*286*